D0991582

THE LORRY DRIVER

INTERNATIONAL LIBRARY OF SOCIOLOGY

AND SOCIAL RECONSTRUCTION

Founded by Karl Mannheim

Editor W. J. H. Sprott

A catalogue of books available in the INTERNATIONAL LIBRARY OF
SOCIOLOGY AND SOCIAL RECONSTRUCTION and new books in
preparation for the Library will be found at the end of this volume

THE
LORRY DRIVER

PETER G. HOLLOWELL

LONDON
ROUTLEDGE & KEGAN PAUL
NEW YORK: HUMANITIES PRESS

434304

Mitchell Memorial Library
Mississippi State University

First published in 1968
by Routledge & Kegan Paul Limited
Broadway House, 68–74, Carter Lane
London, E.C.4

Printed in Great Britain
by C. Tinling & Co. Ltd
Liverpool, London and Prescot

© *Peter G. Hollowell 1968*

No part of this book may be reproduced
in any form without permission from
the publisher, except for the quotation
of brief passages in criticism

SBN 7100 3498 9

CONTENTS

v

For
Twerkalüs
with love

ACKNOWLEDGEMENTS

I wish particularly to thank the following: Dr George F. Thomason, Department of Industrial Relations, University College, Cardiff, my supervisor while I was writing my Ph.D. thesis, of which this book is an edited version; Professor M. P. Fogarty and other members of the above department for their continuous assistance; Dr and Mrs Newson of Nottingham University and Mr Norman Dennis of Newcastle University for help on particular points. I have a great debt to the lorry drivers and textile workers who displayed a remarkable tolerance. Thanks are also due to officials of the Transport and General Workers' Union, the Ministry of Labour, the Road Haulage Association and to the managements of the firms who gave help with the study. I am grateful for financial support from the Department of Industrial Relations, University College, Cardiff; the Charles Henry Foyle Trust, Birmingham; the Sir Richard Stapley Educational Trust, London; the John Hampden War Memorial Fund, Thame, Oxon.; and Mr and Mrs B. A. Hollowell.

I

INTRODUCTION

A study in occupational sociology, like this one of the status and role of the lorry driver, will not be primarily concerned with the structure and economic operation of a particular industry. It is inevitable, however, that the industry will have its effect on the occupational role, and that the consequences of industrial structure will be apparent in the analysis of the observed behaviour and recorded attitudes of a sample of this group of workers.

Any insight into a social system poses the immediate problem that sociology is about real interactions and relationships while analytic schemes run the risk of producing characterless quintessences. The actor, who is in reality a bundle of activities, has to be discussed in terms of statuses and roles. In this work inferences for theory are made directly from illustrations of what lorry drivers actually did or said. It seems very important not to diverge too greatly from the observed and reported realities of the action situation, but it is of much greater importance to produce an analytical framework for replicatory purposes. The realities have to be placed in a context which is capable of being tested in a scientific way for its validity. An important criticism which has been made of some of the earlier community studies in Britain is that they did not produce any generalisations or propositions capable of being tested, though their value to sociology is proved by the frequency with which they are cited.

THEORETICAL CONSIDERATIONS

The central theme of this book is that actors are alienated by structural constraints upon them which remain and persist even though they are unwelcome to the actors. This is not a new notion. Various 'great men', sociological and otherwise, have discussed this problem. What we shall hope to do is to illustrate such alienation as exists amongst these particular actors and attempt to explain it in terms of the constraint hypothesis. At this stage the term 'alienation' is discussed to avoid ambiguity. Alienation and anomie are concepts in sociology which can easily be confused.[1] Alienation is subjective in that it refers to individuals' mental states, whereas anomie refers to a more objective condition in society. There are however subjective and objective aspects of both concepts. Our problem is to produce an analysis where alienation is discussed in terms of role structure.

The actor's orientation to his situation is the base of the theoretical considerations here. The actor interacts with other actors within the guidance of norms. Each actor is a 'bundle of statuses and roles'.[2] Status is the position of the actor in the social system relative to other actors, while what the actor is expected to do in his relations with others is termed his role. An operational definition of role has been provided by Gross *et al.*

> A role is a set of expectations ... [Expectations are] a set of evaluative standards applied to the incumbent of a particular position.[3]

This definition enables the concept of role to be used empirically in the analysis of the lorry driver and his social system. What we are interested in is the way in which the lorry driver resolves a series of actual or potential conflicts. We assume that the lorry driver is an actor in a stable structural system or rather a series of integrated sub-systems. Here we make the assumption of role congruency, that is to say expectations are clearly defined, are not conflicting, and are completely fulfilled by the actors in the system. Having made these assumptions we can

---

[1] See the discussion in Mizruchi, E. H. *Success and Opportunity*, Free Press, 1964. pp. 25–60.

[2] Parsons, T. *The Social System*, Routledge & Kegan Paul, 1951. p. 26.

[3] Gross, N., Mason, W. S., McEachern, A. W. *Explorations in Role Analysis*, John Wiley, 1958. p. 60.

now return to our discussion of alienation and anomie. The assumption of a completely institutionalised system is the very opposite of the assumption of anomie.[4] The anomic situation is essentially one in which the rules have been suspended or upset in some way and actors are not afforded the guidance of the normative order. In other words the familiar and sufficient constraints of social structure no longer exist.

We are saying that actors need constraints in order to have social relationships. Our hypothesis at this stage may seem to have become rather awkward—we suggest that constraint is necessary yet it is alienating. Weber's famous definition of social action will help us here.

> Action is social in so far as, by virtue of the subjective meaning attached to it by the acting individual . . . it takes account of the behaviour of others, and is thereby oriented in its course.[5]

We are brought into the realm of alienation here through the notion of double contingency involved in interaction. The actor is not able to develop a subjectively meaningful response in certain situations. Seeman, in an attempt to clarify the usages of the concept of alienation discusses 'meaninglessness' by relating it to Mannheim's idea that the 'functional rationality' gives the individual no clear insight into events, even those in which he is involved. The second usage of alienation which seems most relevant here is powerlessness. Its relevance seems to derive from the proposition that an environment designed for functional efficiency is unlikely to give the individual the ability to determine events by his own behaviour.[6]

In effect we are saying that the actor requires the constraint of the normative order but the substantive rationality is not always able to accept the constraints of the functional rationality of large scale industrial societies. The contention is that it is the lack of social legitimacy in the orientation of the actor that causes the constraints to induce alienation. It is not only the inability to play a particular role but the extent to which the

[4] Parsons, T. *op. cit.* p. 30.

[5] Weber, M. *The Theory of Economic and Social Organisation*, Free Press, 1964. p. 89.

[6] Seeman, M. 'On the Meaning of Alienation', *American Sociological Review*, Vol. 24, 1959.

actor feels cheated of a role which he could play. This powerlessness or inability due to external constraint applies when the role is not allowed to be played out in the light of the actor's self concept of that role. In the next section we discuss the methods through which it is intended to demonstrate the effects of constraints upon actors.

The view of alienation here is that it is a social-psychological phenomenon. We are dealing with the expectations of actors but we are also concerned with the realism involved in the structural situation. The constraints in social situations will be related to the social-psychological indices of the actors. The types of constraints placed upon actors will be identified conceptually and then the indicators of alienation will be discussed.

Marx puts the notion of alienation most clearly when he says

> In what does this alienation of labour consist? First that the work is external to the worker, that it is not a part of his nature, that consequently he does not fulfil himself in his work but denies himself, has a feeling of misery, not of well being, does not develop freely a physical and mental energy, but is physically exhausted and mentally debased. The worker therefore feels himself at home only during his leisure, whereas at work he feels homeless.[7]

For Marx the alienation of the worker occurred on four counts. The worker is alienated from the work process, from the product, from himself and from his fellows. Capitalism produces a form of work organisation which is objectively alienative. This is a very gloomy view as it relates to industrialism in general rather than only to capitalism. Durkheim[8] writing some fifty years later, offers a view affording more optimism. He refutes the attack on the division of labour as a phenomenon which of necessity diminishes the individual personality. Why is it, he asks, that man's personality should be detri-

---

[7] Marx, K. *Economic and Philosophical Manuscripts*, quoted in Bottomore, T. B. and Rubel, M. *Karl Marx Selected Writings*, Penguin, 1963. p. 177.

[8] Durkheim, E. *The Division of Labour in Society*, Free Press, 1964. pp. 402–5.

4

mentally affected by his functioning as an organ of society rather than in activity which is more extensive? His view is that the individual is emancipated by the division of labour and his personality is enriched through his 'nature' being allowed to develop along particular lines in an untrammelled way. Marx in his polemic against capitalism shows the importance of looking at society from the standpoint of a particular value in that the main lines of the argument stand out. What emerges most clearly from Marx is that the form of organisation under capitalism is a constraint which alienates the worker. Under the heading of 'work process' as an alienating form of constraint we shall identify two sub-types of constraint forms—that of the socio-technical system and of organisational form.

The concept of socio-technical system is discussed in much greater detail in a later chapter. It will suffice here to say that constraint in socio-technical systems is considered to be largely due to the element of technical determinacy in the system. As we have noted, man's loss of control in the work process has been discussed at length by Marx. More recently Blauner has suggested that control over work and thus the powerlessness varies with the specific type of technology in question. He is forced to the conclusion that alienation 'remains a widespread phenomenon in the factory today' but

> For most factory workers the picture is probably less black and white than for workers in the automobile and textile industries, where they tend to be highly alienated and the printing and chemical industries, where freedom and integration are so striking.[9]

Blauner is optimistic about alienation in automated industry, a conclusion which is based on his findings on the attitudes of workers in automated chemical industry. Craft industry produces least alienation with only 4 per cent of the workers finding their jobs dull in the printing industry. This figure increases to 18 per cent in textile manufacturing and 34 per cent in the car industry, while the figure for unskilled assembly line workers is the high level of 61 per cent.[10] These findings

[9] Blauner, R. *Alienation and Freedom*, Chicago University Press, 1964, p. 183.

[10] Blauner, R. *op. cit.* p. 175.

would lead us to suspect that technical determinism is an important independent variable. Alienation increases to a high level as the industry becomes more based on mass production techniques as in the case of the assembly line. Automated production involves a relaxation from the technical constraints and also there is, in time of crisis, a mastery of, and involvement with, the machinery. This reduces the alienation at this level of the technical process. Our argument that technical determinacy, at least up to mass production level, is a potential alienator of workers is not without opposition. Baldamus, for instance, holds that a certain kind of technical determinacy has at least some kind of objectively definable utility for workpeople. He says of the conveyor belt:

> The enormous relief from strain achieved by this method has not been recognised, in fact many people still associate an element of coercion with the conveyor belt.[11]

This view is definitely not borne out in the findings of Walker and Guest in their study of assembly line workers. It is the loss of control over the pace of the work and its lack of interesting content which produces a high degree of alienation amongst this group.[12] The view is taken at the outset that technology in certain forms operates as a constraint on workers which induces alienation.

The other sub-type of constraint form involved in the work process which will be dealt with is that of the organisation. Organisational systems provide objectively differential constraints on actors depending on the type of system. While Max Weber saw bureaucracy as the most rational type of organisation as that it was 'indispensable' for the 'needs of mass administration',[13] he was pessimistic about some of its effects.[14] As Burns and Stalker comment:

> Bureaucracy is often said to have played the part in Weber's

[11] Baldamus, W. 'Types of Work and Motivation', *British Journal of Sociology*, Vol. II, 1951, p. 48.

[12] Walker, C. R. and Guest, R. H. *Man on the Assembly Line*, Harvard Un. Press, 1952.

[13] Weber, M. 1964, *op. cit.* p. 337.

[14] Gouldner, A. W. 'Organisational Analysis' in Merton, R. K., Broom, L. R., Cottrell, L. S. *Sociology Today*, Basic Books, New York, 1959. p. 402.

sociology that social class did in Marx's. But both men were pre-occupied, beyond these notions, with the idea of 'alienation'—the moral, intellectual and social constraints exercised over men's natural instinctual inclinations by the immense apparatus of the social order.[15]

Instinct is perhaps an unfortunate term in this case because it is not man's innate resistance to social order that is the major concern. We have seen that some kinds of constraint are seen by men as being necessary for existence, notably in the discussion of anomie. Man is not boundless in his desire for freedom, it is simply that the particular type of constraint may be considered perverse. In Thoreau's terms, he may simply be marching to a different sound from the one which surrounds him at the particular time in question. This is however the other side to the question of instinct. The sociologist succumbs to the temptation to argue the ideology of sociology as much as any other professional. It may be that the alienation and anomie concepts are subtle forms of such ideology.[16] Whatever the relative validity of these two points of view, a middle path is taken in this book; that is that certain constraints are acceptable to men who have been socialised in a certain way whereas others are not so acceptable.

Burns and Stalker in their study of industrial organisations provide an illustration. They produced typologies of organisation which they call 'mechanistic' and 'organic' types. At the mechanistic pole, which is a model close to Weber's ideal type of bureaucracy, the structural constraints would be such as to produce a severe limitation on the discretion of the participants involved. The organic type of organisation produces less constraints of an organisational kind on the individual in the context of a value system internalised through training in a particular expertise. We shall attempt to demonstrate the actor's expectations of the structure that they are in contact with and their response to the constraints of these structures— notably organisations—which are a major part of the work

[15] Burns, T. and Stalker, G. M. *The Management of Innovation*, Tavistock, London, 1960.

[16] For an example see Horton, J. 'The Dehumanisation of Anomie and Alienation', *British Journal of Sociology*, 1964. pp. 283–300.

process. In short we shall indicate the subjective effects, in terms of a 'definition of the situation', of the constraints imposed by organisation and by the different forms of organisation.

Social relations amongst peers involve constraint just as the relations between groups, or between an individual and a group. This is so in that amongst a plurality of actors 'the action of each takes account of that of the other and is oriented in these terms' and that there is 'at least a minimum of mutual orientation of the action of each to that of the others'.[17] It is the double contingency which operates in the actor's role set that is constraining to him. Merton has developed the concept of 'role set' to analyse the constraints which vary for the incumbent of a single status.[18] A role involves a person in a network of reciprocal expectations, each other role (except possibly that of peers) has slightly differing expectations for the actor. This network of role-expectations in which the actor is involved is the structural basis for conflict. There are mechanisms in social systems which counter this potential conflict. Cultures assign some roles as more important than others. Differences in power, varying degrees of insulation amongst members of the role set, observability, peer support, and the abridgment of role relations are examples of social mechanisms which Merton asserts provide stability in role-sets. Gross, N. *et al.* in their detailed study of the American school superintendent role, give empirical support for Merton's concept of role set. They strike out at the assumption of consensus on role definition and develop a theory of role conflict resolution involving the perceived legitimacy, sanctions, and moralistic orientation to the conflicting expectations. The matrices of these dimensions produce predictable behaviour in role conflict situations. The predictable behaviours are conformity to one or other of the expectations, compromise or avoidance.[19] Perhaps the complexities of such schemes have tended to lead us a little further away from the proposition that social relations involve constraints upon actors. There is considerable justification for

[17] Weber, M. 1964, *op. cit.* p. 118.

[18] Merton, R. K. 'The Role Set: Problems in Sociological Theory', *British Journal of Sociology*, Vol. 8, 1957.

[19] Gross, N. *et al.*, 1958, *op. cit.*

discussing in detail the nature and direction of such constraints, as we shall see in some examples of occupational statuses.

The constraints of social relations which develop in organisations are one type of role set membership which has been given consideration. For studies of social relations that develop in occupations relatively unorganised in the formal sense, we are indebted to Professor E. C. Hughes and his students at the University of Chicago. Such occupations, albeit they are 'more or less lowly'[20], are held by Hughes to reveal social processes more readily than more sophisticated occupations.

Three examples will serve to give illustration of the way in which social relations are constraining. The apartment house caretaker in the course of his occupation comes into contact with tenants. They constitute the major element in his role set and as such they expect immediate service in a wide variety of tasks. In the case of garbage disposal these services are grudgingly given, but it is the garbage which gives him some knowledge and therefore power over his tenants. His expectation of being recognised in his status is not fulfilled and there is the potential reciprocation of using such knowledge against the tenants. Hughes points out that this is a potential mechanism rather than an actual one.

The dance musician also has a potentially alienative relationship with clients. There is an ideological continuum in this sub-culture which ranges from the 'commercial' to the 'creative'. The man who wishes to play only creative music may find himself only irregularly employed while the musician who is regularly employed may be viewed as having sold out the creative ideal. The creative ideal still exists even amongst nominally commercial musicians and is apparent in the symbolic and ritual devices to separate the musicians from the 'squares' who pay for it. In spite of these social mechanisms the musician is not free from the constraints of his clients. Even artists have to eat and he that pays the piper constrains the creative element in music.

The two above examples of role relations in occupations involve the relationship between the occupational status incumbent and his client. The role set is much larger than this

[20] Hughes, E. C. *Men and Their Work*, Free Press, 1958. pp. 49–54.

and many constraints may emerge from co-workers or colleagues. The classic example of this type emerges in the Bank Wiring Room study. Within this worker group there was a status system based on adherence to norms with sanctions for deviance.[21] Studies of restriction of output usually seem to lead to evidence of social constraints of this kind. Constraints may also emerge on individuals from their occupational groups when the group attempts control of the promotion system, or work opportunity. The dance band musician obtains steady work through the membership of cliques. The members of these cliques sponsor each other for jobs and have mutual obligations over this matter.[22]

The final area of constraint to be discussed is that type which impinges on the individual due to his involvement in, what Merton has termed, a 'status set'.[23] An individual has many social positions, he may be husband, father, member of a social club or political party, lorry driver, and so on. Each of these various statuses will involve the individual in a role set. These statuses may be in widely differing institutional spheres. It is the task of sociology to show the sort of relationship the institutional spheres bear to each other and to show how groups accommodate themselves to the demands made by the differing spheres. We shall attempt to show, through model building, the effects of an occupation, like lorry driving, on family life. The constraints of family life may be beneficial to occupational life in some circumstances, while in others they may damage a person's whole career. By the same rule an occupation is essential for a person to maintain his family but his occupation may produce considerable strain in his family life.

Having outlined the major areas of constraint upon the incumbents of occupational statuses we can progress to an analysis of the occupational status and role of the lorry driver. This is done through a consideration of an ideal typical lorry driver role and a comparison of this pure type with the average type of role as it emerges from the empirical material. There is a good deal of argument about the meaning of Max Weber's

[21] Homans, G. C. *The Human Group*, Routledge & Kegan Paul, 1951.

[22] Becker, Howard S. *Outsiders*, Free Press, 1963.

[23] Merton, R. K., 1957, *op. cit.*

notion of the pure type. In this case the meaning is a construction based on an extension of the major characteristics of the role in question and the compression of these characteristics into one case. It is clear that many of these characteristics will correspond to the motivations of the actors. Thus the 'lorry driveriness' about lorry drivers may correspond to the ideology of the occupation more than to any other aspect of their role. In other words our pure type is likely to involve more frequently the expectations the lorry driver has of others in his role set than the expectations which impinge on him.

The concept of role which we shall use is derived from Levinson's discussion of the unitary concept[24] and as such is a more complex formulation than the one made earlier in this chapter. Role is defined in three ways. There is firstly the idea of role as the actor's orientation, or view of the role he is playing. This is the actor's self-concept of his role, his definition of the situation. The self-concept is socially derived and gives the individual and the group the notion of value of their work to society. The expectations a group develops in relation to the work its members do may be designated as the occupational ideology. A brief definition of an occupational ideology is that it is a relatively stable system of beliefs and values by which the interests of the group are legitimated. Its function is largely that of stabilising or raising the status of the group involved.

The second way of looking at role is that it is the set of expectations of a person who holds a particular status. These expectations are demands made upon the individual and as such they are external to him. We have discussed these in detail under the heading of constraints. The third definition of role involves the actions of a person, his performance or what he actually does. Levinson argues that the way the role concept has been treated by many writers is inappropriate for social reality. These three concepts of role have been treated as components of an overall concept through the assumption of a 'high degree of congruence' between them, where the degree of integration between them, in reality, is a variable.[25]

[24] Levinson, D. J. 'Role, Personality, and Social Structure', in Coser, L. A. and Rosenberg, B. *Sociological Theory*, Macmillan, London, 1964. pp. 284–97.

[25] Levinson, D. J. 1964, *op. cit.*

Introduction

The task is to present the pure type of role of the lorry driver and relate it to the average type. In this way we should be able to emphasise the relative importance of the three aspects of his occupational role. The idea is to see how much of the self-concept gets through into actual behaviour and how much it is changed by the constraints of the structures which surround and make demands on him. As Hughes elegantly states of the apartment house janitor, 'It is the tenant who interferes most with his own dignified ordering of his life and work.'[26]

TECHNIQUES

The choice of suitable indicators of the constraints is the major problem here. Indicators are ideally rates of some kind and the system used has to be comparable with those used in larger populations. This reduces our freedom of choice of such indicators. The indicators chosen to illustrate the constraints of the technology and the organisational form are those of rates of job satisfaction and work satisfaction respectively. To a considerable extent the objectivity of these rates was increased by previous investigations of workers in varying and defined technologies and organisational forms. Out of the reasons given for indicating job and work satisfaction we are able to build a picture of the expectations lorry drivers have of their role set.

The indicators of status set accommodation are derived from responses to direct questions on the lorry driver's family life and his activities as a citizen. In the case of the family the data obtained is built into models to indicate possible courses of action with statistical backing to give evidence of their frequency.

The data was collected by means of observation and through interview. There were four samples involved in all. The first of these was a pilot sample of 20 lorry drivers from one café in the centre of a city. These men were met in a casual way and thus the sample was an accidental rather than a random one. A further sample of 200 lorry drivers was obtained by interviewing in an accidental way in three different cafés and at a dockside loading point. The interview schedule was altered for this sample on the basis of data from the pilot sample. An

[26] Hughes, E. C. 1958, *op. cit.* p. 50.

12

attempt to gain a control group was made by obtaining interviews with a 50 per cent random sample of textile factory
workers. There are problems involving the validity of this
control sample due mainly to variables of urban culture and
employment. After this sample was completed and analysed,
interviews from a further sample of 101 lorry drivers were obtained involving a 50 per cent random selection in two firms
which could be classified as different forms of organisation.
Further interviews were conducted with managements of road
haulage firms of varying size in the area. Some 8 firms in all
were involved.

Chapter II of the book discusses the environment of the lorry
driver in the widest possible way involving the many institutions with which he is, and, perhaps more significantly, those
with which he is not in contact. In Chapter II we gain a picture
of the career of the man as he is or has been acting in the
environment. The life cycles of men illustrate the responses and
adaptations which have to be made to a given environment.
Chapters IV and V describe respectively the social psychological effects of the constraints of technology and organisation.
The lorry driver's family involvement and accommodation to
such involvement is the major illustration of the constraints of
status sets. Chapter VII considers his leisure activities; work and
non-work in the occupation is presented through the method of
indicating zones of interaction. Chapter VIII involves the
pulling together of the various strands of the argument previously presented. The constraints are considered in their
totality and placed in the context of their effects on the status
of the occupation.

II

THE LORRY DRIVER'S WORLD

This chapter discusses the general occupational demands and skill of lorry driving. It also describes the lorry driver's wider work environment with particular reference to the structure of the industry and the institutions which it contains. The conclusion of the chapter deals with the way in which the industry has evolved and the relationship between the institutions with its consequent impact on the lorry driver's role.

DRIVING: THE SKILL AND THE JOB

What is driving? Perhaps the best description is the one in the Highway Safety Research Committee report to the National Research Council made in 1952.

> The driver must first learn a series of complex, co-ordinated tasks involving both hands, both feet, vision and hearing. This co-ordination must be learned to a point where it becomes semi-automatic before he can hope to operate in traffic with any degree of safety. He must also learn to make judgements of changing space-time relationships. He must operate in close proximity to other vehicles of different sizes and speeds, going in the same and opposite directions, and on crossing courses. He must operate on highways and streets which require passing other vehicles with a clearance of one foot to ten or twenty feet, and at various angles. When the time intervals within which he must react, even at relatively low speeds, are considered, it will be seen that he must learn to anticipate conditions and situations . . . the factors of foresight, planning and appreciation of hazards must be involved to a major extent. Actually it seems probable that more continuous attention from moment to moment is required of the

14

motor vehicle driver, than of the operator in any other type of transportation, including the airplane.[1]

The above passage shows driving to be a series of responses as a result of continuous processing of largely unorganised stimuli. Often the responses must be so rapid that learning is as implicit in driving as well as an innately rapid motor response. McFarland *et al.*, sum up the skill of driving in the following passage:

> Driving skill largely consists of the organisation, within the pertinent visual field of the driver, of a correctly bounded stopping zone for the entire repertory of speeds, roads and surface, conditions, and a field of safe travel which is precisely moulded to the actual and potential obstacles in the total field at any given instant.

Thus driving skill requires high sensory ability, particularly in the case of vision, and quick reaction and co-ordination by the driver. The better drivers are above average intelligence,[2] in that truck drivers selected to compete in the Roadeo of American Trucking Associations had an average I.Q. of 112. A further requirement for consistent driving skill is a certain level of individual personal and emotional adjustment. A small study of Canadian taxi drivers[3] indicates that the accident repeater is likely to be aggressive and have had a difficult family background and other signs of failure to adjust to social structure in general.

In view of the physiological abilities required in driving skill it would appear that there is some doubt about the advantages to be gained by experience (and thus age) and the disadvantage incurred through impairment or decline in the level of sensory abilities. Certainly eyesight is impaired with age, as is reaction

---

[1] 'The Field of Highway Safety Research.' Committee on Highway Safety Research of the National Academy of Sciences. National Research Council. Washington D.C. August 1952. Quoted in *Human Variables in Motor Vehicle Accidents*. McFarland, R. A., Moore, R. C. and Warren, A. B. Harvard School of Public Health, Boston. Mass. 1955.

[2] Quoted in McFarland, R. A., Moore, R. C. and Warren, A. B. (1955) *op. cit.*

[3] Tillman, W. A. and Hobbs, G. E. 'The Accidental Prone Automobile Driver: A Study of the Psychiatric and Social Background.' *American Journal of Psychiatry*, Vol. 106 (5), 1949.

time when dealing with a crisis, but there is greater emotional stability with age and also a great deal of knowledge acquired through experience. The older driver can make up for the lessening of his sensory and psycho-motor skills by taking care in the way he drives and by going at a slower pace and also because he has considerable experience by this time and has learned to predict with some accuracy what will happen as he is driving along. Usually certain cues appear and give warning of a situation which the driver recognises from experience as being dangerous. Two examples of occurrences which took place while the writer was engaged in participant observation will serve to illustrate this point. The first of the drivers making the statement is 59 years of age while the second is in his late forties.

The first experience occurred while travelling through the town at the beginning of the shift when my driver spotted a man about 75 yards ahead crossing the road to a traffic bollard. He said: 'Look at that cunt, he'll get on to the island, turn round and walk straight back into the wagon.' As he made this remark the driver slowed down. The man stepped straight in front of the lorry as it was passing the traffic island. The driver braked and the man was, fortunately, only just touched by the lorry unit. There was a severe one-sided conversation between the lorry driver and the pedestrian, who was then approached by a policeman. My driver continued on his way and said: 'I don't know, that's twice that's happened tonight: I was on the way to work and I could see this bloke on a mini-cycle wanted to turn but he didn't make a sign, so just in case, I slowed down. Sure enough, he turned straight in front of me. Well, I didn't hit him because I knew what he was going to do, like, but I was annoyed and I slammed the window down and told him. He'd come off, by the way—sheer fright, I expect. I told him, I said: "You ought to be more careful, mate; if I'd been in a bit more of a hurry, I'd have hit you." Well, he picked himself up and said: "I was driving all right. I've passed my test!" So I told him: "If you drive like that much more, mate, you'll be passing in a fucking hearse!"'

The next incident occurred at about half-past three in the morning running towards the end of the shift. It was on the return journey of a long run, the straight clearness of the road

16

suddenly turned into bends, hills and high hedges. A man came out of a telephone box on the side of the road, and my driver slowed down considerably. Immediately round the next bend was a lorry with a flat tyre which he just managed to avoid. 'I thought that fella might be a driver ringing for a fitter, so I reckoned his wagon would not be very far away!'

In both cases the ability to predict a series of events was the product of the experiences of these older drivers. There can be no doubt that experience and the emotional stability which comes with age are sometimes vital to the lorry driver. The major criteria for selection of lorry drivers by representatives of managements of the road haulage firms, who were interviewed, are responsibility and experience. Some of these management representatives said that they regarded a man's driving experience with various types of vehicle as being of primary importance when considering him for employment. Nearly all of the management representatives considered that drivers needed to be responsible in their job and considered that the driver with family responsibilities was more likely to be so than his single colleague. Some quotations from the interviews illustrate the point.

'He should preferably be married, a married man has a bigger sense of responsibility if he's at all a family man. Although it may be that he wants to get away from his family responsibilities, these drivers I don't like.'

Traffic Manager, Joint Stock Haulage Firm

'Single men have days off, married men don't. I prefer a man who has a family for almost the same reason.'

Manager-Director, Road Haulage Family Firm

'I like a married man with two or three children, he becomes a steady driver.'

Owner Manager, Small Haulage Firm

'We prefer a married man with a family rather than the young tearaways for the responsibility required.'

Manager, Medium-sized Haulage Firm

'This (conjugal status) can mean something. I prefer a married man, he has to remember the well-being of his family.'

Manager, Large Road Haulage Family Firm

17

'The single fellow is no good, he's no responsibility like the married man. The young men are fiddling around all night and can't get up. A married man is more responsible and has less cheek, works better and is a better time-keeper. The young fellow spends all night looking for it.'

Owner-Manager, Small Haulage Firm

In short we can say that the skill involved in driving requires the individual to be quick thinking and quick acting, but at the same time he should be a careful individual, who uses his experience, and is reliable and predictable.

THE LORRY DRIVER'S JOB

There is one thing that is certain about almost any job an individual could obtain as a lorry driver, and that is that the job will not consist entirely of sitting in a cab driving from point A to point B. A lorry driver in the course of a week is probably, a driver, a fitter mechanic, a labourer, a clerk and he may even in some cases be a canvasser for his firm. The amount of time spent by lorry drivers in waiting outside factories, docks and warehouses is considerable. As this section is a general survey of the lorry driver's job, the occupation should be viewed in terms of its hazards, its responsibilities, and the skill involved, with perhaps a conclusion on the overall difficulties met by the lorry driver.

The dangers in the occupation stem largely from the fact that the lorry has to be driven on busy roads, some of which are taking more traffic than was ever intended. The report on road accidents in 1962 by the Ministry of Transport states that:

Goods vehicle drivers and passengers killed (death within 30 days of the accident) and seriously injured which necessitate detention in hospital and certain others in 1962 was 5,760. This was 481 or 9% more than in 1961. This compared with an increase between 1960 and 1961 of 8% but whereas between the two earlier years goods vehicle mileage increased by 6%, between 1961 and 1962 it increased by only 1%. This suggests therefore, that, on the basis of the distance travelled, the casualty rate among goods vehicle occupants increased markedly between 1961 and 1962.[4]

[4] *Road Accidents 1962*. Ministry of Transport and Scottish Development, H.M.S.O. London, 1963.

18

Table II in the report shows that there were 182 goods vehicle drivers killed in 1962 and 2,878 seriously injured in the same year. Examples of such reports are unfortunately all too easily found in the daily press. Some are given below:

TWO MEN DIE AS LORRY FALLS INTO CANAL

After salvage operations lasting several hours, an eight-wheeled lorry and trailer which plunged into the Manchester Ship Canal . . . was lifted by a 60 ft. floating crane and taken away for police examination. The trailer had broken in half . . . The two men who died when the lorry plunged 40 ft. into the canal were . . . the driver, aged 34 and . . . his mate, aged 28 . . .

The Guardian, 23rd October, 1963

LORRY DRIVER IS KILLED

The driver of a heavy lorry was killed and another injured when their vehicles were in collision on the main Abergavenny to Hereford road . . . last night. The accident happened near a series of bends, notorious for accidents, when a lorry carrying tinplate going towards Hereford met a lorry owned by . . . The dead man, whose lorry carried a load of potatoes, was freed from his cab by firemen.

Western Mail, 15th October, 1963

Perhaps even worse than these short reports on the deaths of lorry drivers, is the report contained in *The Observer* of Sunday, 27th January, 1964, below a picture of an injured driver in hospital:

MOTORWAY MADNESS

The following interview at the Luton & Barnstable Hospital appeared on BBC Television News on Wednesday night:

Interviewer 'Mr. Lammiman, how are you feeling this morning?'

Mr. Lammiman 'Only fairly comfortable; a little bit of pain . . . not too bad.'

Interviewer 'Just what did happen on the M.1 yesterday?'

Mr. Lammiman 'I left Nottingham for Smithfield with a load of meat on. Of course, you know it was thick fog and I was having to go very steady—well less than 30 miles an hour, which was quite enough really considering—up the near-side lane, and we left Luton junction and I was following within a couple of lengths' distance of another lorry, when he started to slow up and another lorry went flying past me. Then another went too, and I heard a "bang, bang, bang, crash", saw the other one's

tail lights in front come on; so I threw all my brakes on and I stopped just near him, moving over a little to the left. The next thing, there's a crash behind me and something shoved my old lorry right through the back of this one in front of me, taking me and taking everything through the back of the wagon.'
Interviewer 'So, you've lost your leg, in fact?'
Mr. Lammiman 'So I've lost my leg.'

The Observer, 27th January, 1964

TABLE 1

Vehicles Involved in Accidents 1962

Type of Vehicle	No. of vehicles in fatal & serious Accidents	No. of Vehicles in all Accidents	Vehicles involved per million vehicle miles	
			Fatal & Serious Accidents	All Accidents
Mopeds	1,674	6,169	2·3	8·5
Motor Scooters	7,470	28,253	4·8	18·1
Motor Cycles	19,306	55,150	6·2	17·9
Cars & Taxis*	51,094	185,060	1·0	3·7
P.S.V.	4,898	24,086	2·0	9·8
Goods Vehicles:				
Less than 1½ ton U.W.	11,759	43,907	1·2	4·5
1½–3 tons U.W.	3,295	11,256 ⎱	0·9	2·8
Over 3 tons U.W.	6,176	16,792 ⎰		
Other Vehicles	1,740	5,752	—	—
All motor vehicles	107,412	376,425	1·4	4·8
Pedal Cyclists	10,700	45,153	1·9	7·9
All Vehicles	118,112	421,578	1·4	5·0

Source: *Road Accidents 1962*. Ministry of Transport and Scottish Development Department. H.M.S.O. London, 1963.

Such descriptions require a sense of proportion. Horrifying as they are, Table 1 above shows that the lorry driver has least involvement in accidents of any class of road user who has a vehicle, particularly the heavy, and presumably long-distance driver.

The number of fatal and serious accidents amongst users of

* 98 per cent cars.

heavy goods vehicles is particularly low, being 0·9 vehicles involved per million miles compared with the average for all motor vehicles of 1·4 per million miles. Again, the number of deaths (182) amongst lorry drivers due to accidents in 1962 can be seen in perspective when Table 8, in the Road Accidents 1962 report by the Ministry of Transport is considered. This table shows that in 1962, 6,709 people were killed in road accidents (182 lorry drivers) and 83,915 people were seriously injured (2,878 lorry drivers). Men are killed in coal mining and fishing in great numbers, and it is not suggested here that lorry driving is a very dangerous occupation relative to others; the suggestion is rather that it is a dangerous occupation to some extent due to the possibility of accidents.

The other big danger in lorry driving is that of being beaten up and, perhaps, even murdered by thieves who are out to steal the driver's load. Examples are quoted below:

LORRY DRIVER MURDERED BY BANDITS

A lorry driver was fatally shot during an armed raid on the Royal Arsenal Co-operative Society depot at . . . today . . . A fourth bandit was holding a sten gun when (a named driver) arrived to collect his lorry. The bandit shot him through the head.

Headlight, January, 1963

DRIVER FOUND TIED TO A TREE

The driver of a lorry loaded with shoes stolen on the A.1 near Huntingdon was found tied to a tree in Wanstead by a passer-by. The driver said he stopped his vehicle to look at his lights, when some men attacked him, gagged him, put him into a car, and later left him tied to a tree.'

Headlight, July, 1962

CIGARETTE LORRY AMBUSHED

An articulated lorry loaded with cigarettes, worth about £30,000, was stolen in Palmers Green, London, by four men who overpowered the driver and bundled him into a small van. The lorry, minus load, was found several hours later at Whetstone. The driver . . . was flashed down . . . and attacked when he pulled up.

South Wales Echo, 28th November, 1963

Figures of lorry thefts in the Metropolitan area are quoted in *Headlight,* December 1963.

21

The Lorry Driver's World

TABLE 2

Thefts of or from Goods Vehicles in the Metropolitan Police District

| | January to June | | |
	1961	1962	1963
Number of Cases	2,100	2,500	2,000
Value Stolen	£439,000	£354,000	£288,500
Value recovered	£34,000	£24,000	£19,500
Persons charged	173	143	103

The number of cases has fallen from 2,100 in January to June 1961 to 2,000 for the same months in 1963, so has the amount of goods in value terms. Perhaps this is due in part to the formation by the Road Haulage Association of an Observer Corps of mobile volunteers to protect vehicles which are 'parked up'. An article in *The Times*, entitled 'London Lorry Gangs Moving Out', says:

> One incidental effect of the drive against lorry dragging (stealing a vehicle and transferring the load) apart from the move north, could easily be an increase in hi-jacking (a method of stealing a load which involves persuading a driver to stop and then, almost always, attacking him).
>
> *The Times*, 2nd February, 1963

The success of the Observer Corps is again reported:

OBSERVER CORPS FINDS 34 STOLEN VEHICLES

Since it began to operate in July, 1962, the Observer Corps in London has recovered 34 vehicles—20 loaded and 14 empty. This was reported to the Vehicles Safety Committee.

Road Way, Journal of the R.H.A., May, 1964

The occupational hazards are not as great as they might seem on reading local newspaper reports. The driver of the heavy lorry is less likely to be involved in road accidents than any other road user. According to the *Headlight* figures the chance of meeting up with lorry thieves seems to be slightly smaller than formerly. A further 'hazard' if it may be so termed, is the risk of stomach disorders through taking meals at odd times or eating too much of the fatty food which transport cafés provide in quantity and relatively cheaply.

The responsibility of the lorry driver is mainly that involved with getting his vehicle and load to the appointed destination at the appointed time. To do this he has to avoid accidents like those already discussed, and he also has to avoid 'hijackers' or other kinds of lorry thieves such as those who take lorries from cafés and unload them some distance away. The lorry driver has to be particularly careful when he has cigarettes or 'treacle' (whisky) on board. The police often make special arrangements for the drivers of such vehicles. A further responsibility which has not been discussed is that which the lorry driver has to the rest of the road-using-community and, as the examples will show, the rest of the non-road-using-community. This is particularly a responsibility of the lorry driver, since he has usually a very big and dangerous load.

DEATH ON A HILL

A lorry loaded with 10 tons of concrete pipes ran out of control on a steep hill in Porth, Glamorgan, yesterday and crashed into a post office van, killing 29 year old . . . (a named man).

Daily Express, 10th October, 1963

CRASH NO. 5—AS COWBRIDGE ACTS

Cowbridge's fifth road crash in a month occurred early today when a tyre blow-out caused a car to leave the road and demolish part of a front wall of a house. Today the mayor said his council had asked for a meeting with the Ministry of Transport to discuss immediate safety measures, including a possible 20 mph limit on heavy transport.

The List:

September 13:
Runaway lorry hit a car at Eastgate traffic lights, killing the car driver and smashing the garden walls of several houses.

September 16:
Lorry hit a house at almost the same spot.

September 20:
Another lorry hit a house on the opposite side of the road.

October 15:
Lorry hit a bus and ended up in front room of a house owned by a former mayor. Lorry driver slightly injured.

South Wales Echo, 16th October, 1963

The Lorry Driver's World

The lorry driver has a responsibility to see that the vehicle which he drives and its load are safe for the road.

DEATH CRASH DRIVER ACCUSED: WARNED BRAKES WERE
HOPELESS—PROSECUTION

The day before a fatal crash in Cowbridge in which a car was crushed by a heavy lorry, the lorry driver was advised to park the vehicle because of the condition of the brakes, it was alleged today . . .

'Had he taken the advice of the other lorry driver and gone home by train and reported the matter to his employers, this accident, with its dreadful results, need never have happened.

Here you have a lorry on the road driven by a man who knew that he was doing wrong.'

South Wales Echo, 17th December, 1963

COWBRIDGE DEATH-CRASH DRIVER GAOLED, BANNED

(The named driver), who has vowed never again to enter the cab of a lorry following a death crash in Cowbridge, was today gaoled for four months and banned from driving for six years.

South Wales Echo, 22nd January, 1964

The lorry driver must make sure his load is secure, that is, that it is put squarely on the vehicle and covered with canvas sheeting and rope so that it will not in any circumstances slip during the journey.

FALLING LOAD KILLED MERTHYR MAN. SIX ½-TON CASES SLIPPED
OFF LORRY ON TO CAR AT ROUNDABOUT

An accident at Upper Boat, in which a driver was fatally injured when six cases of aluminium sheeting each weighing half a ton, fell from a lorry on to his car, was described at Pontypridd Magistrates' Court today.

The lorry driver appeared on charges of driving with an insecure load and the owners were charged with permitting an insecure load.

South Wales Echo, 29th January, 1964

RUN AWAY TRAILER TRAPS MOTORIST

Firemen cut into a wrecked car today to free a Cardiff man trapped with head and rib injuries after his vehicle was in collision with a breakaway articulated trailer . . .

South Wales Echo, 6th March, 1964

Thus the lorry driver has a responsible job, the responsibility

24

being necessary in three main areas: the general public, both the road-using community and, as in the Cowbridge example quoted, the non-road-users in the community. He has the responsibility of getting the load and his vehicle intact to the destination.

In skill terms the lorry driver's job must be viewed as being at least as skilled as a machine operator's job. The Registrar General's Occupational Classification, 1960, puts the lorry driver in the Social Class III grouping—the skilled worker group. The necessity of skill is apparent in that the lorry driver has to deal with a continuous stream of data which he must process and act upon very quickly. The skill of the driver has been discussed in greater detail in the first section of this chapter. The edition of *Road Way*, the Journal of the Road Haulage Association for July 1964 notes that:

> Goods vehicle drivers acquired their skill principally by experience of the work. It could not be gained by training methods appropriate to other industries.

Lorry drivers may show their skill by competing in the Lorry Driver of the Year competition. Apart from the skill required in competition, extra special skill is sometimes called for in the every day work of the lorry driver.

DRIVER SAVES FOUR CHILDREN
A lorry driver saw the back wheels of a lorry in front shear off and career towards four children in Enderby, Leicester, yesterday. He accelerated and knocked the two heavy wheels into a ditch. Then he drove on without leaving his name.
Daily Express, 7th July, 1964

All in all the hazards of the occupation and its responsibilities create difficulties for the lorry driver in various ways. The greatest difficulty is that of negotiating the lorry to its destination on crowded roads which seem increasingly full of bad drivers. A further difficulty is the way in which the weather can alter road conditions, particularly in winter, from hour to hour. It could also be possible for the driver to encounter difficulties when he is loading and unloading, such as obtaining the correct amount of loaded goods; having his lorry securely loaded, and 'getting on' with customers in the social sense.

The Lorry Driver's World

One of the biggest difficulties in a lorry driver's occupation would seem to be that of obeying all the rules that he is supposed to obey while doing his job. The lorry-thieving problem is a case in point.

The driver has to obey the rules of management of his firm when he takes out a vehicle belonging to the firm, the rules made by his union, and he also has to obey the laws governing his activities on the road. An article in *Headlight*, the Lorry Driver's magazine, for August 1963 entitled 'The Law and your Job' states that:

> The jungle of Acts and Regulations surrounding road transport makes it advisable for drivers to know how the law requires them to co-operate in producing documents and giving information.

The article discusses the powers which the police have to stop vehicles, and states that under the Road Traffic Acts 1960 and 1962 (section 223 of the 1960 Act) drivers who fail to comply when required to stop by a constable in uniform can be penalised summarily by a fine not exceeding £5. Having seen the above, the article quoted below must produce something of a dilemma for the lorry driver reader.

BEWARE OF BOGUS POLICE

What should a driver do when asked by someone in police uniform to dismount? The answer by the Metropolitan Police is to refuse but to offer to drive to a police station or garage where help is available in case of need. They are concerned with the growing practice of criminals of impersonating police officers to lure drivers out their vehicles.

One of the usual pretexts for asking a driver to get out is that his load is slipping, but a loose load normally slides to the side and should be visible in the mirror. Obviously the driver must use his discretion but he should be well advised to lock himself in the cab before stopping at the signal of a policeman in uniform.

Road Way, January, 1964

The difficulties of the total work situation of the lorry driver are further discussed in a later section on the work conditions in the transport industry, where the ambiguity of the driver's position in a complex of rules is outlined.

THE TYPES OF LORRY DRIVING JOB

One cannot look at a lorry driver as he passes by and predict precisely what his job entails. Many lorry drivers do not work in the road transport industry, a factor which alters their conditions of work greatly. For those who do work in the road transport industry there is a great deal of variation. Many sorts of loads are carried in many different makes of vehicle and to meet the needs of manufacturing industry arrangements have to be made for specialised working. The customers of the road haulage industry are probably the cause of task specialisation within lorry driving itself. Within the road haulage industry the lorry driver may take one of three specialised jobs. The jobs are those of the Shunter, the Trunker, and the Tramper.

(a) *Shunting*

A 'shunter' can be almost any kind of local delivery driver. He may just be called a local or general delivery driver if his lorry is below a certain weight, perhaps three or even five tons. Usually in the road transport industry a shunter is a driver of a vehicle of around fifteen to eighteen tons capacity. He drives a big vehicle but usually only within a certain radius of the depot. More often than not, every shunter on a firm has a trunker whose lorry he takes over and delivers the load that the trunker has brought down overnight. The shunter is a driver who spends perhaps more than half his time in loading and unloading his vehicle. He begins his day by offloading vehicles at factories, warehouses and docks. Once the shunter has delivered his load, which may include several 'drops' (deliveries), he then calls at the places where he can obtain another load for his vehicle. He loads his vehicle and then takes it back to the depot and, if it is at the end of his shift, he checks the oil and petrol and lights to make sure that the vehicle is ready for the night trunker. He may load several vehicles in a day according to the cargo and return them to the depot for the trunkers.

(b) *Trunking*

A 'trunker' is a lorry driver who drives a lorry from point A to point B or perhaps, if he is on a 'changeover trunk', he drives the vehicle (usually an articulated vehicle consisting of a unit and trailer) from point A to a point half-way to point B where he changes trailers, according to a pre-arrangement, with a driver from point B. The changeover point may be at a café and is usually so but not always. Consignment notes are usually exchanged at these points. A changeover trunker returns to home base by the morning, and thus although he is a long distance driver he always sleeps in his own bed every day. However, some trunkers may go from point A to point B, stay the day at point B in transport accommodation, and then bring their reloaded vehicle from point B to point A the following night. The archetype of trunk driver just drives; he does not load or unload his vehicle, nor does he deliver loads to customers, or pick up items for transportation. At the depot he picks up his loaded vehicle, which the shunter has left for him, and delivers a loaded vehicle for his shunter in the morning.

(c) *Tramping*

A tramper (otherwise called a 'rover' or 'roamer') is a driver who, unlike the trunker, has no set route. He starts out from the depot perhaps on a Sunday or Monday morning. He collects a load and loads his vehicle himself. As soon as he collects the load the tramper knows the first destination in his week's work. He may deliver the first load in one 'drop' or there may be several 'drops' in one load. If there is a whole load for point B, then the tramper may pick up another load at point B, which may take him to point C. At point C he may load for point D, and so on, until at the end of the week he gets a load for point A, his home base again. The journey described above is only one possible journey of a tramper, the important point to note is that the tramper has no fixed route normally. He is a lorry driver who really does not know where his week's work will take him. A tramper loads and unloads his lorry and delivers goods to customers. His job is probably more physically arduous, because of the loading and unloading that he does, than the trunker's job. A tramper's job is characterised by more variety and less regularity than is a trunker's job. Another characteristic of tramping is that the tramper may himself be left to his own devices to find and organise a return load, or a load to some other place than by his depot. This is why he has no set programme since, until he gets a load from a clearing house or some other place such as the docks, he will not know where he is to go.

All the three jobs in driving have a great deal in common but they have a good deal that is distinct between them. The local driver or shunter is still within his own community when he works by day. In fact as he is travelling about in his community he probably knows it much better than people in less mobile occupations. The long distance drivers, the trunkers and trampers spend most of their working time away from their community. The trunker goes away at night and even when he is on a 'changeover' he spends most of his time at home asleep. In fact a six-night-per-week trunker may mean that the trunker has very little community life of any kind, either in his own community or another. The tramper spends perhaps as much as a week (more in some cases) away from home and after his day's work he eats and sleeps in transport accommodation. Thus, although all three categories of drivers may be seen by the casual observer to be doing the same job, in fact both working and leisure time conditions are very different between the three.

WORKING CONDITIONS

The first thing that strikes the outsider new to the road transport world is the irregularity of the work times of lorry drivers and also the long hours that he puts in. The irregularity is determined in part by the demands that the customers of the road haulage industry make upon it. The trunker has the greatest regularity of work times and the tramper the least. The trunker goes to his depot at approximately the same time every night and finishes at a regular time in the morning. The shunter's routine is also fairly regular as he is, in effect, servicing the trunker. The tramper, on the other hand, does both shunting and trunking, and he follows the work around. Perhaps it would be enlightening to describe the type of week that a typical tramper might have.

On a Sunday morning at 10 a.m. the tramper leaves his

South Wales depot for Birmingham with a load of steel billets. Assuming that the billets can be 'craned off' and they are all for one firm, he parks up his lorry in Birmingham around 2.30 p.m. ready for a 6.30 a.m. start in order to get his vehicle unloaded first at the factory. He then seeks accommodation which he knows to be suitable. On the Monday he delivers his load and is clear of the factory by 7.45 a.m. and rings the depot. There is a load at such and such a factory for Glasgow. This is a multi 'drop' load for various factories in Glasgow and its immediate area. Dependent on how quickly he can get the load on (1–4 hours) he can then make for say Warrington or Carlisle, where he will stay the night. With a bit of luck he might meet the two drivers from 'X' firm and have a night's chatter in the 'tele' lounge or the pub. After what might be a hilarious night, he fills himself with a monstrous breakfast and leaves for Glasgow about 7.15 a.m. An advantage of tramping is that within reason he starts when he pleases, according to what he has to deliver and where it has to be delivered. If he has stayed in Warrington then the whole of Tuesday is spent in getting to Glasgow, dependent on the type of vehicle he drives. Tuesday night is spent in accommodation in Glasgow and on Wednesday morning the tramper leaves early to counter the effects of having to wait to get his 'drops' done. About 1 p.m. he has cleared his vehicle and goes to either a depot of his firm or a clearing house to get a load. Assuming it is a depot he waits in the depot canteen after reporting until there is a call for Driver 'X' of Welshtown. He hears he has got a load for Newcastle. 'I hope it's a oncer, I've been out since Sunday,' he says. If he is lucky he will get a single delivery for Newcastle and will be able to load for Welshtown. It is now afternoon so he will have to stay in Glasgow for Wednesday night. On Thursday he leaves early to get his delivery made in Newcastle which he completes by 1 p.m. He again reports to his firm's depot. He gets half a load for Birmingham and about six and a half tons for Welshtown and by the time the load is on the vehicle there is about two hours of the legal shift left. He spends the night in transport accommodation about 55 miles south of Newcastle. He rises early on Friday to see if he can get to Birmingham to get rid of his half-load of domestic cleaners which has to be taken off by the caseful. By a good fortune and a bit of running 'on the dodgy' he makes the warehouse in Birmingham and gets the load off. He is lucky it is a warehouse, a factory would not look at him after 3.30 on a Friday afternoon. Back to the depot and the problem now is whether or not he will have to find another half-load for Welshtown. 'My kid's birthday party missed,' he thinks, as the clerk gives him notes to pick up four and a half tons of boxes and bolts from 'Ferrogrind' in South Birmingham. 'Still I might get in there first and get away by nine o'clock.' He stays in Birmingham at the same accommodation as earlier in the week. At 7 a.m. on Saturday the tramper drives into 'Ferrogrind' and up to the loading bay. 'Can't deal wi' yow yit' says the chargehand. 'Aye aye', says the tramper, 'I reckon your blokes would get tired just going for a piss, wouldn't they?' 'Yow fuckin' Welshmen are all the same, carvin' the job up.' The tramper replies, 'I hold a card same as your blokes but I want to get back for my kid's party at four o'clock.' 'Oow, well whoi din' ya say, oi'll ger'em out now.' Within three quarters of an hour the tramper is able to roll his sheets back over the new load and rope it down. By about quarter to nine he is on his way. He stops at the motorway services café and has a tea and two toasts and then continues to Welshtown. After three quarters of an hour waiting in a traffic jam in a neighbouring town the tramper arrives at his home depot at 2.30 p.m.

The tramper in this example is of course theoretical. Had he managed a good set of loads from clearing houses the week could have been much easier but clearing houses are, on the whole, less reliable for 'good' return loads than, say, the arrangements that are made through the depots for the British Road Services drivers. The schedules in the example may be more or less tight than the ones in reality as many drivers may 'flog their logs' (run illegally) or 'do a dodgy' (running further than the firm allows, which usually involves running illegally as well). Some of the schedules allowed are very good from the drivers' point of view. A whole night of 10 or 11 hours may be allowed for a London run, but the Black Country has to be reached and a return journey made in the 10-hour-shift by B.R.S. drivers. The older drivers are constantly aware that schedules are getting tighter. The writer wanted to go to

Birmingham one night and when an old driver (60 years) was approached, the following conversation took place:

Writer 'Any chance of a trip to Birmingham or will I get in the way when you have a kip?'

Driver 'Sleep! sleep! We haven't got time to stop for a shit on this job, I'll have to bake it now until morning.'

Writer 'Well, am I on then or not?'

Driver 'Aye, pick up your clutter and let's get out of here.'

In the private firm sample, the trampers did the biggest mileage, often illegally although it never would appear so to the outsider, and the trunkers had a relatively easy mileage schedule of an average of 162 miles for the eleven-hour-shift. At the B.R.S. depot the trunk runs expressed as an average for all the trunkers was 181 miles per ten-hour-shift. The trampers at B.R.S. had to keep much closer to the legal amount than those at the private firm.

There are two main aspects of working conditions which are important to the lorry driver and these are the hours that he is allowed to work, and the complex of rules within which he does his job. The hours of work are laid down by law.[5]

No one may drive for more than $5\frac{1}{2}$ hours (Act 1960, 75.1 (i)) without having a break of at least half an hour for rest and refreshment.

No one may drive for more than a total of eleven hours in any 24 hour period commencing 2.00 a.m. (73).

Any time spent by the driver on other work in connection with the vehicle or load is counted as driving time.

These three statements on the legal hours of the lorry driver refer to the simplest possible situation. There are such things as twelve and fourteen hour 'spread-overs'. The legal working hours of the lorry driver are almost in themselves a legal specialism. The *Headlight* magazine runs a special legal advice page for drivers which deals with hours, pay and other questions.

[5] Kitchin, L. D. *Road Transport Law.* Iliffe Books Ltd. (14th Edition) London. 1964.
Road Traffic Act 1960.

The age of the drivers is also regulated by the 1960 Road Traffic Act. No person under the age of 16 is allowed to drive a motorised vehicle on the road. A motor cycle and certain other vehicles may be driven by persons between the age of 16 and 17. Over 17, a person may drive a light goods vehicle (up to 3 tons) but a person may not drive a heavy goods vehicle (over 3 tons) until he is 21 years of age. The regulations of insurance companies often provide that a person under 25 may not drive a heavy vehicle or they cost the firm more in premium payments. This means that the working conditions of younger drivers will be perhaps more favourable than those of the older drivers, as they are not able to go long distance lorry driving.

The second important aspect of the work situation which affects the lorry driver is the complex of rules of the work situation. Table 3 shows summaries for offences in the industry.

TABLE 3

The Number of Summonses relating to Goods Vehicles Carriers' Licences, or Drivers of Goods Vehicles, issued by the Licensing Authorities or by the Police in co-operation with the Licensing Authorities

Offences	Prosecutions	Convictions	Adjourned or dismissed sine die	Withdrawn
Using vehicle without carriers' licence	2777	2676	83	18
Breach of conditions of carriers' licence	2077	2013	52	12
Offences relating to records	4559	3953	309	297
Offences relating to records	8778	8505	206	67
Offences under Motor Vehicles (Construction and use) Regulations 1955	3474	3352	113	9
Failing to display an identity certificate	65	61	3	1
Using a goods vehicle whilst a prohibition notice is operative	21	18	3	—

Source: Annual reports of the Licensing Authorities. 1962–3.

One of the chief offences that drivers commit it seems, are offences against hours of work laid down by Parliament. There were 3,953 convictions for offences relating to hours of work. Reports of such offences are often found in the press.

HAULAGE FIRM FINED £58 AT ABERCARN

A Crumlin haulage firm were fined a total of £58 by Abercarn magistrates today when they admitted 29 charges of allowing goods vehicles to be driven for more than the permitted hours.

South Wales Echo, November 11th, 1963

LORRY DRIVER HAD A HARD DAY'S NIGHT

A lorry driver wanted Friday afternoon off to take his wife out. So he worked through Thursday night to get his work done in time. The family outing cost him £10 in fines, plus a five guinea advocate's fee at Aylesbury Magistrates' Court.

The Bucks Herald, August 14th, 1964

In connection with the hours-of-work regulations the lorry driver must have so many hours away from his lorry in every twenty-four. This prevents drivers sleeping in the cabs of their vehicles and saving their expenses allowances for lodgings. Also closely connected with the hours of work regulations are the offences relating to the keeping of records. If a driver can 'flog his log sheets' he can work over his hours and get home early, as in the case above, which is known colloquially as 'doing a dodgy' or being 'on a dodgy'. The table shows that the chief offence that a lorry driver commits is that of failing to keep his records properly, 8,505 convictions were made in 1962–3 for offences relating to records.

Another set of convictions occurs relating to the driving of vehicles which are in a dangerous condition. Eighteen such convictions were made in the year 1962–3. Three quotations below show that the lorry driver can be in an ambiguous position with regard to rules made and enforced by the different agencies, in this case the agencies are the firm and the transport ministry. John Barry in the *Sunday Times* article of 23rd August, 1964, quoted below says:

A £30 a week man is not going to jeopardise his wage by getting a name as a 'trouble-maker', always reporting faults in the lorries he drives. I spoke to one driver who was kept on low wages in his

34

firm's sheds after annoying the foreman with complaints, and I was told of similar cases.

'It's all very well getting noble and public spirited when it's someone else's job at stake', said Mr. Joe Kelson, editor of *Headlight*. 'But if a man has a wife and three kids, he's not going to stick his neck out by kicking up a fuss over what he drives.'

Sunday Times, 23rd August, 1964

DRIVER REPORTED BRAKES INEFFICIENT

A lorry driver who found his brakes were not working properly drove his articulated lorry to the police station and reported the matter. As a result his *former* employers were convicted by Bolton Magistrates for using a lorry and trailer with inefficient brakes. But the company was given an absolute discharge, as it had taken the vehicle off the road as soon as the defect was pointed out. (The driver) stated that the vehicle's footbrake was nearly useless and the trailer brake would not come off the floor. Asked why he did not report this to the firm he replied, 'I was fed up to the teeth. When I made complaints repairs were not carried out, except when I did them myself.'

Headlight, April, 1963

DRIVE DANGEROUS LORRY OR LOSE JOB

When driver (named) was summoned at Hull for using a lorry with dangerous parts and tyres, inefficient brakes, silencer, windscreen wipers and speedometer, having no horn and failing to maintain the lights, he told the magistrates it was a case of 'drive or be sacked'. He had since been sacked because of the case. His employer, who was fined £11 for permitting the offences, told the court that if the lorry was faulty the driver should have reported it, and the matter would have been put right.

Headlight, April, 1963

Thus in the work situation the lorry driver is surrounded by a complex of rules which often ensnare him when he tries to obey the rules of all the agencies. The drivers' view of their work situation is often very critical and sometimes dramatic, as the letter quoted below in full shows.

LIABILITIES OF BEING A LORRY DRIVER

Sir,

It is obvious that your correspondent, who was surprised that an insurance company should offer lorry drivers a policy against loss of wages caused by legal withdrawal of their driving licences, is not a professional driver. If he were he would treat the present plight of the lorry driver, and indeed any of us who rely upon our driving licences for a living, with far less levity. The motoring correspondents of a number of journals have recently pointed out that it is now possible for a driver to be disqualified for making mistakes and not only for deliberate offences on the road, so that those licence holders who spend their working lives at the wheel are necessarily most at risk.

Many lorry drivers are at the additional disadvantage in that they drive vehicles which are not their own property and which they do not maintain themselves. Thus a driver might be unaware of mechanical defects in his vehicle until, having been stopped by a Ministry of Transport inspector for a spot check, he is prosecuted for being in charge of a vehicle in a dangerous condition.

Often a driver is in no better position if he appreciates that his lorry is defective. Drivers working for some firms, usually those without a trade union organisation, can be faced with driving vehicles which will put them in danger of prosecution or losing their jobs. A driver who resigned from a firm in these circumstances, incidentally, would be liable to be refused unemployment benefit, on the grounds that he had deliberately quitted his job, and would have to apply for National Assistance.

Driving a lorry is becoming increasingly difficult and dangerous on our crowded roads. The need which has arisen for this insurance cover indicates the new hazard which the driver must face, that of the 'Russian Roulette' of disqualification. Bearing in mind these factors, together with the fact that the lorry driver is still paid a wage little more than that of a labourer for a tough and responsible job, it would perhaps be more appropriate for fellow motorists to extend sympathy and support rather than to sneer.

Yours faithfully, etc.

The Guardian, 6th June, 1964

Accidents, defective vehicles, hours of work and the work schedule are very closely related to one another. The actual length of the runs which a driver can do in a single shift (though there are legal exceptions to the eleven-hour rule) of eleven hours are noted in the *Headlight* Wages Calculator. The time mileage chart for 30 mile per hour vehicles (the maximum hourly mileage permitted for such vehicles in 1962) shows that the driver can go 242 miles in an eleven-hour-shift when the average speed is reckoned at 22 miles per hour. For the B.R.S. driver the number of miles in a ten-hour shift would be 220 miles. The maximum speed permitted has been increased to 40 miles per hour but lower speeds are still prevalent. There are exceptions to this as illustrated below:

The average speed for schedules was 16 m.p.h. in about 1956; now it is 22–24 m.p.h. and quite a few firms tell their drivers bluntly; 'you can do 40. So do it till you get there'.

One East London haulage firm makes its drivers do the 440 mile round trip to Stockton in a single 11 hour shift. It can just be done legally—police have tailed the lorries all the way to make sure. But the driver can have only a 30 minute break in Stockton. A Cardiff firm sends its drivers on four trips to London and back each week. For this they get £16 per week. Some firms pay less.

By slogging, an experienced driver with a good record can earn perhaps £30 a week. He will not touch the £16 a week job. So 'the cowboys' take over—the new boys 'just off the minis', the sacked 'C' licence drivers, the rough necks, the maniacs. The only firms that will have them are the small precarious ones—and the drivers need work so they do as they are told.

Sunday Times, 23rd August, 1964

TABLE 4

*Hours of Work in Road Transport of Men-Manual Workers
Compared with Certain Other Industries*

Industry or Firm	Hours Weekly
Agriculture	53·1
Construction	49·8
Road Passenger Transport (Except L.P.T.B.)	49·6
All Manufacturing Industry	46·8
Road Haulage Contracting (Except B.R.S.)	56·4
Estimate B.R.S.	50·0
Average for All Industries (Except Agriculture)	47·6

Source: *Statistics on Incomes, Prices, Employment and Production*, No. 8. 1964. Figures for October 1963 of Average Hours Worked for Men—Manual Workers.

A summary of working conditions must give due emphasis to the complex of rules and to the long hours worked by lorry drivers. A source of information on the hours is contained in the Ministry of Labour publication from which most of Table 4 is derived.

The estimate for B.R.S. drivers' hours is a very vague guess, but it is probably better to err on the low side rather than risk creating an artificially high level merely for the purposes of the argument. Even so, weekly hours in the road transport industry are considerably higher than the average for all industries (except agriculture).

PAY IN THE ROAD GOODS TRANSPORT INDUSTRY

The high hours worked in road transport have an effect on the driver's extra-occupational life which is discussed in a later chapter. The particular relevance of hours here is firstly that if the schedules imposed on the driver by his firm are heavy, then the driver's chances of breaking the rules of the Ministry are increased. Secondly, the high average weekly hours make the earnings of lorry drivers look artificially high. It is difficult to say what a lorry driver is worth but it is possible to arrive at an estimate of what he gets in his wage packet.

TABLE 5

Statutory Minimum Remuneration.
R.H. 74 Weekly Rates and B.R.S. Weekly Rates (42 hours)

Age	Carrying Capacity of the vehicle	R.H. 74			B.R.S.	
		London	Grade 1	Grade 2	London	Prov-inces
Under 19	1 ton or less	134/0	132/0	130/0	134/9	132/9
19 and under 21	1 ton or less	160/3	158/3	156/3	161/0	159/0
21 and over	1 ton or less	197/6	192/6	188/6	199/6	193/6
All Ages	Over 1 ton–5 tons	197/6	192/6	188/6	199/6	193/6
,, ,,	Over 5 tons—10 tons	205/6	200/6	196/6	207/6	201/6
,, ,,	Over 10 tons–15 tons	212/6	207/6	203/6	213/6	208/6
,, ,,	Over 15 tons–18 tons	220/6	215/6	211/6	221/6	216/6
,, ,,	Over 18 tons	230/9	225/9	221/9	231/9	226/9

Source: *Headlight* Wage Calculator based on the Road Haulage Wage Council Order R.H. 74.

The lorry driver is an hourly paid worker whose wage rate is determined by his age up to the age of 21 and by the carrying capacity of the vehicle he drives when he is over 21. A driver under 21 years may not drive a heavy goods vehicle but once over the age of 21 the carrying capacity of vehicles driven is not regulated by law. The weekly rates vary by area and also by the type of firm for which the lorry driver works. There are also special wage rates for certain types of load which are classified as indivisible. Table 5 shows most of the differences in the minimum weekly wage rate due to the suggested variables, at the time the study was made.

Table 5 shows that the lorry driver is paid according to the weight of the vehicle he drives up to a maximum of about £11 10s. per 42 hour week for a vehicle of over 18 tons. B.R.S. drivers get paid a slightly higher rate than the drivers in private haulage firms and they also have a bonus which private haulage drivers may not have, which is equivalent to 15 per cent of weekly earnings.

TABLE 6

Men Manual Workers Average Hourly Earnings
Index: April 1960 = 100

Industry	April 1960 (pence)	October, 1962 (index)	April, 1963 (index)	April, 1963 (pence)
Agriculture	46·8	115·8	118·2	55·3
Food, Drink, Tobacco	64·0	117·8	121·9	78·0
Chemicals and Allied	72·4	115·9	111·3	86·4
Motor Vehicle Manufacturing	96·3	109·1	113·9	109·7
All Manufacturing Industry	75·0	113·2	115·3	86·5
All Industry Except Agriculture)	70·5	114·9	117·3	82·7
Road Haulage Contracting (Except B.R.S.)	58·3	118·7	123·2	71·8
Estimate B.R.S. (50 hrs. weekly)	—	—	—	75·5

Source: *Statistics on Incomes,* etc. No. 6, September 1963. Ministry of Labour.

How do the hourly earnings of the lorry driver compare with those of workers in other industries? A basic rate of £10 15s. 6d. for a driver of a vehicle with carrying capacity of 15–18 tons does not seem very high. Table 6 shows that hourly earnings in lorry driving are significantly lower than those in the chemical and motor manufacturing industries, and slightly lower than in food, drink, and tobacco manufacture and lower than hourly earnings in all manufacturing industry. On the other hand earnings per hour in road transport are considerably higher than in agriculture.

Of note here is the fact that the table shows that the B.R.S. driver has average hourly earnings which are nearly fourpence above those of his colleague in private enterprise. Earnings over the week however, reverse the picture. While the hourly earnings of the B.R.S. driver are higher than those of the

TABLE 7

Men Manual Workers: Average Weekly Earnings
Index: April 1960 = 100

Industry	April 1960 s	d	October, 1962 (Index)	April, 1963 (Index)	April, 1963 s	d
Agriculture	194	6	121·7	116·1	225	11
Food, Drink, Tobacco	260	8	115·5	119·1	310	7
Chemical and Allied	286	8	112·9	117·1	335	8
Motor Vehicle Manufacturing	380	5	100·4	108·1	415	0
All Manufacturing	296	4	110·3	112·1	332	4
All Industry						
(Except Agriculture)	282	1	112·5	114·5	323	1
Road Haulage Contracting						
(Except B.R.S.)	269	11	118·3	122·8	331	4
B.R.S. Estimate	—		—	—	315	6
(Over 50 hours)						

Source: *Statistics on Incomes*, etc. No. 6, September 1963. Ministry of Labour.

private-enterprise driver, the probability is that the B.R.S. driver earns less per week than the private-enterprise drivers. Table 7 gives an estimate of a B.R.S. driver's weekly earnings for a 50-hour week with a vehicle carrying capacity of 15–18 tons to be some 15 shillings a week less than his 'private-enterprise' colleague. The table also shows that the weekly earnings in lorry driving are less than weekly earnings for all manufacturing industry but the difference is not as marked as the difference in hourly rates between those engaged in manu-facturing and those engaged in lorry driving. Lorry drivers can apparently make up their weekly earnings by doing a good deal of overtime. The difference between B.R.S. and private haulage earnings can be explained through the fact that B.R.S. drivers can work only a limited number of hours. The private haulage driver can work more hours provided his management is not too mindful of the law. Private haul-iers may pay a special bonus.

All in all the lorry driver is not highly paid when his basic rate and hourly and weekly earnings are compared with those in the chemical and motor industries. On the other hand by

TABLE 8

Growth of Road Transport

Industry	Estimated Million Tons Carried			Estimated Ton Mileage (*Thousand Millions*)			*No. of* Licensed Vehicles (*Thousands*)		
	1958	*1963*	% Inc.	*1958*	*1963*	% Inc.	*1958*	*1962*	% Inc.
Road Haulage	448	530	15·4	13·1	18·0	27·1	174	193	9·3
'C' Licence Transport	613	770	20·4	12·1	17·0	28·8	1048	1226	13·7

Sources: Table 33. *Highway Statistics* 1963. Ministry of Transport Statistical Paper No. 3. H.M.S.O. London 1963.

Appendix H. *Annual Reports of the Licensing Authorities* 1962–3. H.M.S.O. London 1964.

working a considerable amount of overtime the lorry driver can attain average weekly earnings which are only slightly below the average for all manufacturing industry. The tramper or any driver who stays away overnight is entitled to claim subsistence of about 18 shillings to cover his bed, breakfast and evening meal.

THE ROAD TRANSPORT INDUSTRY

The road transport industry in Britain is a growing industry, Table 8 indicates this in terms of tons carried, ton mileage, and numbers of licensed vehicles.

The increase in the size and work done by the road haulage industry is not so great as the increase in the carriage of goods in 'C' Licence vehicles. Nevertheless the growth of numbers of both types of licence is considerable, and as a result it would be reasonable to expect a disproportionate amount of younger men in the industry. The important point to note is that the road haulage industry has fewer vehicles and thus carries proportionally more goods than are carried under 'C' licence. Further, most of the vehicles in the road haulage industry are of a size over three tons, about 34 per cent being three tons carrying capacity and under. The essential differences between licences in the road haulage industry and the 'C' licence are described in the section below on the legal position, recent history, size and structure, of what is called, in the official handbook, 'the road goods transport industry'.

Late in 1962 there were 10·5 million vehicles licensed to use Great Britain's roads. Of these 1·4 million were goods vehicles, and 92,000 were public road passenger vehicles (i.e. buses, trolley-buses and taxi-cabs).

The Road and Rail Traffic Act, 1933, based upon the recommendations of the Royal Commission and of an expert's report (The Salter Report) of 1932, established a system of licensing for road haulage vehicles, which is still in operation, designed to restrict vehicle operations to proved needs and to eliminate wasteful competition. A licence has to be secured from the licensing authority (the chairman of the appropriate body of traffic commissioners) before a goods vehicle can be used on the road. There are three types of licence: the 'A' licence for general public haulage; the 'B' licence for public haulage limited to certain goods or certain areas and covering also the carriage of the licensee's own goods; and the 'C' licence for the carriage by traders solely of their own goods. Applications for 'A' and 'B' licences are examined by the licensing authorities to see if they are necessary in view of existing transport services, and competitors may raise objections. There is a right of appeal to the Transport Tribunal against the decision of the licensing authorities. The 'C' licence is granted on application as of right. All goods vehicle operators are bound by the regulations concerning the fitness and loading of vehicles, the movement of large vehicles likely to obstruct traffic, the keeping of records, and driving hours and rest periods of their employees.

Under the Transport Act, 1947, the British Transport Commission took over 'A' and 'B' hauliers predominantly engaged on long distance haulage; vehicles operating under 'C' licences and those used for carrying certain specialised traffic were not affected. After the change of Government in 1951, the Transport Act of 1953 required the B.T.C. to dispose of the bulk of its road haulage undertaking. In 1956 this process was halted by the Transport (Disposal of Road Haulage) Property Act, which enabled the Commission to retain under its control more vehicles than were permitted under the 1953 Act. Altogether the Commission disposed of 20,000 vehicles. From September 1956, British Road Services (B.R.S.) were a division of the Commission and conducted their business through the medium of five companies which together owned about 16,000 vehicles: British Road Services Ltd., (general haulage); B.R.S. (Pickfords) Ltd., (special traffic and some contracts), B.R.S. (Contracts) Ltd., B.R.S. (Parcels) Ltd., and B.R.S. (Meat Haulage) Ltd. All the companies' vehicles are subject to the licensing system.

Since January 1963, these organisations have been operating as companies incorporated under the Companies Act, with their own Boards. As a result of the 1962 Transport Act, they are grouped under the newly created Transport Holding Company, responsible to the Minister of Transport.

The number of licensed vehicles in the road goods transport industry rose from 1·2 million in 1955 to 1·4 million in 1962. The percentages with 'C' licences were 78·3 in 1955 and 80·4 in 1962. Of the other 192,000 vehicles with 'A' and 'B' licences, about 13,800 are operated by British Road Services and the rest are operated by some 63,000 hauliers. There are only a few operators with large fleets of vehicles in any of the licence categories. 'C' licence vehicles include a large number of small vehicles used locally in the delivery of groceries and other goods. Other vehicles in this class are engaged in long distance carriage of traders own goods. A sample survey made by Traders Road Transport Association in 1958 indicated that 'C' licence operators with fleets of over 100 vehicles were probably fewer than 3% of the total number of operators, but accounted for over half the 'C' licence vehicles in use in the country.[6]

The major institutions of the industry are the firm, the relevant Government departments, the trade unions, and the management association. Other small but growing institutions of the industry are the numerous drivers' clubs, such as the Headlight Drivers' Club and the Bedford Drivers' Club. These clubs issue badges and often offer wage calculators and legal advice and insurance to their members. A very important institution in almost every lorry driver's life is the transport café. Important to nearly every private enterprise tramper is the transport clearing house, as is also the 'transport house' where he obtains his accommodation.

(i) *The Firm*

The firm in the industry is one of two main types, either public or private. The biggest single group of firms is the nationalised British Road Services, which consists of five separate firms. The remainder of the industry is made up of many private hauliers of whom only a few have large fleets of vehicles.

(a) *British Road Services (B.R.S.).*[7] The size of B.R.S. is not left obscure, the group owns 16,000 vehicles which are operated from some 500 depots and branches throughout the country. These vehicles run 300 million miles per year and carry a total yearly tonnage of 16 million tons. The business done in a

---

[6] *Britain: An Official Handbook.* H.M.S.O. London. 1963. The most comprehensive textbook on the transport industry in Britain is: Savage, C. I. *An Economic History of Transport.* Hutchinson University Library. London, 1966.

[7] Information about B.R.S. as stated here is obtained from the driver's introduction to B.R.S., a handbook called *Welcome to B.R.S.: The Driver's Handbook*; the *British Road Services (Male Wages Grades) Group Pension Fund*, explanatory booklet; and interviews with representatives of the management of B.R.S.

year totals about £50 million. To operate these vehicles, to maintain them and carry out the administration work necessary to run the business, B.R.S. employs a total of 35,000 men and women, 8 out of 10 of whom are directly engaged on the driving, loading and operation of the vehicles and their maintenance.

The essential features of B.R.S. are that it has a highly developed management system and hierarchy; it has a high degree of formalisation of rules; the trade unions play an official part in the organisation through a joint consultative scheme; its driving rules are specialised and defined, it allows only a 10-hour-shift in any 24-hour-period for its drivers as opposed to an 11-hour-shift in private firms and, lastly, pay for drivers per hour is officially higher at B.R.S. than in private firms. There is also a contributory pension fund for male wage grade staff of the firm. The disciplinary code is highly formalised and there is an appeal system. The working conditions of drivers are clearly defined wherever possible.

(b) *The Private Haulage Firms.* Many of these are small in size. Most of the information contained below is based on interviews with private road haulage firms' managements in the South Wales area, and on an article in the *Sunday Times* of 23rd August, 1964. There were some 63,000 private enterprise road haulage firms in 1962 and so it would seem that there is at least a possibility of a wide range of types within this vast number. Eight interviews were held with representatives of management of road haulage (A and B licensed firms) firms in South Wales and only slight generalisation is possible from these interviews. The range in size of the eight firms engaged in private haulage or, as they stress themselves 'free enterprise' road haulage, is from one which employed 3 drivers to one that employed 100 drivers. Two of the firms employed under 10 men. Two firms employed over 20 but under 40 men, and two more employed between 40 and 50 men. One firm employed 80 men and the biggest firm employed 100 men. At the time of the interviews the 'freight' section (general haulage section) of the B.R.S. depot, which was located within five miles of each of these firms, employed 124 drivers. The manager of a firm employing 42 men said that his firm was 'medium size'—a big firm is one which has 'in excess of 100 vehicles'.

The outstanding feature of the managements of these firms is that they are either made up of members of a single family or a single individual, who is both owner and manager. In other words, if the small firms are run and owned by several people, then these people tend to be of the same family. Five of the eight firms had managements with this characteristic. With the variance in the managements of firms in the road haulage industry it is likely that the conditions for employees will also vary. The chief advantage of working for a private enterprise firm seems to be that managers are known as individuals and can be identified by the drivers who can approach them and explain any difficulties. Examples of statements by managers on this aspect are quoted below:

> 'We have the ability to give the older men lighter work, on lighter vehicles or in the shed, or we can switch a man onto a delivery where they use a forklift truck (to off-load the vehicle). In a big organisation this would be hard to do. We are small and we can keep control of the situation. I know the men by their first names and I know their wives and kids.'
>
> Owner-managing director of family firm

This sort of intimacy also occurs in small branches of large 'public' (in the sense that the firm is a private enterprise joint stock company) firms. The manager of a South Wales branch of such a firm says:

> 'We find that the drivers from B.R.S. that have come to us, come to us because of the fact that they have lost their individuality. I know all the drivers here and also I know most of their families. I know how many children they've got and whether they've got troubles at home. They say the management at B.R.S. doesn't know them, which doesn't lead to happy working.'
>
> Branch Manager, Joint Stock Road Haulage Company

Closely connected with managements' view of the necessity of a close knowledge of the individual driver, is the view that lorry drivers are individuals and that they have responsibilities and have to be trustworthy as individuals.

> 'With a factory a manager has a better chance of controlling his men. He can watch them, they have to clock in and out and they have a foreman whereas with our "fellas" once they're away you

46

don't know where they are. If you've got six lorries all over the place, you don't know where they are. The driver's the boss when he leaves, you're the boss to guide him away but after that he's the boss.'

Manager-Owner of small firm

'The lorry driver is a much more independent person than you would normally find since he is on his own once he leaves the depot.'

Transport Manager, Joint Stock Road Haulage Company

'This job [being manager in transport] is bound up with people. Your success is bound up with the way you handle men. We employed a firm of management consultants. The lorry driver as such is a bit of a gipsy—the home life is not so hot in lorry driving. The lorry driver has more freedom than other people. He has a sense of power which you can't have in a factory or office.'

Manager and Director of family firm

'You should run the firm as a family unit. I will help them if I can but when a man is doing a job I leave him alone. One of my drivers I see once a week. He's always on time and he completes his full day's work. If a man knows what he's doing then there's no object at all in me telling him. So long as he is doing it okay then I leave him alone but if not then I'm on to him. If they have a tidy wagon and there are no shortages then I give them a bonus. If you spoke to ninety per cent they'd tell you that they feel hemmed in in a factory, they like the outdoor life.'

Owner-Manager of small firm

'The professional lorry driver is an individual in the strongest sense. Although he is subject to rules from the company and the Ministry of Transport, for the greater part of his working life he is not under direct supervision, which I think is why so many of them follow the life. I've actually known during my B.R.S. days, men who've gone into factory life and most of them have invariably returned to transport, only after a short period of indoor work, under constant supervision. Added to that there are the tramp drivers, which we don't have ourselves, which we see a lot of. In the case of a very small company they (the trampers) practically operate on their own for weeks on end, travelling to all parts of the country.'

Branch Manager, Joint Stock Road Haulage Company

These quotes of managers of private road haulage firms

indicate that they see the lorry driver as a workman who likes to have individual recognition by management. At the same time, managers of private firms find that it is advantageous to know their drivers well as these drivers are away from the depot for most of the time and are on trust with valuable vehicles and loads. The management structure of B.R.S. is such that individual recognition of the lorry driver may not be as great as in the private firm. The effect of this lack of recognition on the job and work satisfaction of the lorry driver is discussed later. A further point, which is important in the lorry driving ethos, is the fact that many firms in the industry are small and thus it would be possible for the driver to own his vehicle or even build up his own fleet of vehicles. This possibility of the opportunity to go into business on his own account, added to the amount of discretion that he has in his job, may well produce in the lorry driver less of a socialistic outlook than that of many other manual occupational groups of the same level.

(ii) *The Trade Unions*

There are two trade unions which cater for the lorry driver. These are the Transport and General Workers' Union, (T.G.W.U.), and the United Road Transport Workers' Association of England (U.R.T.W.A.E.). For lorry drivers north of the border there is the Scottish Horse and Motormen's Association with approximately 20,000 members. The T.G.W.U. is a general workers' union whose membership includes people from a wide variety of occupations. The report of the T.U.C. 1963 states that the membership of the T.G.W.U. was 1,330,962 in 1962. An estimate of the number of members who were lorry drivers is difficult to make. The union organises lorry drivers employed both inside and outside the road haulage industry. The U.R.T.W.A.E. in contrast to the T.G.W.U. is a union whose membership is almost exclusively made up of lorry drivers. The membership of the union in 1962 was 10,000. This union is known colloquially as 'The Manchester Union'. All in all, it is very difficult to say how many lorry drivers are organised but a reasonable estimate would be that at least half of the private haulage men are not in unions.

The lorry driver seems to be a difficult person to organise. An official of the T.G.W.U. stated that many drivers in private enterprise haulage firms do not like trade unions or strikes. Further, this official said, in an interview with the writer, that many of the firms were small and scattered widely over rural areas. This makes it very difficult for the union officials to recruit the drivers employed by visiting firms. A further complicating factor is the individualism and concept of opportunity amongst lorry drivers which sets up something of a barrier for the union organiser.

The T.G.W.U. is the main organisation (the U.R.T.W.A.E. plays a lesser part) which represents lorry drivers in negotiations over wages and conditions of employment through the negotiating machinery of the road haulage industry. The union also provides a legal service for drivers who get on the wrong side of the law. In spite of these benefits many lorry drivers are outside of union organisation. The pamphlet, published by the T.G.W.U. in 1962, which summarises wages and conditions applying to road haulage workers, tells the union member:

> You should keep in mind the fact that there are still Road Haulage employees enjoying the benefits of the work of the Union and who are not yet members. No opportunity should be lost to convince these non-members that it is to their advantage to join because this gives more power to the arm of the Trade Union representatives in their activities.
>
> *Transport and General Workers' Union: Summary of Wages and Conditions Applying to Road Haulage Workers, 1962*

An article in the *Sunday Times* on the scandals on the road haulage industry also makes the same point:

> '. . . The 'C' licence fleets are mostly closed shops—another reason why standards are better—but in the haulage business, only the biggest firms have anything like 100 per cent membership. London has a better solidarity than anywhere else because the London dockers are adamant in their refusal to work with any driver who cannot produce a card. But most other parts have apparently become more easy going in the last five or six years, so the only weapon of compulsion is blunted.'
>
> *Sunday Times*, 23rd August, 1964

ii i) *The Road Haulage Association*

The Road Haulage Association represents the independent road haulage firm and is an organisation which is joined voluntarily by road hauliers to further their interests as a group. The road haulage association is a body which acts on the administrative rather than the technical side of the road haulage industry, particularly with regard to licensing of vehicles and new entrants into the industry. As the representative body of the private haulier the Road Haulage Association publishes its own journal called *Road Way* monthly. The British Road Services organisation has recently (1964) shown the desire for closer connection with the R.H.A.

(iv) *The Ministry of Transport*

The Ministry of Transport is the executive body which has the duty of dealing with all aspects of transport in Britain. The Minister of Transport implements the policy on transport enacted by Parliament. The lorry driver comes into contact with the Ministry and its enforcement of rulings in that he has to fill in log sheets (showing his hours of work) and he is subjected to 'silent checks' on the movement of his vehicle. Also he can be stopped by officials at any time for a vehicle roadworthiness check. Many vehicles have been found to be in a condition which can only be described as a scandal to the safety of the public. The subject of unsafe vehicles has been mentioned earlier in this chapter but an illustration of the kind below gives emphasis to the issue.

> In fairness to the lorryman, Mr. Marples [Minister of Transport] pointed out that the police were only stopping lorries that looked possible offenders . . . Among the stopped lorries, there were bad brakes, loose or worn steering gear, broken springs, fractured chassis, and faulty lights. One gravel tipper had 22 faults.
>
> *Daily Express*, 14th July, 1964

The major institutions in the road haulage industry form the basis of the complex of rules which provide the source of ambiguity in the working life of the lorry driver. There are, however, more minor institutions with which the driver has a more voluntary association. Probably the foremost of these institutions is the transport café, which may or may not also provide accommodation for trampers and other long distance 'C' licence drivers.

(v) *The Transport Café and Transport Accommodation*

The transport café is used perhaps two or three times in a shift by lorry drivers. A stop is usually made for tea after two or three hours on shift; then a stop for a substantial meal is taken during the half-hour legal break after five and a half hours. A further tea break is then taken later in the shift. Tea breaks are taken when there is time. It is quite possible for a driver to go five hours without a cup of tea. The older drivers do not frequent the cafés so much as the younger ones, who can 'clog it' to gain the extra twenty minutes required. Many older drivers prefer to 'tootle along' and stop briefly in a layby for sandwiches and tea from a flask.

A detailed examination[8] of several transport cafés in a small area of Lancashire was made around 1953–4. The investigator, Soloman, came to the conclusion that the transport café is essential to the welfare of the lorry driver and that, as inspection by health authorities is 'noticeably lacking', the Ministry of Transport should at least approve the cafés and preferably supervise them.

Things have changed since Soloman made her study. The cafés have become larger, more impersonal, cleaner and more expensive, though the improved facilities probably justify the increase in prices.[9] There is still a wide range of cafés when they are classified in terms of these characteristics. Many cafés of the old type produce plain food—cooked meals of the beef, boiled potatoes and two vegetables variety ('a beef dinner'),

[8] Soloman, E. 'Transport Cafés: Their place in Modern Society.' Social Studies Dissertation. (Unpublished) Teacher's Certificate. Padgate Training College. 1954.

[9] Peter Dunn writing in *The Observer*, 16th February, 1964, entitles his article 'A caff on the motorway—or lorry-men steer clear'. He says, 'Three lorry drivers (in picture) stick to cups of tea at Top Rank's pull in on the M2. All three, including the coal driver with his back to the customer in a fur coat, think the motorway caféterias are too posh and expensive for them and want Mr. Marples to give them motorway caffs.'

apple tart and custard and the favourite bacon sandwich. In some of the newer cafés, the food is less plentiful and more on the fatty side (bacon, fried egg and chips), especially at night. Some drivers the writer met had stopped their patronage of the motorway cafés because of the 'lack of life' in them, as well as the greater expense. According to the November 1964 edition of *Headlight* a commercial organisation is to provide better facilities for the lorry driver. These will include showers and rest rooms for his exclusive use. This will be the height of luxury for the tramper and a significant improvement of facilities which are generally provided for him. In all fairness to the proprietors of transport houses there cannot be a great margin of profit from the price that drivers pay for evening meal, bed and breakfast. Drivers usually try to save enough from their subsistence allowance for meals during the day. Transport accommodation varies in quality, from the small house where several drivers may sleep in one room to the large transport 'hostel' where drivers have their own cubicle bedroom, hot water, and television lounge. The writer heard many tales of accommodation where proprietors or proprietresses made drivers as comfortable as was possible, but every now and again he met drivers with views on accommodation of which the following tale is typical:

> 'I was running with [a named driver] and he said about these digs in Newport. We went there and she almost pulled us inside, and I'm not surprised now that she did. I said to my mate "I'm not all that keen on this place." Well, he was a scruffy old bugger and he didn't mind, so I went upstairs. I took one look at the bed and came straight down again. I told her, "I'm off." She said, "What's the matter?" I said, "Well the place is scruffy and the bed's worse." She said, "The bed's all right, I've changed the sheets." I said, "Well, you should have changed the oil as well, cheerio." '

On the whole, however, the lorry driver has better accommodation than previously but there are still some establishments which could be improved considerably.

(vi) *Clearing Houses*

These are firms that gather information on loads and store

quantities of goods which arc waiting for shipment. The tramper who wants a return load to his home town may call at one of these firms and if he is lucky will get such a load. The house receives payment from the shipper of the goods, takes a percentage and pays the remainder to the transport firm whose driver and vehicle carries the goods. The writer heard grumbles from trampers concerning the difficulties of getting loads from these houses but their advertisements seem to proliferate in the *Headlight* magazine.

(vii) *Drivers' Clubs*

In competition to some extent with the T.G.W.U., are the more occupationally oriented drivers' clubs. These clubs, of which the 'Headlight Drivers' Association' and the 'Bedford Drivers' Club' are prominent, provide legal advice and insurance facilities. The Headlight organisation also inquires from time to time into the quality of transport accommodation. This organisation publishes a monthly magazine especially for lorry drivers called *Headlight*. *Headlight* contains both national and international news of the lorry driving world; legal advice on lorry drivers' questions; wages news; and also of some importance, accommodation advertisements. The magazine has a slight bias to the right of centre in politics, which probably reflects the general mood of the lorry driver employed by the private firm. This magazine does a good deal to identify lorry drivers as an occupational group and to provide some sort of ideal code of behaviour. This is discussed in a later chapter.

CONCLUSION

The picture of the lorry driver presented in this chapter is that of a skilled workman with a responsible job and one which can be dangerous. The type of skill required, together with expansion of the road haulage industry, tends to skew the age distribution of the lorry driving population towards youth. On the other hand, some of the most desirable characteristics a good lorry driver should possess are considerable experience and emotional stability, a maturity and reliability that usually only come with age. The interplay of these two factors, physical ability and maturity, turn out to be important determinants of the lorry driver's career pattern, which is the subject of Chapter III.

For all his skill and responsibility, the lorry driver is not all that well paid. His basic rate of pay varies according to age up to 21 years and then by carrying capacity of the vehicle. Average hourly earnings are well below those in 'All industry' (exclusive of agriculture), although average weekly earnings approach the average for all industry since the lorry driver works long hours. An eleven-hour-shift is prevalent amongst private haulage drivers and B.R.S. drivers have a ten-hour-shift. Working conditions in the road haulage industry vary a great deal from firm to firm. It would seem that the drivers of goods vehicles with 'C' licences have better conditions than drivers in the road haulage industry. Conditions in British Road Services are laid down with the agreement of the union and are clearly defined. The trade union is an accepted part of the industrial relations system at B.R.S. but this is not always the case in the private firms. This fact and the regional location and employment position make for variation in working conditions in private firms. There is less variation in wage rates than in a free market as firms can be prosecuted for paying below the minimum required by the Road Haulage Wages Council Orders. However, many private firms pay over the rate or give excellent bonuses which make some lorry drivers' earnings very high.

From this summary, the lorry driver emerges as something of an 'individualist'. His job, the driving itself, is done in semi-isolation where communication is by signals because of the boundary of the cab. The managements interviewed generally believed that lorry drivers like to have a large area of discretion in their job. This area of discretion arises from the separation of the driver from his depot and management for most of his working hours. The amount of discretion varies according to the type of driving job the driver has, whether it is shunting, tramping or trunking. Paradoxical to this substantive discretion is the fact the work situation is a complex of rules which emanate from various agencies. The driver's individualism may make him much more conscious of the rules in the total work situation. This consciousness will also vary between firms, the discretion of the driver will be less in the nationalised B.R.S. with its formalised set of rules, than in the smaller private haulage firms. The private firms can have a less formal system and allow greater discretion since the managements can have a personal knowledge of the drivers they employ.

It is possibly the way the industry has evolved which has created the individualism amongst lorry drivers. The chaotic conditions of the 1920s have subsided with the regulations imposed by the 1933 Road and Rail Traffic Act. In spite of this Act, the rapid growth of the industry since the war, coupled with the freeing of road haulage in 1953 has produced conditions in which the many rules and regulations are evaded. The evidence is that, in Gouldner's terms, the rules of the Ministry of Transport have to be seen as 'mock bureaucracy'. Either the lorry drivers do not obey them, or the firms do not, or there is collusion between the two parties to evade them. This collusion takes place in the private enterprise road haulage firms, whereas B.R.S. are on the whole extremely observant of the rules.

The trade unions are only weakly equipped to deal with the abuses that go on. The lorry driver is difficult to organise, particularly by a general union as big and diversified as the T.G.W.U. The emergence of more specialised associations, known generally as 'Drivers' clubs' are representative, at least to some extent, of competition for the trade unions. The clubs attempt to help the lorry driver without attempting to restrict him formally, although informally, attempts are made to induce him to behave in a way which is agreeable to the community as a whole.

There is an objective situation in the work environment which makes for the inability of the lorry driver to achieve and maintain a status ranking in the eyes of the general public. The existence of 'mock bureaucracy' through collusion of the managements of smaller private firms and their drivers in order to compete in what is a very competitive industry has produced scandals. The lorry driver may well be driving an ill-maintained vehicle and is very likely to be 'flogging his log' by working hours which are over the legal maximum. If managements see the lorry driver as an 'individualist', and attempt to conform with such expectations, then the lorry driver will inevitably see a deficit in terms of the social reputation of his group.

III

THE LORRY DRIVER'S CAREER

An incumbent of a particular status and its accompanying roles may be in that status only temporarily or for a lifetime. If a person remains in an occupational status or a particular set of occupational statuses we say that he makes a career in that occupation. Is lorry driving a career or are lorry drivers people who have taken up the occupation temporarily as a fill-in of some kind? If lorry driving is a career, in what sense is it so? The answer to this latter question depends very much on the definition of career which is adopted.[1]

E. C. Hughes in stating Mannheim's view of career, that it is a 'predictable course through a bureaucracy', says that this is career in the narrowest sense. Wilensky takes the view that the important element in career is the predictability of movement between jobs.

> A career viewed structurally, is a succession of related jobs, arranged in a hierarchy of prestige, through which persons move in an ordered predictable sequence. Corollaries are that the job pattern is instituted (socially recognised and sanctioned within some social unit) and has some stability (the system is maintained) over more than one generation of recruits.

The opposite view of these very narrow definitions of career is taken by Hughes who says:

[1] Hughes, E. C. 'The Study of Occupations' in Merton, R. K., Broom, L. and Cottrell, L. S., *Sociology Today: Problems and Prospects*, Basic Books Inc., New York, 1959. p. 455. Wilensky, H. L., 'Work, Careers and Social Integration', *International Social Science Journal*, No. 4, 1960. p. 554. Miller, D. C. and Form, W. H., *Industrial Sociology*, Harper Bros., New York, 1951.

Career in the most general sense, refers to the fate of a man running his life cycle in a particular society, at a particular time.

Like Hughes, Miller and Form prefer to give the term 'career' a much wider application but at the same time they do suggest that the career progression of an individual can be analysed in terms of five periods. Each of these periods isolates a broadly different relationship of the individual with his work.

The individual starts off in the 'preparatory period' in which the chief formal activities are confined to the schoolroom; this is transformed into the 'initial work period' in which part-time jobs are usually held while the individual is still being educated. Then comes the rather turbulent period of job changing in an effort to obtain realisation of goals—'the trial work period'. The 'stable work period' follows, when the worker has realised or rationalised his goals. The 'retired work period' is the period between finishing working and death.

As Miller and Form admit, there are many permutations and combinations of these periods, and they are only likely to be able to describe careers in the most general terms. Progression is not a function of age alone, there can be progression both vertically and horizontally at many age levels but this does not upset the general applicability of Miller and Form's analysis. The general implication is that the mobility is vertical but this, of course, need not be so.

As soon as the term 'career' is discussed in the widest possible use of the word the problem of the 'predictability' element occurs. Careers in the generic sense have a great deal about them that is predictable, but at the same time, there is a great deal that is not. Careers in the generic sense are certainly not 'predictable course(s) through a bureaucracy'. Nevertheless, as Hughes says,

> The career includes not only the processes and sequences of learning the techniques of the occupation but also the progressive perception of the whole system and of the possible places in it, and accompanying changes in the conception of the work, and of one's self in relation to it.[2]

For the purposes of analysing the career of the lorry driver certain assumptions are made. These are that:

[2] Hughes (1959) *op. cit.* p. 456.

1. Career is a progression, either vertical or horizontal through time, of the individual, in relation to jobs of work. This progression is usually from less to more desirable positions, although any one position may vary in desirability with factors like age.

2. Careers fall into broad patterns if particular occupations are investigated. It becomes possible to distinguish the broad general characteristics of career progression, and this may be done either by the members of the occupation, or by outsiders, or by both.

3. For the term career to become meaningful in the social-psychological sense, some element of predictability is necessary; this predictability being largely in relation to the individual's knowledge of choices of available positions within a given occupational system, and following the generally characteristic progression.

The findings will, as far as possible, be expressed in terms of the modal characteristics of the population of lorry drivers under investigation. It will not be always possible to describe a career curve in these terms, especially at the beginning and end of drivers' careers. The description of the lorry driver's career will be in terms of his passage through his total working life. Having stated the theoretical and methodological assumptions underlying the analysis, the main features of interest are: the early career, career continuity in lorry driving, career progression, and the end of the career.

TABLE 9

Occupations in the Pre-Lorry Driving Phase

Average Years in Type of Occupation	Trunkers	Trampers	Shunters
Static	3·03	3·91	3·08
Static but working with vehicles	0·03	0·52	0·13
Mobile	3·18	2·89	3·24
Total Average Pre-Lorry Driving Years	6·24	7·32	6·45

THE BEGINNING OF THE LORRY DRIVER'S CAREER

Due to legal restrictions no person may drive any kind of lorry until he is 17 years of age, and he may not drive a 'heavy' vehicle until he is 21 years of age. This means that every lorry driver must have an enforced trial work period in which a job other than lorry driving will be done. This period, according to Table 9, is between 6 and 7 years.

Occupations are classified into three types: static; static, but working with vehicles; and mobile occupations. The occupations in the pre-lorry driving phase may well be close enough to lorry driving to ensure that lorry driving is seen as a natural continuation. It is only the tramper who seems to have had more experience in static than mobile occupations in the pre-lorry driving phase. It appears that a mobile occupation on first leaving school points to lorry driving as an occupational choice in the later career which is fairly natural. In each type of driving job around half the average years of the pre-lorry driving phase have been spent in mobile occupations.

The most usual first occupation of a lorry driver is, as might be expected, that of lorry or van driver's mate, 17 per cent of the sample started their working life in this way. 10 per cent of the sample were errand boys when they first left school, while a further 16 per cent of the sample had first jobs which are classified as mobile.[3] All told, mobile occupations were taken as first jobs by 43 per cent of drivers in the sample. A further 6 per cent started off in a static job but working with vehicles in a garage. Between 45 per cent and 51 per cent of the drivers started off in static occupations such as factory work in general, bakery worker, etc. It might be expected that these men had less reason to become lorry drivers as they are less likely to meet the lorry driver in their early career and thus do not get the 'call of the road'. On the basis of these findings it is not possible to say that lorry drivers will tend to have a mobile first occupation. He is nearly as likely to have a mobile first occupation as not.

A comparison with the factory sample however, does indicate that the lorry driver is much more likely to be mobile in his first job than the factory worker who has had a static job for most of his career. In the factory sample only 10 people have ever had mobile jobs. While this constitutes 22 per cent of the

[3] See Appendix, Table 1. The First Jobs of Drivers.

sample, the years spent in mobile occupations, expressed as a percentage of the total career years in the sample is 4 per cent (39 years out of a total of 981 years). This comparison provides much stronger support for a hypothesis of the socialisation through physical mobility amongst lorry drivers, whether it is through taking a non-driving mobile job such as an errand boy, or by driving a light lorry at 17 years of age.

CAREER CONTINUITY

Can it be said that lorry driving is a career in the sense that a lorry driver tends to stay in his occupation or is it less of a career because he moves into and out of the occupation? Before any progression can exist in the career, there has to be continuity.

The most frequent age[4] for starting in the actual occupation of lorry driving is 17 years. Trampers tend to start later, the mode amongst them being 19 years. The mean average age for beginning in lorry driving in the sample is between 21 and 23 years. The mean average number of years spent in lorry driving varies according to the type of driver. Trampers, whose average age is 38 years, have spent least years, 12 years and 4 months, while trunkers and shunters (whose group mean average age is 44 and 46 years respectively) have both spent 21 years on average in the occupation.

The number of years spent away from the occupation is also indicative of career continuity. This again varies by the type of driver. The trunkers have on average spent 30 per cent of their total careers away from lorry driving, trampers 49 per cent, and shunters 37 per cent. A consideration of years away from the occupation once the driver has entered lorry driving provides an even stronger argument for saying there is great career continuity. The percentage of the total career spent in lorry driving after first entry ranges from 90 per cent for trampers to 96 per cent for shunters. The years spent away after first entry when expressed as a percentage of total career are 6 per cent for trunkers, 10 per cent for trampers, and 4 per cent for shunters. The average numbers of years spent away

---

[4] See Appendix, Table 2. Aspects of Lorry Drivers' Careers.

after first entry are 1, just over 2, and just over 1 for the three types of driver respectively.

While it is not a case of 'once a lorry driver always a lorry driver' it certainly appears that once in their occupation lorry drivers do, on the whole, stay in it for considerable periods. The same cannot be said of the men in the factory sample.

The career continuity in terms of single occupations is very low compared with the career continuity of the lorry drivers. There are several men in the sample who have had long periods in coal mining. Even in coal mining, men start as collier's boys, then become colliers, and then move to lighter surface jobs. It is most likely that there is a more marked 'age–strength' effect in mining than in lorry driving, which forces men to the surface again. The longest continuous career in the sample is that of a fitter, who reported some 45 years in fitting of one sort or another. Even in this man's career however there was a variety of occupations ranging from apprentice fitter up to chief engineer, and back down to general factory maintenance fitting. The biggest single set of occupations in the sample were those in factory work other than fitting in factories. Although there is considerable continuity here, in that the 41 men who had been engaged in general factory work, as opposed to fitting, had been so for 10 years on average, there were many different occupations held under this very general classification.

In lorry driving there is a career continuity which is present to a great enough extent to enable consideration of a career progression or career cycle in meaningful terms.

THE CAREER PROGRESSION

It seems reasonable to suppose that the various types of lorry driving job will be done by men with certain biographical characteristics. Each of the types of driving job are so different from the others that definite selection of jobs by certain men will be, at least in theory, possible. Once the lorry driver has taken up his occupation there is a definite progression through the different driving jobs. This progression is indicated in three ways: the present average age of the men in each type of driving job, and the average age on first entry into the different jobs; the driving experience of those men in each category; and lastly in terms of aspiration to the various categories of driving job.

AGE AND CAREER PROGRESSION

It was suggested in Chapter II that certain sensory, psycho-motor, and physical abilities were necessary in a lorry driver's job. Clearly the effects that age has on these abilities will be important determinants of career cycles in lorry driving, and will heavily influence the selection of the types of driving job at various age levels. The progression through the driving jobs is from local driving or shunting, to tramping, then trunking, and finally shunting. Shunters in the sample have a higher mean age (46 years) than trunkers (44 years) or for trampers (38 years) but there is a bi-modal distribution of shunters by age.[5] The shunters who have had no driving job other than shunting are on average much younger than the shunters who have also had experience in tramping or trunking.

TABLE 10

The Age of Shunters

Shunters who have been	*Average Age (Years)*	*No. of Shunters*
Shunters only	33·69	13
Shunters and Trampers	49·50	12
Shunters and Trunkers	45·33	3
Shunters, Trampers and Trunkers	56·90	10
All Shunters	45·71	38

The progression in terms of present ages of the drivers in various groups is from shunting, to tramping, to trunking and back to shunting. The psycho-physiological determinants of

[5] See Appendix, Table 2. Aspects of Lorry Drivers' Careers.

this progression are largely through changes in the level of the abilities required for driving, with age. As age increases, an impairment of the efficiency of all the senses is usual.[6] Eyesight is not as good in later life as in youth, and reaction times tend to become longer. There is, to a great extent, however, the existence of a compensating emotional and personal stability and also the learning of cues for danger in middle age. The age–strength threshold is also reached by the time the driver is 40 to 45 years of age. The driver will overcome the age–strength threshold difficulty by moving out of tramping and into trunking. Trunking, being a night driving job, is heavy on the eyes, and also requires quick response to meet crises particularly on runs where the schedules are tight.[7] This eventually means a movement back into shunting. There is a case for suggesting that the selection of types of driving jobs is to some extent a function of psycho-physiological changes with age.

Driving Experience and Career Progression

An examination of the experience of the drivers in the sample in the various driving jobs supports the supposition that drivers progress by age from local driving or shunting, to tramping, trunking and finally back to shunting. This progression is shown in diagrammatic form as Figure 1. If the supposition about the age progression is correct, it is to be expected that trunkers will, for the most part, have held both shunting and tramping jobs, and that trampers will have held jobs in

[6] Griew, S. *Job Re-design. Employment of Older Workers I.* O.E.C.D. Paris 1964. Chapter 6 'Ageing and Skilled Performance' and Chapter 3. 'Age and Physical Working Capacity'.

[7] 'Dark adaptation—the ability to see more quickly after varying periods of time in the darkness—is slower, both for the younger and older age groups. The linear correlation between age and the final level of dark adaptation is actually so high that it may be used to predict age with narrow limits of error.' ($r = 0.89$). McFarland, R. A. and Fisher, M. B. *Journal of Gerontology*, Vol. 10. 1955.

The findings of Shock, N. W. (1952) that the efficiency of the homeostatic mechanism is impaired with age, which is particularly important in the ability to adjust in occasions of stress, are quoted in McFarland, R. A., Moseley, A. L. and Fisher, M. B. 'Age and the Problems of Trunk Drivers', *Journal of Gerontology*, Vol. 9. 1954.

shunting but not in trunking. Shunters have already been presented as being divided into two categories, the younger age group has had little experience other than shunting, and the older age group of shunters have very likely had experience in either trunking or tramping or both.

With all three types of driver interviewed, the mention of entry into the various types of driving followed the supposed pattern. For all three types of driver the age on entry into shunting or local driving is lower than the age on entry into tramping. Both these entry ages were lower than the entry into trunking. The order of age progression is that trunkers progressed through all the categories at an earlier age than trampers, who progressed through at an earlier age than the shunters. Trunkers have, for the most part, had some experience in the other types of driving. Over three-quarters of the trunkers have been trampers or shunters at ages lower than their entry into trunking. Trampers on the other hand have much less experience of trunking (only 18 per cent of trampers have been trunkers) than shunting (82 per cent of trampers have been shunters). For shunters the percentage who have been trunkers is 34 per cent compared with 58 per cent who have had experience as trampers. The lower percentage of shunters who have been trunkers may be explainable in terms of the job content in relation to age; it may be that a trunker gets set in his ways and out of practice at lifting heavy weights which the job of shunting demands. It may be that a trunker is physically incapable of doing a shunting job after being a trunker for so long. Many trunkers probably retire from lorry driving altogether after they are no longer able to go trunking. The attitude to shunting, as a job, will be the key to discovering why more trunkers do not return to shunting.[8]

Aspiration to the Various Types of Driving Job

How far do lorry drivers have a 'perception of the whole occupational system and their places in it'? To what degree is any particular driving job recognised as the 'top' driving job? The vertical axis in Figure 1 is essentially an indication of

[8] See Appendix, Table 2. Aspects of Lorry Drivers' Careers.

prestige. Trunking is shown as the job with the highest prestige, while tramping holds second place, and shunting has the lowest prestige, as it is either the first or the last job held.

There seems to be some kind of recognition of the prestige of driving jobs and the career progression by the lorry drivers themselves, though this is not entirely unambiguous. This perspective is the basis of the indicator used for the prestige axis. However the recognition is not completely in pure career terms but rather in terms of the relative advantages and disadvantages of the different kinds of driving. For instance, there are domestic and social advantages of having a trunking or shunting job as opposed to being a tramper.

> 'The trunk work is for the convenience of my wife—there was difficulty at home, my wife had an operation; and from "shunt" to "trunk" is a step up.'

Money enters in also:

> 'Fortnight about (i.e. shunting for a fortnight and then trunking for the following fortnight) is a better paid job.'

Trunking may also be more secure:

> 'Years ago if you were a trunk driver they kept their trunk drivers—when the depression was on you would be the last to go and service would count.'

The progression from trunking back to shunting is also mentioned. In this case a trunker predicts that this is the way his career will go, but for this man the family factor was also relevant.

> 'The girls will have finished school and I'll apply for a lighter job when I'm about 55.'

Another trunker who was talking about the status of lorry drivers gave a clue to a different kind of progression.

> 'The wife tends to think that lorry drivers are fucking bums and what disturbs me is that she must think the same of me. The progression used to be local, tramp, trunk, and that's as far as you could go, but not today—shunting is the top job.'

This last statement implies that shunting is the job which is aspired to as opposed to trunking. On the other hand, the

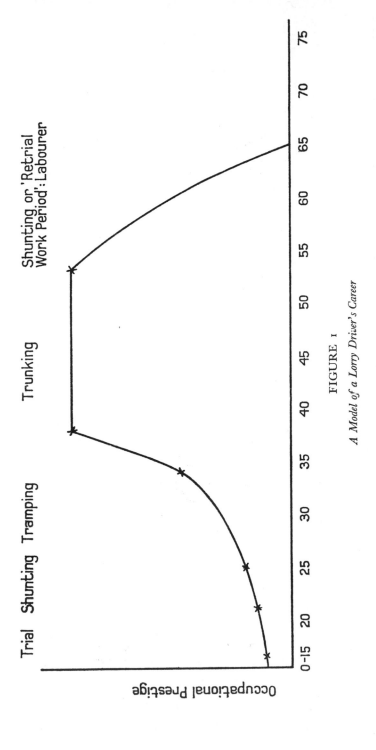

FIGURE 1

A Model of a Lorry Driver's Career

FIGURE 2
Determinants in the Lorry Driver's Career Pattern

Age	15–20 years	21–25 years	26–35 years	36–55 years	56–65 years
	Trial Work Period	Shunting (1)	Tramping	Trunking	Shunting (2) or Retrial Work Period
Situation	Incumbence in a non-driving mobile occupation or an occupation from which driving is a 'visible' occupation.	More a local delivery driving job than a real shunting job, where trunkers are serviced. If the driver is between 17 and 21 the vehicle driven will be under 3 tons.	Driving heavy goods vehicles to all parts of the country on a schedule determined by where the work is to be found. Loading and unloading as well as driving.	Set journeys: night work with the possibility of staying one day in two away from home compared with 4 days to the week in tramping.	Shunting on local work, 'servicing' trunkers' vehicles; often loaded and unloaded by cranes.
Factors in movement into an occupation.	General but the 'trial work period' is enforced by legal restrictions on the ages of drivers.	Gaining experience before insurance restrictions are lifted. Socialisation.	Socialisation: learning to load various types of goods, to sheet and rope a load and unloading. Also where to pick up loads.	Trunking; a job for experienced drivers.	Needs a lighter local job such as shunting where loads handled by crane. May move into labouring of one kind or another since transport firms may not have any jobs other than for drivers.
Factors in movement out of an occupation.	The 'visibility' of driving making it a natural next move. Also possibly alienation from other occupations (See Chapter VII)	Long distance work is more adventurous and less monotonous than local work. The driver has by now family responsibilities which can be financed by long distance work. Long distance driving is a natural progression from short distance work.	The age-strength threshold is reached. The driver can no longer load or unload easily. Family and community pressure. The comforts of home and companionship of friends in home community, the loneliness of wives and the desire for family life.	Psycho-physiological changes—vision—the homeostatic mechanism. Night work. Domestic problems: wife needs company. More community life required by the driver himself.	Retirement.

following statement by a trunker indicates that some trunkers at least, perceive their type of driving job to have the most skill and prestige.

'Trunking—there's less traffic at night. You can keep to your time, and you're with your own class of people—you all know one another.'

Certainly, the figures used to illustrate career continuity show a similarity between trunkers and shunters, which tends to put in doubt a hypothesis that trunking is the driving job for the lorry drivers with the greatest career orientation. The aspirations of lorry drivers to the various types of driving job will show whether in fact the recognition of a 'top' driving job exists and to what extent it exists. If the aspiration pattern does not fit in with the progression, then the drivers' perspectives of the various types of driving job should reveal the reason for this.

There is a strong identification with present occupation: 67 per cent of trunkers think the best job is trunking; 52 per cent of trampers think tramping the best driving job; and 58 per cent of shunters think shunting the best job.[9] Overall, however, trunking is the preferred job, with 40 per cent of the sample mentioning it. Shunting is next with 35 per cent and tramping least favoured with 25 per cent of drivers in the sample preferring it. In the private haulage firm tramping is definitely the least favoured job and trunking definitely the most favoured. At B.R.S. shunting is the most favoured job and tramping and trunking are favoured equally. Within the occupational categories the most noticeable thing is the lack of preference for tramping. No shunters say they prefer tramping, while only 4 (11 per cent) of trunkers opt for tramping. On the other hand, 16 (32 per cent) of trampers prefer trunking, and 16 (42 per cent) of shunters prefer trunking.

Indication of the progression being aspired to is apparent from the table but rather tenuously so. More trunkers prefer shunting than prefer tramping. More trampers prefer trunking than shunting, and shunters prefer shunting and trunking but not tramping. This information, coupled with a knowledge of

[9] See Appendix, Table 3. The Best Type of Driving Job.

the relative present ages of the types of driver, shows an aspiration pattern along the lines of the suggested progression from shunting and local, to tramp, trunk and back to shunting.

There is not a complete congruency between the aspiration pattern and the suggested career progression. Tramping can be worse in some firms than in others. At B.R.S. 31 per cent of drivers prefer tramping, whereas in the private firm only 15 per cent of the drivers prefer tramping. One tramper at B.R.S., who had been employed by the private firm as a tramper, when asked what he liked about working for his present firm said:

> 'You get a fair crack of the whip—you're required to do a certain amount of work a day and you get paid for it and no more; with a private firm you're expected to work all hours. On B.R.S. if you have an accident, they will see to it—with a private firm you're out, and you don't have to take out faulty vehicles on B.R.S. I was on for (X private firm) for "x" months and I was there a week without getting out of my overalls. I just had four hours' kip while waiting to load or tip.'

The shunter's aspirations should vary by age, if he follows the pattern which fits in with the career progression. Although this is by no means completely true, the overall picture is that of the younger shunter aspiring to a long distance job to a greater extent than the shunters aged 41 years and over.[10]

At this stage in the argument it appears that there is a 'top' driving job, in that trunking is modally preferred. It is by no means exclusively preferred. There are obviously many other variables affecting the aspirations of drivers besides that of the lorry driver's perception of his place in an occupational system. Job content is one such variable affecting aspiration; personality and family responsibility are others. In this connection drivers were asked which type of driving job they preferred, why they had this preference, and also to give their reasons for not preferring the other types of job.

The main reason for liking trunking seems to be that it is a straightforward driving job with no loading and unloading and that it is done at night when the roads are clear.

[10] See Appendix, Tables 4 and 5. Aspiration and Type of Driving Job Held and Shunters, Age and Aspiration Pattern.

'Trunking—you run from depot to depot, you don't touch your own load, and you know what you're doing and where you're going.'

Money, and the skill and comradeship involved in trunking are also given as reasons for liking trunking.

Trunking is disliked because of the lack of variety in it.

'You do the same run over and over, it gets monotonous; if you're on the same run you get over confident with the road whereas if you're on a different run you keep your eye open all the time.'

This characteristic is mentioned mainly by trampers who get a great deal of variety, both in terms of runs and of different loads carried. Many drivers dislike trunking because it involves working at night with obvious consequences for their social and domestic life. Trunking is also considered bad for health. The absence of physical activity is considered to be fattening, while night driving has adverse effects on the eyes.

Tramping, in contrast to the monotony of trunking, is mainly liked for the variety it affords, both in the types of loads carried, the different parts of the country which are seen, and also because tramping is a job where more social contacts can be made than in trunking. Autonomy is a big factor in tramping even when the job is viewed as clashing with domestic life.

'You're your own boss while you're away, and you run the job to suit your own feeling.'

'I shouldn't like it. I'm a married man with children, but it's the freedom.'

Another interesting feature of the view of tramping is that it is seen as a job which is skilled since it involves the successful performance of a number of separate tasks.[11] Trunking is viewed as a highly skilled job in terms of driving:

[11] This point is demonstrated in the differences between the three technical levels in coal mining. Unmechanised mining and fully mechanised mining means that the miner must perform several tasks. *Organisational Choice*, Trist, E. L., Higgin, G. W., Murray, H., Pollock, A. B. Tavistock Publications Ltd., London 1963.

Also Georges Friedmann *The Anatomy of Work*. Heinemann, London 1961, offers job rotation as a solution to the problem of diminishing returns to the division of labour through alienation.

'and some of these trunkers are the best drivers of the lot.'

but a tramper takes into account the art of loading a lorry, when he considers the total skill level.

'You load your own motor and you know what's on the motor.'

There is also the variety and interest taken in actually finding a load to take back, which gives some satisfaction, although loading and unloading generally are more likely to be a source of dissatisfaction than satisfaction in a tramper's job.

'and you get the experience of finding different loads.'

The major complaint about tramping is that it keeps the driver away from home too much and interferes with his domestic life.

'I loved it [tramping] but now its just the same as going away from home. I made some wonderful friends on tramping and I've still got them. A Newcastle bloke sent down a message by one of our drivers asking how I was getting on, and the foreman at "X" Firm in Watford never misses.'

A tramper like the ex-tramper above may lead two lives in the social sense in that a lot of his friends will be friends he has met at work. This compensates to some extent for being away from home so much, but it does not always stop comments about bad accommodation. The loading, unloading, and waiting around also makes some lorry drivers dislike tramping, but by far and away the biggest reason for disliking tramping is the fact that it takes the tramper away from his home and family for long periods.

Shunting is liked, on the other hand, because of its regularity and the fact that it is a local job which allows the driver to have a domestic life.

'Shunting is best they're home every night, and they know what time they're going to be home.'

The worst features of shunting are considered to be that it is a heavy job:

'Shunting is mostly manual labour.'

which is often done against a tight schedule:

'Shunting is very awkward, you're running to time all the time as you have to have the wagon back for the trunker.'

72

Some lorry drivers in the sample, most of them trampers, say that they find local work does not interest them, it is monotonous going around one small area all the time.

In modal terms trunking is the 'top' lorry driving job, but the many different factors, which drivers take into account when thinking about which job is best, make for some ambiguity in the prestige system.

'A skilled lorry driver starts right at the bottom and goes right through the lot—you start at local and you get to trunk. The modern idea is to get handling the bigger vehicles earlier. Night trunk or night tramp has disadvantages, with home life, but with the actual job it is better as the traffic is not so dense. With family ailments you may have to drop money and take a job local. Shunting is too heavy for me at the moment.'

The reasons given for entering the various jobs reinforces the impression of multiple factors in the types of driving job preferred.

TABLE 11

Reasons for Changing Jobs Given in Employment Histories

Reasons for Moving into	Shunting (for First Time)	Tramping	Trunking	Shunting (for Second Time)
Money	7	16	5	1
Preferred Job	9	12	12	4
Domestic Reasons	1	1	9	8
Just a Job	46	21	4	—
Accidents or Illness	—	—	2	4
Changes to or within Firm	7	25	20	9
Learned to Drive	15	5	—	—
Other Reasons	9	6	—	—
Not Known	14	9	7	—
TOTAL	108	95	59	26

There seems to be little significance in the differences of numbers of drivers moving into certain types of driving because they prefer that kind of driving job. The greatest significant movement in this sense seems to be that of shunters who move into shunting for a second time but even so these numbers are very small. The most significant aspect of Table 11 is that it shows that many drivers start driving because it seems the next logical step in their career after the trial work period. Hughes[12] implies that the individual has limited choice in this sense when he says:

> 'They [occupations] vary also in their demand for full and lasting commitment and in the age and life-phase at which one must decide to enter training for them. Some occupations are more visible to young people than are others, and effective visibility varies also by class and other social circumstances.'

This argument clearly has some relevance when it is considered that the greatest part of the lorry drivers moving into lorry driving for the first time, either in shunting, local work, or tramping, give the reason as being just a job that they took at the time. In many cases driving was an occupation which they took up in the armed services during war-time or national service. These kind of reasons given for taking the job (i.e. 'Just a job' and 'learned to drive') amount to 56 per cent of the reasons given by drivers for taking up shunting for the first time. With tramping such reasons amount to 27 per cent of the total, while for trunking the figure is much lower at 7 per cent. Thus about half the drivers seem to start in occupations which are for the most part unskilled but in some way connected with driving or the mobility involved. They then seem to drift into driving since this seems to them the logical next step, in the sense that it is the most visible occupation to them. Changes within the firm or movement between firms are the biggest single reason for drivers moving into tramping and even more so into trunking.

While it is noticeable that not many drivers are like the ones quoted below, in that they for the most part do not take up lorry driving out of a positive desire,

> 'As a kid you like lorries.'

> 'Where I live there was a bus garage and I was always itching to drive. I took a bus out once, you should have seen the headlines in the local paper "12 Year Old Boy Drives Bus in Bare Feet." Yes, I always wanted to drive.'

[12] Hughes, E. C. (1959). *op. cit.* p. 456.

It is apparent that the reason of positively preferring the job is given by a larger proportion of drivers in the trunking categories than the other categories. This may be a sign of increased socialisation into the occupation. 20 per cent of drivers who moved into trunking did so because they preferred the job.

'That's bettering yourself' (moving from tramping to trunking)

'Seniority—I moved on to trunk' (moving from tramping to trunking).

This is compared with 8 per cent for shunting (first time); 13 per cent for tramping, and 11 per cent for shunting (second time). An interview with the freight manager at B.R.S. revealed that:

'All trunk positions within the depot are advertised; usually about six trampers apply. We have agreed with the trade union to take the senior man (i.e., the man with longest service with the firm) provided that he's suitable. We are not always able to select the most suitable man due to the union ruling. Usually, if a man has given suitable tramping service and he's not accident prone, then it's all right.'

This would indicate that there is a definite preference for the trunking jobs as there is careful institutional regulation of their allocation. A further point of interest are the reasons which are given for movement into tramping. Sixteen drivers say that they moved into this type of driving job because it offered more money, as it is a long distance driving job. It seems again a natural progression to move from local to long distance driving but family commitment obviously affects the lorry driver here. Tramping is done with full sized vehicles which again means more pay for the driver, and the job seems to be held between the ages of 25 and 35 years. These years are often those of maximum family responsibility for the driver.[13] It is through the tramping that the driver gains the

[13] An increase in the number of children in a household will reduce the standard of living of individuals in the household unless the family income is increased, Fogarty (1961) says,

'A three child working class family needs 2 to 3 times the income of a single person, in cash or kind, to enable it to keep up the same living standard.'

experience to do the job with the highest prestige of all, trunking. However, tramping may be taken up at a time when the driver is newly married which may cause difficulties in his relationship with his wife. Through tramping the driver is able to build a home in the economic sense but not so much in the social or emotional sense.

THE END OF THE DRIVER'S CAREER

The indication from Figure 1 showing a model of a most usual lorry driver's career is that the end of the driver's career means a fall in occupational prestige. This can happen in two ways: either the driver moves out of trunking into shunting and loses the prestige of high income and the long distance job; or he leaves lorry driving altogether and takes up another job, which usually involves a drop in income and also some re-

---

The differences between living standards in the childless household and the dependent family household are not eradicated by 'Social income'. Jackson, J. M. (1961). See also Robertson, D. J (1961) section on Family Incomes, p. 170–71. Brennan, T. (1955) and Williams, G. (1956) both qualify the position on income and family needs. Brennan states that the 'old established unit of "bread winner and dependent family" has disappeared as the typical family structure'. Only one in six households is in the situation in which there is only one earner and any dependant at all child or adult. Williams suggests that it is only for 18 years out of a total working life of 50 years that most wage earners have dependants. She says,

'In more than 60 per cent of families the family is completed within the first ten years of marriage.'

This suggests that the family responsibility of the first ten years are likely to be heaviest between 25–35 on average.

Wilensky (1960) has a straight forward passage on the relationship between the family as a consuming/producing unit at different stages of the age/career cycle of the principal earner.

Fogarty, M. P. *The Just Wage*. Geoffrey Chapman, London 1961. (See especially Table 3. Coefficients of Working Class Family needs. p. 169). Jackson, J. M. 'Wages, Social Income and the Family' *Manchester School of Economics and Social Studies*. Vol. 29, No. 1, 1961. Robertson, D. J. *The Economics of Wages*. Macmillan and Co., London 1961. Brennan, T. 'Household Structure and Family Income.' *Scottish Journal of Political Economy* 1955. Williams, G. 'The Myth of Fair Wages' *Economic Journal* 1956. Wilensky, H. L. 'Work, Careers and Social Integration' *International Social Science Journal*. No. 4. 1960. pp. 449–50.

training or learning of a new occupation. This is a modal picture and as such it does not exclude a gain in status through realised aspiration, such as becoming a foreman, traffic manager, or perhaps even owning a fleet of vehicles.

The evidence from both the café sample and the firms sample is that there is a dropping out of the occupation when drivers reach 50 years of age. The café sample contained no driver over the age of 60 while the firms sample showed a more even age distribution but still a slight falling out after 60.

TABLE 12

Percentage Age Distribution by Firm and Driving Job

Age-Group	Trunkers	Trampers	Shunters	B.R.S.	P.H.	Total
21–30	5	29	16	19	20	20
31–40	30	25	24	19	36	26
41–50	43	32	18	31	18	26
51–60	19	14	29	21	26	23
61–70	3	—	13	10	—	6
Per Cent	100	100	100	100	100	100
Number	37	44	38	62	39	101

Table 12 also illustrates very clearly the age factor in the career progression. After about 50 if a lorry driver stays in the occupation it is likely to be as a shunter. Age and lorry driving is also to some extent a function of the type of firm that a driver works for. The table shows that it is much more difficult to stay at work as a lorry driver in a private firm than at B.R.S. This is interesting in that it is suggestive of considerable differences in working conditions between the two types of firm.

The first possibility for the end of the lorry driver's career is that he will spend it in lorry driving as a shunter. The career of the local driver shown in Table 13 is one of a man who is 70 years old and who, in an interview with management was especially mentioned as a man who did an excellent job.

77

TABLE 13

Ending a Driving Career in Driving

Occupation	Types of Firm	Dates	Reasons for Leaving
Not Given	—	1905–15	—
Artillery Driver	Army	1915–19	Demobbed
Local Driver	Private Haulier	1919–48	Nationalised
Tramper	B.R.S.	1948–51	Appendix taken out—heavy work on tramp
Trunker	B.R.S.	1951–2	Appendix trouble
Local Driver	B.R.S.	1952–63	—

The second possibility is that the lorry driver may end his working life in a job other than lorry driving. Within this possibility there are two separate paths which may be taken. The first of these is a downward mobility due to an 'enforced' retirement from the occupation while the other is a voluntary retirement due to a realised ambition. It is more likely that the driver will suffer 'enforced' retirement (retirement due to a physical need or to family and community pressure) than that he will realise his ambition. Such drivers take a downward path in prestige terms. They get a job which is 'static' and they have to make some sacrifices, perhaps in money terms or perhaps in more general social and occupational prestige terms. The more general lowering of prestige is through having to undergo a 'retrial' work period of some kind although this does not always mean a drop in income. The career of the 58-year-old, ex-trunker in Table 14 is a case in point.

This particular man was lucky enough to obtain as much money in his labouring job as in his driving job but he still suffers in prestige terms as illustrated in the following conversation with the writer.

Writer 'So it's from tea boy to tea boy is it?'

Ex-Driver 'What do you mean tea boy to tea boy?'

Writer 'I mean that you made tea in your first job and you're making tea now.'

Ex-Driver 'Making tea aye I do, I don't mind that but the trouble is you can't tell these young fuckers here anything.'

TABLE 14

Ending a Driving Career outside Driving:
Downward Mobility

Occupation	Type of Firm	Dates	Reason for Leaving
Horse Stable Boy	Private Haulier	1918–22	His old woman started to be boss—she wanted me to fuck her—she didn't get enough
Lorry Driver	Building Contractor	1922–3	Shortage of work. Too far away
Miner	Colliery	1923	Didn't like underground
Quarryman	Quarry	1923	No work (Redundant)
Lorry Driver	Building Contractor	1923	No work (Redundant)
Plant Driver	Sand & Gravel Merchant	1924–6	I had a row because they put me on the shovel, I was a very surly lad when I was about 30; they could fuck it or fight it, but when you're older you have to be more careful
Transport Trunker	Heavy Haulier	1926–7	I didn't want to take a hard tyred wagon out
Driver	Retailers	1927–9	Not Given
Lorry Driver	Sand & Gravel Merchant	1929–32	Not Given
Driver	—	1932–40	Not Given
Lorry Driver	Private Haulier	1940–2	Had a row
Trunker	Private Haulier Van Dept.	1942–8	Nationalised
Trunker	B.R.S.	1948–63	I promised family I'd finish if I could get another job with as much money
Labourer	Garage	1963	—

Writer   'How come?'

Ex-Driver   'Well you know on a (named make of lorry) it won't lock round all the way will it. I had just finished greasing her for a (named firm) and one of the drivers down here—they do nothing but take these wagons back to firms after we've greased and repaired them—he comes up and says "I'll take her off." I said, "Aye you'll need to bring her half off on one lock, go back

79

and then lock her over again and then come straight". "No," says the driver, "I'll get her out in one", I says "You please yourself." Well out he came and caught the side of the tank on the steelwork at the side of the garage. Well (a named firm) don't like their petrol bowsers all scratched and dented. He was still in the cab and I went over to him and said, "(the customer— a named firm) will give you a prize for the fucking marvellous job you've done on that tank and paint work." I didn't hang around to see what he thought about it, but there you are see, you can't tell them anything, you're only a fucking greaseboy to them.'

TABLE 15

Ending a Driving Career outside Driving:
Upward Mobility

Occupation	Type of Firm	Dates	Reasons for Leaving
Apprentice Sawyer	Timber Mill	1928–31	There was a slump on— I only had apprentice's wages and I needed the money
Dumper and Digger	Brickworks	1931–9	Called up
Driver	Army	1939–46	Demobbed
'C' Tramper	Brickworks	1946–51	The man in the office got awkward, so I had an argument and left
Tramper	B.R.S.	1951–2	Asked by the management to change about
Trunker/ Shunter	B.R.S.	1952–5	Promotion
Foreman	B.R.S.	1955–8	Depot closed—unfit because of coal workings
Yard Foreman	B.R.S.	1958–61	Depots amalgamated
Foreman	B.R.S.	1961	The vacancy occurred
Senior Foreman	B.R.S.	1961–3	—

Many other drivers on leaving driving go 'into the sheds' and load and unload lorries, or become 'yard men' sweeping up and doing odd jobs such as filling lorries with diesel fuel, or acting as gatemen. In the writer's experience these men like to hear from the drivers what has gone on 'up the road' during a shift.

Some drivers get out of driving before retirement is 'forced' upon them in that they are upwardly mobile in occupational terms through the realisation of ambition or perhaps just through chance or 'visibility' as in the case of the senior foreman at a B.R.S. depot in the Midlands.

Some drivers get junior managerial jobs away from the transport industry altogether while others are lucky enough to get on in the transport industry as with the man above. The interviews with representatives of management revealed that three of the representatives of managements of nine firms had in fact been lorry drivers. Two of these now owned their own firm while the third was a traffic manager. The certainty is however that many more drivers have ambitions than actually realise them.

In the firms sample almost exactly two-thirds of the drivers said that they expected to spend the rest of their working lives in driving, while 29 per cent said that they did not so expect and 4 per cent said they did not know one way or the other. Of the 29 drivers in the sample who say that they do not expect to spend the rest of their working lives in lorry driving, 10 give the desire to find an alternative occupation as the reason:

'No—I have ambitions to be a representative.'

'No—not all driving; as I get older I may go into a factory.'

While 3 other drivers in the sample say they will give up driving for domestic reasons:

'No—I'll have to pack it up sometime to have some family life.'

'It's hard to say: if the opportunity arose that I could get an inside job with equal pay and be home with the family every night, I'd not refuse it.'

Other drivers are quite certain that they will leave driving but do not indicate what they will do instead.

'No, I'd like to get inside.'

For some drivers age and physical condition is an important consideration when answering the question on expectation.

'Yes, but I expect to drop back, you can't keep on night tramp. When I'm about 60, I'll be better off in a local job.'

'No but I'll stay in transport, but as you get older you don't want to keep driving up.'

'No—its a job for a younger man, I shall not try to cling on if I'm failing in any way—with the eyes for instance.'

The end of a driver's career is likely to be marked by a fall in status:[14] either because the driver takes a local job of shunting and thus suffers a drop in income, or because he leaves the transport industry and the occupation of driving altogether and has to learn another occupation.

CONCLUSION

We have shown that the lorry driver is consistent in his attachment to his occupation. Within the occupation he progresses through a series of statuses, from short to long distance work and, if he is lucky, back to short distance work in the industry. The socialising agencies are largely internal to the occupation, excepting the ever present physical visibility factor. Men in factories, on building sites, and in warehouses are able to see lorry driving as an occupation which they could take up. In the case of the lorry driver's mate, to become a lorry driver would seem a natural progression. Once in the industry handling the 'big stuff' carries more prestige as does driving long distance. The family undoubtedly plays a big part here as more money can be earned at tramping than shunting, and the tramping phase tends to come when the lorry driver has a young family. The experience at tramping gives him the ability to do the top night trunking jobs. It is in this sense that the lorry driver's career is structured, he has a definite career pattern which he is likely to follow. There is also some evidence that his definition of the situation is that this is the progression he will follow. The conception of career amongst lorry drivers is more blurred when the end of the career is discussed. There is a divergence between expectations of the lorry drivers on the one hand, and the age statistics on the other. While the road haulage industry is still young there can be no really

[14] A similar process occurs with fishermen. See 'Fishermen on the Beach', Chapter 12 in *The Fishermen*. Tunstall, J. McGibbon & Kee. London. 1962.

objective proof that lorry driving involves a retrial work period towards the end of the career. However, it would seem that there is a discrepancy between the numbers of lorry drivers who expect to remain in driving after 55 years of age and the number for which the industry has room.

IV

THE MOBILE TECHNICAL SYSTEM

The structure of the road haulage industry and its evolution present an environment in which regulations are difficult to enforce. Managements of road haulage firms seem to know how the lorry driver sees his role and in most instances are prepared to meet his expectations. Management views the lorry driver as a worker who likes the discretion involved in his job. The job presents, in an objective sense, a good deal of discretion to him. This chapter attempts to discover what the subjective side of the picture is, in other words, to discover whether the lorry driver in fact has the expectations that managements perceive that he has.

The indicator used to show expectations is based on a concept of job satisfaction. We assume that the way in which the lorry driver talks about his job will provide the evidence from which expectations can be inferred. In attempting to measure job satisfaction we find ourselves in as great a number of difficulties as those who have attempted to conceive of alienation for empirical or operational purposes.[1] Blauner operationalises job satisfaction by counterposing it to alienation. He refers to Bendix and Lipset's statement:

> The Marxian theory of why men under capitalism would revolt was based on on assumption of what prompts men to be satisfied or dissatisfied with their work.[2]

[1] For example: Nettler, G. 'A Measure of Alienation', *American Sociological Review*. Vol. 22, 1957. Seeman, M. 'On the Meaning of Alienation', *American Sociological Review*, Vol. 24, 1959.

[2] Blauner, R. 'Work Satisfaction and Industrial Trends in Modern Society', in Galenson, W. and Lipset, S. M. *Labour and Trade Unionism*, John Wiley. London. 1960.

84

Thus while keeping in mind the difficulties of measuring job satisfaction and making meaningful inferences we shall use it to infer the expectations the lorry driver has. In Chapter II we have seen that managements view him as an 'individualist'. Chapter III indicates that there is a good deal of conformity to his expectations in that the lorry driver tends to have a career in lorry driving. The assumption is that if his expectations were not met he would tend to come and go from the occupation.

Starting with Blauner's analysis we find that job satisfaction is a purely empirical notion, derived from the findings of numerous surveys on job attitudes. Blauner identifies four major variables in job satisfaction levels. These are occupational prestige, integrated work groups, occupational communities, and most important of all, control. Control is divided up into three areas: control over time work pace and physical movement; control over the social and technical environment; and control represented as the product of freedom from supervision. In this chapter we are interested in seeing whether the job situation, presented as a socio-technical system is objectively one which can meet the lorry driver's expectations. On the subjective side we want to know what his expectations are, and whether he sees the expectations as being met or not.

NORMAL JOB SATISFACTION

Blauner's article contains a more or less explicit notion of a 'normal' level of job satisfaction. This takes the form of a percentage figure which may be viewed in the same sort of way as a normal body temperature reading on a thermometer. Although there may be cultural factors in the different levels of job satisfaction which are revealed in different groups and 'the methodological limitations make it hard to accept the findings of any one of these studies by itself', Blauner concludes that 'it is much harder to reject the weight of cumulative evidence.' The normal level of job satisfaction for Blauner is 80 per cent satisfaction and he says further that such a level is hardly surprising as:

> Under 'normal' conditions there is a natural tendency for people to identify with, or at least be positively oriented toward, those social arrangements in which they are implicated.

There are obviously going to be variations about the 'normal' level of job satisfaction. Blauner states that the purpose of his article is to illustrate the types of variable relevant in deviance from the statistical norm. The major visible variable is occupational prestige but this is not explanatory as prestige includes all the other relevant variables, particularly control. As the prestige of occupational groups reduces so does the element of control, which the incumbents of such groups possess. Professional and managerial groups tend to have high levels of job satisfaction and control, while unskilled manual worker groups have less control and lower levels of job satisfaction.

Blauner's survey of job satisfaction studies is extremely useful in the sense that he enables some standard or level of 'normal' job satisfaction to be taken into consideration. However, much of the material is based on significantly differing methods used to estimate job satisfaction between the quoted studies themselves, and thus the findings of specific studies are, disappointingly, of less use than would otherwise be so. The concept of a 'normal' level of job satisfaction is extremely useful for present purposes but an index method, for estimating the levels of job satisfaction in individual studies, is used, and this is constant throughout almost all of the studies quoted. The levels of job satisfaction are presented graphically in Figure 3.

Figure 3 shows two axes, one, the vertical, indicates job satisfaction, and shows the arbitrary position of Blauner's 'normal' level, while the horizontal axis shows the types of work being done. There is a consideration of manual work in terms of a range from unit through batch to mass production in one half of the diagram. On the other half job satisfaction in non-manual occupations is indicated. Lorry drivers are fitted into this diagram both in full samples, and also by occupational category, that is trunking, tramping or shunting. Before a comparison of the various worker categories is made the level of job satisfaction in lorry driving and its estimation will be discussed.

A job satisfaction index[3] is derived by weighting the numbers of responses in the categories 'like it a lot', 'merely like it',

[3] This method is that used by Wyatt, S. and Marriott, R. *A Study of Attitudes to Factory Work.* Medical Research Council. Special Report Series. No. 292. H.M.S.O. London. 1956.

'neither like it nor dislike it', 'merely dislike it' and 'dislike it a lot' by +2, +1, 0, −1, −2, respectively. The products of the weights times the numbers are then added with regard to signs and divided by the total sample. Maximum possible job satisfaction would thus be at the point of +2 on such an index where all the people in the sample liked their job 'a lot'. At the other extreme where everybody disliked their job a lot the minimum job satisfaction level would occur at −2. For convenience, Blauner's 'normal' level of job satisfaction is arbitrarily located as being three-quarters of the way along the range at 1·0.

The horizontal axis is designed to illustrate the different possible types of production, from unit to mass production. Process production as a type is omitted from this continuum. Persons in work groups which are not strictly definable as being in any of the above related production categories are entered on the graph as the 'Other. The three types of production mentioned on the axis are taken from the definition of Woodward.[4] She designates unit production as being the type where single units or goods, in varying degrees of technical complexity, say from a wrought-iron gate to a diesel locomotive, are produced to customer specification. Batch production occurs wherever runs of a product of a certain type occur, short runs indicating small batch production, and long runs indicating large batch production. Mass production occurs where there is a continuous run of production, but where there is still a separation of the units which are being produced, as on a car line, although there is almost complete homogeneity. Process production is production in a continuous flow and where there is no separation of the units.

THE COMPARATIVE LEVEL OF JOB SATISFACTION
IN LORRY DRIVING

The comparative levels of job satisfaction indicated in Figure 3, show the lorry driver in general to have a higher level of job satisfaction than all the other work groups investigated, except

---

[4] *Management and Technology.* Joan Woodward. Problems of Progress in Industry. 3. D.S.I.R. H.M.S.O. London. 1958. Figure 1. p. 11.

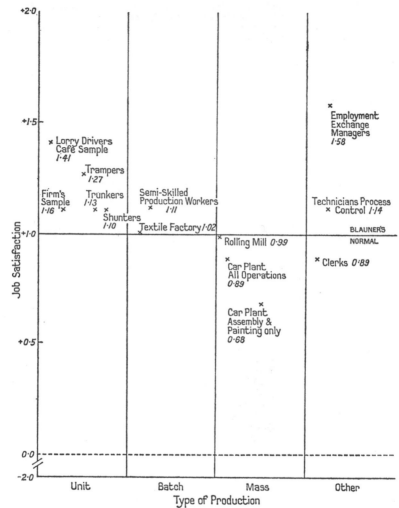

FIGURE 30. *Comparative Job Satisfaction*

Sources: LORRY DRIVERS. Café sample 200 drivers. Firms' sample 101 drivers. Trunkers, trampers and shunters are taken from Firms' sample. See Appendix, Tables 6 and 7, on Job Satisfaction.

SEMI-SKILLED PRODUCTION WORKERS. Chadwick-Jones, J. K. 'Report to Firth-Cleveland Fastenings Ltd.' Cyclostyled. Department of Industrial Relations. Cardiff, 1963.

TEXTILE WORKERS. Thomason, G. F. 'Work Satisfaction and the Image of Management.' Cyclostyled report. Department of Industrial Relations. Cardiff, 1963.

MASS PRODUCTION WORKERS. Wyatt, S. and Marriott, R. *A Study of Attitudes to Factory Work.* M.R.C. Special Report Series. 292. H.M.S.O. London, 1956.

the employment exchange managers. Unfortunately the group of technicians in process control number only 7 but the remainder of the samples are of reasonable size for the purposes of comparison. Only in two cases is there an overlap between the level of job satisfaction amongst lorry drivers and other types of work. When the firms' sample is broken down by occupational category then the shunters are found to have a lower index of job satisfaction than the semi-skilled production workers, while trunkers with a higher index than shunters rate lower than the technicians in process control. All the lorry driving groups rate lower than the employment exchange managers. This is rather to be expected in view of the considerable prestige difference between the two groups.

The very comprehensive surveys carried out by Wyatt and Marriott in three factories all reveal lower levels of job satisfaction than is to be found in the batch production worker groups and considerably lower than the lorry driver work groups. It seems clear that there is a factor of technical determinism in the job operating to produce the job satisfaction differences. As the level of technical determinism increases, limiting the discretion of the worker in his occupational role, then the level of job satisfaction amongst the manual workers who are in the Registrar General's 'skilled' category falls off. In the batch production groups it still remains above the normal but the mass production groups are below normal and in the case of the car assembly worker job satisfaction falls well below the normal level. The position of the car assembly worker on the job satisfaction scale is consistent with the findings of Walker and Guest who found that the central motive for working on the assembly line was the money which could be earned. The jobs on the assembly line consist of tasks so broken down that there can be little intrinsic satisfaction with the job.

'There is nothing more discouraging than having a barrel beside you with 10,000 bolts in it and using them all up. Then you get a barrel with another 10,000 bolts and you know that every one of

TECHNICIANS PROCESS CONTROL. Personal communication, G. F. Thomason.
EMPLOYMENT EXCHANGE MANAGERS. Survey for Durham University Business Research Unit, 1965.
CLERKS. Dale, J. R. *The Clerk in Industry*. Liverpool University Press, 1962.

those 10,000 bolts has to be picked up and put in exactly the same place as the last 10,000 bolts.'[5]

As well as the lack of discretion in the job there is another factor which causes discontent in assembly line work. This is the pacing of the line technology.

> So demanding is the line that one worker, echoing others complained: 'You get the feeling, everybody gets the feeling, whenever the line jerks everybody is wishing 'breakdown, baby!'[6]

It is clear that lack of discretion at job level through machine pacing is polarised in assembly line work. While in batch production the more usual forms of work organisation are not so restrictive on the incumbents as is the assembly line, they are more restrictive than the 'unit' production organisation of the kind Woodward suggests. Lorry drivers seem to fall into the area of the type of organisation present and necessary for 'unit' production. It is apparent that the tramper has the highest level of job satisfaction as measured by the index. It may be argued that this is due directly to the socio-technical system which allows his maximum freedom from control (he gets his own work in many cases) or it may be argued that it is the possibility of job rotation which pleases him. The probability is that it is a combination of both these factors which produces a high level of job satisfaction amongst trampers. We should not allow our hypothesis in favour of open socio-technical systems to obscure Friedmann's[7] argument in favour of job rotation. In fact the two factors closely co-exist in some cases as in the pre-mechanised and fully mechanised systems of coal getting,[8] where a direct advantage of the socio-technical systems in these two cases is the possibility of job rotation. It is necessary to make a comparative survey of socio-technical

[5] Walker, C. R. and Guest, R. H. *Man on the Assembly Line*, Harvard University Press. 1952. p. 54.

[6] Chinoy, E. *Automobile Workers and the American Dream*. Garden City Doubleday. 1955. p. 71.
N.B. Both these quotations are to be found in Blauner, R., *op. cit.* 1960.

[7] Friedmann, G. *The Anatomy of Work*, Heinneman, London. 1961.

[8] Trist, E. L., Higgin, G. W., Murray, H., Pollock, A. B. *Organisational Choice*, Tavistock Publications Ltd., London. 1963.

systems, if we are to accept the hypothesis that the technical dimension is important in determining job satisfaction levels.

A socio-technical system comprises a technical system, which is a combination of tasks, and a social system, which is a pattern of statuses and roles. While the equipment and process layout may limit the type of work organisation which is possible, it cannot entirely describe the way status incumbents are related to each other while they are carrying out their roles. The two components of a socio-technical system are interrelated but also separate.

> The technological demands place limits on the type of work organisation which is possible, but a work organisation has social and psychological properties of its own that are independent of technology.[9]

Since the problem is to examine the effect of technology on job satisfaction, socio-technical systems have to be examined for the extent to which the technical element determines the behaviour of actors. Organisations have been considered separately from their environment, that is as 'closed' socio-technical systems. Later developments have resulted in the demonstration of the organisation's relationship to its environment through the concept of an 'open' socio-technical system. These concepts are adapted for our purpose of examining technical determinacy.

As it is used here, a closed socio-technical system is a system in which the actor has his behaviour determined to a great degree by the technical component. An open socio-technical system is one where the actor has some degree of choice in his behaviour. Such a choice may involve whether or not to do something at one particular time or another. By contrast, in the closed system the technical expectations are more imperative. In the event of unfulfilled expectations the closed system

---

[9] Rice quoted in *Organisational Choice*. Trist, E. L., Higgin, G. W., Murray, H. and Pollock, A. B., Tavistock Publications, London. 1963. p. 6. For a very detailed discussion see Emery, F. E. *Characteristics of Socio-Technical Systems*. Tavistock Institute Document No. 527. January 1959.

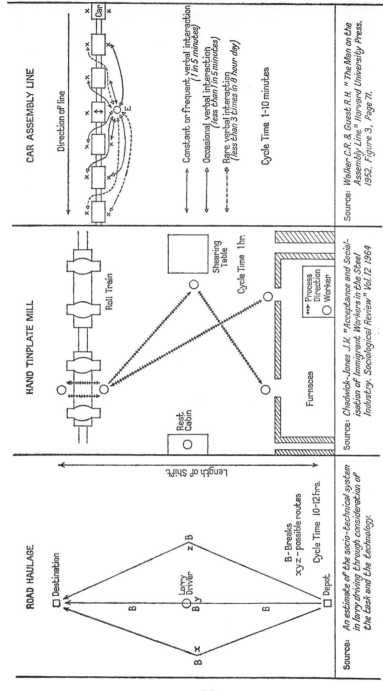

FIGURE 4. *Types of Socio-Technical System, Indicating Different Levels of Technical Imperatives*

CAR ASSEMBLY LINE

Direction of line

→ Constant or frequent verbal interaction
(1 in 5 minutes)

↔ Occasional verbal interaction
(less than 1 in 5 minutes)

⇢ Rare verbal interaction
(less than 3 times in 8 hour day)

Cycle Time 1-10 minutes

Source: *Walker C.R. & Guest R.H. "The Man on the Assembly Line" Harvard University Press. 1952. Figure 3, Page 71.*

HAND TINPLATE MILL

Roll Train

Shearing Table

Cycle Time 1hr.

Rest Cabin

Furnaces

→ Process Direction
○ Worker

Source: *Chadwick-Jones J.K. "Acceptance and Social-isation of Immigrant Workers in the Steel Industry. Sociological Review" Vol.12 1964*

Length of Shift

ROAD HAULAGE

☐ Destination

Lorry Driver

Depot

B B - Breaks
xyz - possible routes

Cycle Time 10-12 hrs.

Source: *An estimate of the socio-technical system in lorry driving through consideration of the task and the technology.*

will quickly break down. The conceptual framework is thus a continuum of technically derived freedom or constraint ranging from the open to the closed socio-technical system.

Three socio-technical systems are compared in Figure 4, that of the car assembly line, the hand tinplate mill work group, and the socio-technical system in lorry driving which is constructed from data on the technology and work situation.

At one end of the scale the situation of the car worker indicates a maximum control of worker behaviour by technology. Every few minutes the line brings work for the man to deal with and this results in very restricted predetermined work behaviour. The car worker must work very rapidly indeed to get time off from the assembly line. This can be done by working back up the line at a rate faster than it can produce new work. Generally the worker is tied to the line in the sense of being in one position. Technology places considerable limits on worker behaviour. The diagram shows that the car worker, E, can interact, in the sense of verbal communication, with only four people. His interaction with others is limited to a much greater extent.

The tinplate worker group is much more flexible in terms of technological limitations and although it is doubtful whether there is a great quantitative difference in verbal interaction it is clear that the technology allows a much greater freedom of actual physical movement than the assembly line. It is in technologies of this kind that work groups can restrict output. American studies by Roy, provide evidence of this kind of worker control in the work situation. Similarly and more recently in Britain, Lupton[10] has made a very detailed study showing such restriction. Much of what Woodward calls 'unit' production and also 'batch' production is arranged in this type of work group. The mining industry in Britain is a good illustration of the effects of differing socio-technical systems. Particularly since the war years mining has undergone

[10] Roy, D. 'Quota Restriction and Goldbricking in a Machine Shop'. *American Journal of Sociology*. March 1952. pp. 427–42.
Lupton, T. *On the Shop Floor*. Pergamon Press, Oxford. 1963.
Gouldner, A. W. *Patterns of Industrial Bureaucracy*. Free Press. 1954. pp. 140–41. Remarks that the miners had much more freedom from technological control than the factory workers in the Gypsum plant.

major technical changes. Briefly it has seen changes in techniques which have resulted in a cyclical phenomenon in work
organisation.[11] Mining in the first instance or stage was unmechanised and the consequence was the predominance of
small groups with high autonomy. Then came the partially
mechanised Longwall method of mining, where men worked in
shifts of groups which were much larger than the small autonomous group of three or four men on the unmechanised system.
The system had the advantages of a mass production scheme
in terms of output, but the social organisation was not a happy
one. Men were not so predominantly related in terms of face
to face relationships; they were more directly supervised; and
there was no possibility of job rotation as in the smaller group.
Further the men of each shift were disconnected from each
other. This had some unfortunate consequences. Negligence
on some shifts would create tension. The men on the next shift
would arrive to find that the job had not been completed
properly, ready for them to start their particular aspect of the
total task. With further mechanisation the small group tends
to return to prominence. Once again job rotation and worker
decision making are possible. The three stages in mechanisation of mining thus present a similar picture to that arising
out of Figure 4. The mass production technique having the
most unhappy consequences for the miner ties in with Walker
and Guest's car worker study. The relative contentedness of
Chadwick-Jones's tinplate group (had it not been for the
uncertainty in job security Chadwick-Jones reports that job
satisfaction would have been much higher) is comparable
with the increased satisfaction in the fully mechanised mining
group.

The socio-technical system of the lorry driver presents a
marked contrast to that of the assembly worker. The technical
system allows the lorry driver autonomy within very wide
limits. If a lorry driver is given a journey to do, with a delivery
to make at an appointed time at a destination, he is free to
vary things as he wishes. He is limited only by the amount of
time he takes to travel the route compared with the time
allowed. He may vary his route, or he may stop his lorry and

[11] Trist, *et al.*, *op. cit.* See also Goldthorpe, J. H. 'Organisation and
Supervisor–Worker Conflict'. *British Journal of Sociology.* Vol. 10, 1959.

chat to his fellow drivers en route. He is autonomous in that he can control his 'technology' in a way in which the assembly line worker cannot do. He is not hemmed in by the four walls of the factory in the way in which the tinplate worker or Lupton's transformer assembly worker is. The lorry driver has space and changing perspective as well as the ability to determine to a comparatively large extent the way in which he runs the job once away from the depot.

CYCLE TIME AND SOCIO-TECHNICAL SYSTEMS

Control in socio-technical systems, that is the extent to which the worker is constrained by the technology, is thus mainly a product of the cycle time of the operation involved. Baldamus[12] has related labour turnover to the disparity between the existence of 'strain increasing' and 'strain reducing' factors in types of work. Turnover rates are also inversely related to the level of skill and the length of the job cycle. It is possible therefore to say that the shortness of the job cycle is clearly a strain increasing factor which will not be compensated for by the 'traction' of the assembly line or 'object' traction. Wyatt and Marriott[13] suggest that the cycle time may be less important in determining job satisfaction than the type of work done. They also suggest that, given the same type, there will be an inverse relationship between cycle time and job satisfaction.

The three socio-technical systems indicated in Figure 4 show considerable differences in cycle times. The lorry driver has a considerably larger cycle time than the batch production tinplate worker and larger skill than the mass production assembly worker. The various kinds of lorry driver also show different cycle times. On average the shunter will have the shortest of all three kinds of lorry driver since he may make several or few journeys locally in the course of a single day. By contrast the tramper may have what is, in practice, a weekly

[12] Baldamus, W. 'Types of Work and Motivation'. *British Journal of Sociology*. Vol. 2. 1951. In a sense Baldamus is putting forward an alternative view to the one suggested here. He would argue that technical determinism in terms of the traction of the assembly line is a 'strain-reducing' factor producing higher job satisfaction than would otherwise be the case.

[13] Wyatt, S. and Marriott, R. *op. cit.* 1956. p. 23.

cycle of work. The trunker has a cycle of a single shift. If job satisfaction is related to technical determinism, then viewing the job cycle time as part of this determinism, trampers will have the highest level of job satisfaction, shunters the lowest. This is in accord with the evidence.

By comparing the various socio-technical systems evidence is presented that the lorry driver's socio-technical system affords more freedom than those of other workers. The relatively high indices of job satisfaction amongst the lorry drivers would indicate that whatever his expectations are, they are met. The next step is to discuss what his expectations are and to relate them to a major variable, technical determinism in socio-technical systems.

THE BASIS OF THE LORRY DRIVER'S JOB SATISFACTION

For a worker in the Registrar General's skilled status category, the lorry driver has a remarkably high level of job satisfaction. The reason seems to be that the socio-technical system, being in Woodward's 'unit' category, affords the lorry driver more control than a worker in 'batch' and 'mass' production work organisation is permitted.

Job satisfaction in lorry driving is predominantly the consequence of the technical system of the lorry driver's work situation. Autonomy is mentioned most frequently as a reason for liking the job, which reflects not only the objective freedom of the work situation but also the lorry driver's realisation of his freedom.[14]

> 'When you're away on the road, you're like the captain of a ship, you haven't got people telling you what to do and what not to do.'

> 'The freedom of the job as opposed to being in a factory. Any reputable firm will give a lorry driver complete freedom. He's the skipper of the ship and he makes his own decisions.'

The trunker is much more likely to mention autonomy as being of importance in liking the job than the other types of driver. The tramper may well take his autonomy for granted

[14] See Appendix Table 6. The Sources of Job Satisfaction in Lorry Driving.

as he may only see his management once a week or even less. Certainly in the café sample the biggest proportion of the drivers are conscious of the freedom of their work situation as they indicated when they were asked about their breaks during the shift. 61 per cent indicated that the number of breaks they took varied and some of the remarks made are especially illustrative of this socio-technically derived freedom.

'We stop and have tea when we want it—that's why we stick it (i.e. the job)—there's no bosses with it—it's a free life, that's why people like it.'

'I please myself, if I want to get my bloody hair cut I'll stop, which you can't do in a factory.'

For the tramper it is the variety of places, which he travels to and sees, which gives him job satisfaction. Variety of places is the factor second in quantitative importance amongst the drivers in the firms' sample.

'You get a variety and you get into contact with different people. You get different views of the scenery and the country, it's a most healthy job.'

'It gives you a chance to see round, the time goes quicker when you're out than when you're inside.'

The job of lorry driving itself is an important factor in the job satisfaction of the lorry driver. He sees himself as doing a skilled job with responsibility in the 'professional' sense.

'I like seeing the different places and then there's a certain pride in driving that all lorry drivers feel, especially long distance drivers.'

'It's like an art or a profession where a certain amount of skill and judgement is required, plus having the responsibility as an individual.'

The mentions of the variety of people met while actually on the job, and the 'healthy', 'open air' nature of the job are further indicators of the sense of freedom that lorry drivers feel. The cash obtained from the job is seen much less often to be a factor giving job satisfaction. All in all, 109 mentions (63 per cent) of a total of 158 are indications of the drivers' sense of

97

autonomy, to a greater or lesser extent. Only 3 drivers said they could find nothing to like about the job.

The textile factory sample is one of male workers engaged in the production of ribbons and tinsel articles. The work is done in batches and there is a shift work system operating. It should be noted that the sample includes craftsmen but it also includes some men who would be so unskilled as not to fit into the Registrar General's skilled worker category. These two small groups tend to offset each other. The level of job satisfaction in the textile factory is lower than amongst the lorry drivers but above that obtaining in the mass production factories, in particular the car assembly plant.

Even though the question is asked about the satisfaction with the actual job of driving many drivers made comments about the more general work situation. This is not so apparent with the textile factory workers. The factory workers are likely to perceive interest and variety in their actual jobs, and 7 of the 46 report liking the actual job itself. Familiarity with the job, relations with fellow workers, and wages earned are also more important to the factory workers but these are likely to be related to the work situation rather than the job itself. The things which are disliked about jobs by the two groups of worker are also very different. The major dislike of the lorry driver is the ordinary road user whom he considers is not a 'professional' but an 'amateur' driver. The factory worker is likely to say that he dislikes the job itself. Eleven out of 46 replied in this way. There was also considerable mention of monotony (in the sense of no variety) and boredom (in the sense of no interest) by the factory workers. This did not occur amongst the lorry drivers. A further noteworthy difference is that amongst the factory workers' mentions of management and supervision as the source of job dissatisfaction are more frequent than amongst the lorry drivers.

The sample of the two types of worker make responses which reflect their job situation and their expectations of it. The factory worker is more circumscribed by his job than the lorry driver. He thinks in terms of the job alone to a greater extent than the lorry driver. The lorry driver by contrast tends to be unable to exclude the work situation. It is significant that he does not mention the job itself as a primary dislike in the way that the factory worker does. While the lorry driver regards his job as being important in itself, it is the benefits of the relatively 'open' socio-technical system which he sees as significant. He is afforded more satisfaction due to having a mobile work situation than due to his actual job of driving. The rewards for the factory worker are more likely to be in the actual job. This is where the interest and variety in the factory situation stems from, as opposed to the work situation in the case of the lorry driver.

'You do have a variation, there are so many operations you haven't time to get bored.'

'The variety of the work, the different operations, the different colours, shades and patterns you get, you don't get bored.'

The lorry driver is not so likely to mention good relations with his fellow workers as is the factory worker. This would seem to be reasonable in view of the lorry driver's mobile work situation, where he cannot interact as frequently with his fellow workers as can the factory worker. The significant differences between the two groups of worker occur with reference to the autonomy factor and the worker inter personal relations factor.[15] Even if the variety and interest mentions are added together in the factory sample there is no significant difference between the two groups of worker. If the various sorts of variety are separated out, then there is an absolute difference between the lorry driver and the factory worker in terms of mentions of variety of people and places. The factory worker does not mention variety in these terms at all. The factory worker is more likely however, to find more variety in his actual job than the lorry driver is in his actual driving. The lorry driver obtains his variety from the places he visits and the different people he meets. These different people whom the lorry driver meets as he travels about the country seem to be

[15] Autonomy. $X^2 = 14 \cdot 05$. Relations with Fellow Workers. $X^2 = 9 \cdot 86$. Both significant at the 1 per cent level with 1 D.F. See Appendix, Table 7. The Sources of Job Satisfaction in Lorry Driving and Factory Work Compared.

the main source of interpersonal relationships for the lorry driver, rather than his fellow lorry drivers.

THE LORRY DRIVERS' ATTITUDE TO FACTORY WORK

In terms of socio-technical systems the lorry driver's job situation is such as to afford expectations of an autonomous role. As he defines his role, the lorry driver expects to be left very much on his own while he is actually doing his job. In the early part of this chapter we have been concerned to demonstrate that the major source of job satisfaction for the lorry drivers is this autonomy which they feel the situation affords them. In order to be certain of the inferences for their expectations the lorry drivers were asked in a direct way about their attitude to factory work.

The impression that the lorry drivers give is that factory work has little, if any, appeal for them, apart from the wage packet at the end of the week. Two thirds of the drivers say that they would not consider working in a factory *even* for more pay. Trampers, who have the driving job which presents them with the greatest freedom, or in analytic terms the most open socio-technical system, are the category of lorry driver most likely to express a dislike of factory work in this form. 70 per cent of the trampers say that they would never work in a factory even for more money. The trampers' convictions are based on experience since they are more likely to have worked in a factory than any other type of driver. By contrast the evidence over the whole sample is that a driver who has had experience of working in a factory is more likely to be willing to work there than a driver who has not.

Lorry drivers were asked to say what they thought was attractive and unattractive about factory work. 53 per cent said that they could think of nothing attractive, while only 2 per cent thought there was nothing unattractive about working in a factory. By this measure the tramper was again the driver who expressed the greatest dislike of factory work.

Factory work is attractive to a few lorry drivers because it is carried out in a warm dry atmosphere.[16] Participant observa-

---

[16] See Appendix Table 8. Reasons for Liking Factory Work.

tion demonstrated to the writer that the task of sheeting and roping a load on to a lorry in the wind and rain is not a comfortable one.

> 'With the weather we've had I'd like to try it (factory work) but I don't think it would work out.'

Regularity of the job and ease in arranging a domestic routine is another factor which makes factory work attractive to nine of the lorry drivers, and six more say that if they were in a factory job they would have more home life. The two reasons are obviously closely linked.

> 'Your wife would know what time you were coming home so she would cook your dinner, and you'd know that you'd be home every night.'

Seven drivers say that they find the work that they have seen being done in factories interesting.

> 'I'd like to work in a steel works. I've been interested in making steel as I've been looking at it these last few years.'

Conditions and amenities in general are mentioned by three drivers as a reason for liking factory work and short hours in particular are mentioned by three more. There are also a few drivers who think that more money can be earned in a factory job than in lorry driving. Some drivers mention the greater opportunity for promotion, and also the greater security of employment in factory work in general. In the favourable views of factory work it is generally the conditions or the general work situation and surroundings, which are seen as making factory work attractive, not the actual job that would have to be done in the factory. On the unfavourable side,[17] the actual job to be done in the factory is viewed with disfavour, as is the environment. Sixteen drivers in the sample say that the job would be full of routine and monotony.

> 'I left it (factory work) to get back on the road outside. I left the factory with more money to come back. In the factory it's just repetition, the same thing day after day, it's monotonous.'

The major complaint about factory work is that it is indoor

---

[17] See Appendix, Table 9. Reasons for disliking Factory Work.

work. Sixty-five drivers in the firm's sample mention this as an unfavourable aspect, and the proportion of such mentions constitute 57 per cent of the total unfavourable mentions in the sample. Although some drivers like the idea of factory work because it would get them away from the elements, most view a job inside a building as one in which their general perspective would be restricted and thus feel they would lose their freedom.

> 'You're shut up and tied in, there's more open space on a job of driving.'

> 'The walls would start to hit me and bash me about the head.'

> 'You're indoors all day, but with a lorry you're out. The day goes very quickly in a lorry but in a factory, no, you're in one spot.'

Seven drivers mention supervision as being a big disadvantage in factory work.

> 'I like to be free. I don't like anybody stooping over me all the time, and in a factory there's always somebody watching.'

> 'You're supervised. There's always a foreman above you at every minute of every hour.'

These four reasons constitute 100 out of 116 mentions of the unattractive aspects of factory work.

A further question asked the driver to compare his job with a job in a factory. On the whole the lorry drivers preferred lorry driving to factory work. Although 13 (13%) thought the two types of work about equal, two drivers out of every three, in the sample, said that lorry driving compared favourably. Only 18 (18%) said that it definitely compared unfavourably with factory work. Shunters are most likely to indicate that lorry driving is less favourable than factory work (24%) compared with trunkers (11%) and trampers (14%). Trampers are however more likely than any other driver category to compare their job favourably with jobs in factories.[18] This question also reveals the high degree of estrangement of the lorry driver from factory work, and in particular the extreme estrangement of the trampers.

[18] See Appendix, Table 10A. Comparison of Lorry Driving with Factory Work by Firms. Table 10B. Comparison of Lorry Driving with Factory Work by Occupational Category.

A survey of the reasons for a favourable comparison of lorry driving with factory work [19], shows that it is the autonomy at job level which is the chief factor giving lorry driving its advantages. Twenty-nine (29%) of the drivers in the sample mention this and there is a noticeable difference between the proportions amongst the types of driver who mention it. Shunters are less likely to mention it than trunkers, while trampers mention it most frequently of all.

> 'It's better than factory work, when you're out on the road you're your own boss. The boss relies on you. In the factory you have piece work and a foreman over you all the time.'

> 'Better! You're your own boss once you leave the depot, you can say "I'm on my own". You've got a job to do. You know how long you've got to do it in and you get on with it.'

> 'Better! For myself I don't like somebody over my shoulder telling me what to do all the time. I'd rather leave it to my own initiative.'

The other reasons tend to reinforce the findings of the previous question on factory work. Lorry driving is an outdoor job and due to the constantly changing perspective that the lorry driver has in a mobile outdoor job, he feels that the job is one which has variety in it.

> 'Better! There's a certain amount of freedom when you're out on the road and its not quite so boring. There's something different to see all the time. You're travelling and meeting different people, not like in a factory where you're stuck with one machine.'

> 'A lot better, we're out in the fresh air and seeing different parts of the country every day.'

Again, because of the outdoor nature of lorry driving, the lorry driver sees his job as being much more healthy than a job in a factory. Another five drivers mention that there is variety in a lorry driver's job in terms of the actual job itself. This contrasts with the mentions of routine and the monotonous elements in factory work.

The main reasons for an unfavourable comparison[20] of lorry driving with factory work are the weather:

[19] See Appendix, Table 11. Reasons for Favourable Comparison.

[20] See Appendix, Table 12. Reasons for Unfavourable Comparison.

'It's worse due to the conditions we have to work in, the wet weather and the cold.'

or the general conditions in factories:

'Worse, today factory work is a lot better than lorry driving. They (factory workers) have better conditions such as canteens and there are no ropes and sheets and they're working in the dry. But our life is healthier.'

or the better money earned in factories:

'Worse, if you get the right sort of factory, like Fords, you're better off.'

The other factors mentioned in unfavourable comparisons of lorry driving with factory work mainly amount to saying that factory work is easier, 'they are spoon fed', than lorry driving and that it is less regular. One remark, by a driver who considered that on the whole his job was a better one than one in a factory, is interesting in that it is illustrative of the earlier discussions on the lorry driver's career.

'Our job is better, we have to concentrate and we have the responsibility, but as you get older you get more nervous.'

As with the findings of the earlier question on factory work, when the relationship of attitude to experience in factories was considered, the favourable comparison of lorry driving with factory work is much more likely to come from lorry drivers who have in fact worked in a factory than from those who have not.[21] Lorry drivers are also by this measure estranged from factory work to a surprisingly high degree, the greatest extent being amongst the trampers.

The responses made about factory work indicate an indictment of both the jobs which would be done in factories and the total socio-technical system involved. The work situation is restrictive, both in terms of being 'indoors', fixed in spatial terms within the factory, and with a cycle time for the actual job which makes the work routine and monotonous, and also in terms of the supervision restrictions. It is significant that the tramper, with his great amount of freedom in the work

[21] See Appendix, Table 13. Comparison of Lorry Driving and Factory Work in Relation to Employment Experience in Factories.

situation, is the type of driver who is most of all estranged from the factory work situation.

All this is not to say that the lorry driver never thinks of taking another type of job. Once he has begun in road haulage the lorry driver tends to have a more or less continuous career. Two in every three drivers say they expect to spend the rest of their working lives in the occupation. In spite of this nearly one in two drivers do aspire to some other occupation if they were given the opportunity to change. There is a considerable difference in the job satisfaction index amongst those who said they would change (0·87) and those who would not (1·43). If they could start life all over again 58 per cent of the lorry drivers had made up their minds on occupations other than lorry driving, usually in the general area of engineering. There is however comparatively little aspiration to occupations above that of social class III manual.

CONCLUSION

In contrast with occupations which can be organised on a factory basis the lorry driver has a role in a relatively open socio-technical system, An open socio-technical system has been defined as one in which the technology permits a good deal of discretion by the actors involved. Closedness in socio-technical systems is usually, though not of necessity, represented by the determinacy induced by the technical components of the system. Thus we say that assembly line work is more 'closed' in terms of socio-technical system than 'batch' or 'unit' production. The lorry driver has a high level of job satisfaction when compared with workers of similar status. This level is to be explained in terms of socio-technical systems. The assembly line worker has a low level of job satisfaction in his closed system than has the batch or unit production worker in his relatively open system. The tramper has the most open socio-technical system of all and has the highest level of job satisfaction. By comparison the driver with the least open system, the shunter, has the lowest level of job satisfaction of all the types of lorry driver.

The evidence on the relationship of the lorry driver's level of job satisfaction to the type of socio-technical system is strongly reflected in other ways. The lorry driver's attitude to factory work indicates his expectations of a work system. Operationally factory work can be represented as a closed socio-technical system to the lorry driver. His view of factory work is such that the implications are of almost complete dislike of factory work. To the lorry driver there is nothing or very little which is attractive about factory work, while the unattractiveness is made clear in terms of the lack of physical mobility, the confining nature of work in factories, and the actuality of close supervision. If the career of the lorry driver is one way of assessing the persistence of remaining in the occupation, the concepts of socio-technical system and job satisfaction are useful in an attempt to explain this persistence.

V

ORGANISATION AND THE
LORRY DRIVER

The last chapter showed how the lorry driver's technology leads to expectations of discretion in his work role. Job satisfaction is found to be inversely related to the level of technical determinacy as indicated by the length of the work cycle, the physical-spatial effect, and other possible technical determinants of behaviour in socio-technical systems of various kinds. The greater the level of technical determinacy in the system the less satisfied the status occupants in those systems seem to be. The lorry driver by virtue of working in what has been termed 'an open socio-technical system' comes to expect the same freedom from organisational constraint. This chapter is a discussion of the organisational aspect of control, what Blauner would call 'freedom from supervision',[1] and consisting of substantially the same notion as that expressed in Jacques' 'time span theory of responsibility'.[2]

It is not supposed that the aspects of job satisfaction and socio-technical system should be linked and compared with equally tightly linked constructs of work satisfaction and organisation in the sense of comparing the components of two mutually exclusive entities. The separation between the two sets of aspects of a lorry driver's occupational life is firstly for the purpose of analytical convenience but secondly there is evidence of the necessity of a distinction between job and work

[1] Blauner, R. 1960. *op. cit.* p. 347.

[2] Jaques, *The Measurement of Responsibility.* Tavistock Publications. 1956. pp. 32–5.

satisfaction due to their being derived from the separate sources of socio-technical system and organisation respectively. The argument which is presented by Herzberg *et al.*[3] is weakened by the possibility of overlap but presents a reasonably convenient basis on which to organise facts and arguments. The suggestions of Herzberg *et al.* are that job satisfaction and work satisfaction are distinct in that it will be the job itself that will produce the positive satisfaction, with particular reference to responsibility and advancement (more in the sense of personality development, such as the growth of skill and other self-actualisation processes than movement in a hierarchy) as well as the 'work itself'. These factors representing job factors are termed the 'motivators'. The 'hygiene' factors, such as company policy, administration, supervision and working conditions, 'represent major job dissatisfiers with little potency to affect job attitudes positively.'

The distinction seems to be a reasonably valid one except that the factors in motivation and hygiene are not always mutually exclusive. In fact for the purposes of this analysis such a blurring is the basis of the problem. Blauner[4] makes the distinction between the 'control' factors in the actual job reasonably clear by his use of three categories with only slight blurring in the area of 'control over the social and technical environment'. The difficulty with Herzberg's[5] analysis is that the factors in the variable 'control' may be either motivators or hygiene factors. Is responsibility as such a matter of the actual job or is it a product of the total work situation? The analysis contained in this chapter and the one preceding is based on splitting the context of the total work situation into two areas. In Chapter IV the actual job and the socio-technical system with its implications for control in terms of the length of the job cycle was discussed. In this chapter control is viewed from the standpoint of job prescription and discretion by factors outside the area of technological determinacy. It will therefore be assumed that the 'responsibility' aspect and other self-actualisation process in work have also to be looked at in terms

[3] Herzberg, F., Mausner, B., Snyderman, B. B. *The Motivation to Work.* Chapman and Hall Ltd. London, 1959. See in particular pp. 81–2.

[4] Blauner, R. 1960. *op. cit.*

[5] Herzberg *et al.* 1959. *op. cit.*

of freedom afforded by hierarchial structures in organisations. Blauner makes the distinction between the two areas explicit by saying that 'control from direct supervision' concerns 'not the aspects of the work process under control, but rather the locus of control'. He goes on to say that the Hoppock survey indicated that both railroaders and truckdrivers have high levels of job satisfaction ranking only below professionals and artists in the case of the railroader, while the truckdrivers ranked at approximately the same level as salesmen. This level is due for the most part to freedom from direct supervision.

Control here refers to the extent of job prescription, that is to say the amount of discretion which the individual is allowed in his job merely through the dictates of organisational hierarchy. This definition follows that of Smith and Tannenbaum[6] who say that control is thought of as being 'any process in which a person (or group or organisation) determines or intentionally affects what another person (group or organisation) will do.' Smith and Tannenbaum suggest that control is important in the level of morale of the members of organisations and that there is a conflict of interest between management and workers in the general area of control. The discrepancy between managerial power and the power of employees should not be too great if a high level of morale is to exist. The discrepancy is not, however, accompanied by demands for radical changes in the distribution of control, as in the European Anarcho-Syndicalist tradition, but is rather in the direction of more control at all levels. Control and discretion vary with the type of organisation under discussion, and possibly with the extent to which forms of organisation are a reflection of socio-technical systems, with a particular emphasis on the extent to which the technical system is reflected. Before this important aspect is discussed it will be necessary to suggest how control will manifest itself. Control will indicate a direction of behaviour; a particular kind of behaviour in a certain situation rather than another kind, which is a result of determination by others in the organisation. Essential here is the notion of a person with a role where he either has a choice

[6] Smith, C. G. and Tannenbaum, A. S. 'Organisational Control Structure'. *Human Relations*. Vol. 16. 1963.

in behaviour pattern or not. This choice will be termed discretion which in its turn will be indicated by the responsibility that the status occupant has.[7] To summarise: In relating the notion of control to the work situation in the road haulage industry we have to consider the extent of the responsibility and discretion in the lorry driver's role and the extent to which these are enlarged or diminished by the organisation which employs him.

ORGANISATIONS AS SOCIO-TECHNICAL SYSTEMS

Any discussion concerning the extent of freedom from control in the sense of organisational hierarchical determinism must essentially consider the extent to which organisations as a whole are products of technical systems. Is organisation merely a particular kind of socio-technical system? The evidence is that, even if organisations may not in fact be thought of in this way, there is a close connection between the type of technical system and the resultant form of organisation. More or less emphasis can be found in the writings of sociologists on the importance of the technical system as a determining feature of organisation. Parsons places low emphasis on the technical system itself in his analysis but this may be due to the level of abstraction involved in his discussion. Resources can be 'mobilised' and there seems to be less emphasis on the limitations imposed by the dictates of technical system than those imposed by the 'centrifugal tendency of the sub-units' (human) in organisations. However there is an implicit recognition as he says:

> The technical man can reasonably be held responsible for the results of his operations; he cannot, however, be 'dictated to' with respect to the technical procedures by which he achieves these results.[8]

and:

[7] Jaques, E. *The Measurement of Responsibility*. Tavistock Publications. 1956. Responsibility is basically determined by the length of time discretion is allowed to continue without a check by a higher participant.

[8] Parsons, T. 'A Sociological Approach to the Theory of Organisations' in Etzioni, A. *Complex Organisations: A Sociological Reader*. Holt, Rinehart, Winston Inc. 1964. p. 45.

Certain of its (i.e. the organisation's) special features will derive from goal primacy in general and others from the primacy of the particular type of goal.[9]

Other writers on organisations tend to be more explicit about the relationship of the technical system to the total organisation as a system. Trist *et al.*, discuss enterprises as 'open socio-technical systems' with technical demands limiting the work organisation which is possible, but at the same time stressing that a social psychological system arises with properties which may be independent of the technology.[10] The notion of an 'open' socio-technical system indicates the possibility of the need of the system to adapt and change in accordance with the market demands and also presumably new technologies. Burns and Stalker produce what is almost a formula for describing organisations, taking into account almost every aspect of the determining characteristics of organisations except perhaps the geist or pervading spirit of the organisation which presumably grows up in an autonomous fashion. Burns and Stalker's view of management systems may presumably be extended to mean 'organisation' if 'informal' behaviour is also included both at management level and also at worker level, where it tends to be viewed as a countervailing force to management. Such management systems are viewed as a dependent variable in response to four main independent variables; the rate of technical change, the rate of market change, motivational aspects of lower participants, and the relative capacity of the directors of a concern to 'lead' which is their ability to relate the external system demands to goal attainment by the organisation. This is perhaps the most all embracing view of factors in organisations and their relationship to the determination of patterns of behaviour of the incumbents. The use of the term organisations here, to cover what has been described as a 'management system', is possible as informal behaviour as such may be subsumed under the headings of motivational aspects of lower participants and the ability of managements to lead.[11]

[9] Parsons, T. 1964. *op. cit.* p. 35.

[10] Trist, *et al.* 1963. *op. cit.* p. 6.

[11] Burns, T. and Stalker, G. M. 1961. *op. cit.* p. 96.

Joan Woodward's study is an example of an extreme view of the technical factor in the determination of the final structure of organisations. She also argues that the technical system is of predominating importance in the determination of human relations. The technical system, as it varies with unit, batch, mass, and process production, means that a different kind of co-operation is required which has an effect on the final structure of the organisation. There seems to be no need to discuss these in detail; it will suffice to note that 'pressure' on employees increased up to mass production and then decreased. Pressure is lowest in unit and process production. In unit production 'it was traditional that they (the employees) were unlikely to work well "with a gun at their backs" ', while in process production the 'exercise of control was so mechanical and exact that the pressure on people was again at a minimum.'[12]

A general pattern emerges from the studies quoted. There is a close relationship between the technical system and the final emergent organisation. Whether this brief discussion enables organisations to be described as socio-technical systems is still open to question, but in discussing the nature of control we should be ready to consider several sources determining such control. Control may be purely a function of technology as in Joan Woodward's process and unit production systems. Control may be an indirect product of technology buttressed by management hierarchy, as it tends to be in mass production. At the other end of the scale control may be purely hierarchical, as in the case of an administrative state bureaucracy under stable conditions.

ORGANISATIONS, CONTROL AND WORK SATISFACTION

In the same way that differences in cycle times mean a difference in control for the worker by his actual job in a particular technical system, there are also differences in organisation structures which will also give a differential amount of control. There are several views of organisations which are worth looking at in this context.

[12] Woodward, J. *Management and Technology*. D.S.I.R. Problems of Progress in Industry No. 3. H.M.S.O. London, 1958. p. 29.

Weber's ideal type of bureaucracy is a construction[13] based on maximum rationality in orientation to goal attainment. The functional division of labour and hierarchical characteristics of such a form reduce the discretion of task roles to a minimum. Such a form exhibits a polarisation of prescribed content in the task roles of the incumbents. The prescribed elements exist both in terms of the results expected and, what is more important in the context of the discussion, the limits set on the 'means by which the work can be done'.[14] This is not to say that task roles in bureaucracies have no discretion. Discretion exists but is prescribed by the organisation. Weber was himself pessimistic[15] about the effects of such a type of organisation on human personality for this very reason of restriction. Such doubt on the ultimate value of this kind of organisation in a final analysis of the human condition is expressed by Herzberg *et al.*

> The profoundest motivation to work comes from the recognition of individual achievement and from a sense of personal growth in responsibility. It is likely that neither of these flourish too well in a bureaucratic situation. Rules determine what is to be done and how it is to be done . . . Since this is true of almost every level of organised authority one might predict a decrease in the available amount of motivation as the rigidity and complexity of bureaucracy increase.[16]

This form of organisation is however non-existent in the empirical sense, but Burns and Stalker show two forms of management systems one of which, the 'mechanistic' system approximates to the Weberian bureaucratic form. The other form, the 'organic' system is a construction closely approximating to Gouldner's natural system[17] approach based on

[13] Weber, M. 'The Essentials of Bureaucratic Organisation: An Ideal Type Construction', in Merton, R. K., Gray, A. P., Hockey, B., Selvin, . C. *Reader in Bureaucracy.* pp. 21–2. Free Press, Glencoe. 1952.

Jaques, E. 1956. *op. cit.* pp. 32–5.

[15] Gouldner, A. W. 'Organisational Analysis' in Merton, R. K., Broom, L. and Cottrell, L. S. *Sociology Today: Problems and Prospects.* Basic Books, New York. 1959. p. 402.

[16] Herzberg, *et al.* 1959. *op. cit.* Chapter 13. 'In Perspective.'

[17] Gouldner, A. W. 1959. *op. cit.* pp. 400–28.

reciprocity of interaction between status occupants. The 'organic' construction is shown to be more fluid internally and relevant to changing situations. The internal fluidity means greater freedom from control in the sense of more discretion in the task role. The organisations involved are in the electronics industry which had to adapt to changes in technology compared with the 'mechanistic' system model, which was derived from a study of a firm, involved in synthetic textile manufacture, operating in relatively stable technical and market conditions.

In a sense the 'organic' form of Burns and Stalker is an anomaly if the definition of organisation retained is that of a social system characterised by a primacy of orientation to goal attainment. The orientation in the organic system is a pure technical one rather than one in which technical development is a means of attaining the ends of the organisation. Whether or not this assertion of anomaly can in fact be borne out in the empirical sense remains to be seen but the implication is one of split orientation, with a possible primacy of orientation to science or technical matters. In this case control is not so much dictated by the centripetalising effects of hierarchy but rather by the dictates of a cosmopolitan expertise. One thing is clear, in terms of organisational determinacy the task role in the 'organic' form is less prescribed by the hierarchy than is the case in the 'mechanistic' form.

Another view of organisations is the 'formal' and 'informal' postulate of the Human Relations school of thought. In this mode, the control is conceived of as being an equilibrium source between groups with *opposing* interests. In such a situation a worker would be rational enough to drop his control through informal processes. He is given an explanation of the facts and he will behave in accordance with the organisationally acceptable rationality. His interests have never really been divergent from those of the organisation. The situation is that the worker does not have the status to warrant being informed and, so long as he perceives a conflict of interest, then his attempts at control will take such irrational forms as restrictive control by informal groupings. The function of such informal activities as mechanisms of control by lower participants in organisations, in the sense of a countervailing power, is not one which has been shown to exist in satisfactory empirical terms. It has been related to specific factors as in Lupton's study,[18] but this is really only one area in which the worker can assert his control. A further view[19] is that informal relations are a necessary concomitant of formal organisation in that the everyday tasks of the status occupant provide exigency for the autonomous generation of discretionary behaviour unprescribed by managements. Further, such behaviour has been shown to be functional in goal attainment in organisations.[20] Smith and Tannenbaum[21] have indicated that although lower participants seem to have a 'realistic' view about control in economic organisations, morale is increased if the discrepancy between management's power and their own is not too great so it is quite possible that informal groups have a function of countervailing power in organisations.

The third relevant analytical mode for any discussion of control is that of 'compliance'. This is the central element in organisational structures which Etzioni uses as a comparative base for his study of organisations. Compliance seems to be useful as a basis to discuss control as it takes into account the checks and balances in the system as well as the differential hierarchical power. Compliance for Etzioni refers to 'a relation in which an actor behaves in accordance with a directive supported by another actor's power, and to the orientation of the subordinated actor to the power applied'.[22] From this definition, which indicates compliance in terms of power and involvement in organisation, Etzioni builds up a theory of organisations. The different types of compliance relationship produce different types of organisation. Organisations occur mainly, though by no means exclusively, in terms of the congruent compliance relationships. For example a prison will

[18] Informal process stabilises the earnings level thus giving the worker a steady income. Lupton, T. *On the Shop Floor*. Pergamon Press, Oxford. 1963.

[19] Selznick, P. 'An Approach to the Theory of Bureaucracy'. *American Sociological Review*, Vol. 8. 1943.

[20] Blau, P. M. *The Dynamics of Bureaucracy*. University of Chicago Press. 1955.

[21] Smith, C. G. and Tannenbaum, A. S. 1963. *op. cit.*

[22] Etzioni, A. *A Comparative Analysis of Complex Organisations*. Free Press, Glencoe. 1961. p. 3.

have highly alienated lower participants and in such a case coercive power is probably the only effective power. Industrial organisations have a compliance relationship which is broadly 'utilitarian', that is one which is based on remunerative power of those in the hierarchy and the calculative involvement of the lower participants. This is not to say that all work organisations can be subsumed under this heading. Blue collar workers will tend to have a primacy of 'utilitarian' compliance pattern whereas white collar workers are predominantly utilitarian with normative compliance as a close secondary pattern. Professional workers, on the other hand, show a primacy of the normative pattern with utilitarian compliance as a secondary pattern.

The difference in classification between professional workers and blue collar workers is due primarily to the difference in the involvement of the two types. The professional worker is 'morally' involved while the blue collar worker is more or less calculatively, or perhaps even, alienatively involved. A prostitute is probably alienatively involved with her clients, while the jazzman may well come in the category of moral involvement with his work. An audience which forces him to play dance music will however soon produce a calculative or perhaps even alienative involvement.[23] For the purposes of the present analysis Etzioni's typologies are useful, since it will enable us to see the type of organisation which will produce the greatest amount of moral involvement in lorry driving, and which types will produce the purely calculative, and perhaps even alienative involvement. It is suggested that the lorry driver will have a particular orientation to the organisations in the road haulage industry and in particular to the power system in such firms, since we have already seen in Chapter IV that it is the autonomy in lorry driving as a socio-technical system which is the primary source of job satisfaction. We shall therefore expect that a firm which shows an 'organic' form of organisation will secure the optimum involvement with organisational goals as its tendency to a relative primacy of normative power (even though remunerative power still predominates) will suffice in securing a moral involvement. Conversely this may

[23] Becker, H. S. 'The Professional Dance Musician and His Audience'. *American Journal of Sociology*, Vol. 57. 1951.

be interpreted as seeing moral involvement present in the lorry driver's orientation and therefore not allowing the other forms of power to exist as they have a 'neutralising effect' with consequences for work satisfaction. The following hypotheses can be made about organisation and work satisfaction in lorry driving.

1. The level of work satisfaction will differ between lorry drivers, workers in small batch production schemes, and workers in mass production schemes.

2. The sources of satisfaction in work will be different for the lorry driver than for the factory worker.

3. Organisation will play a major part in the lorry driver's work satisfaction. The more mechanistic the organisation, and the less responsibility and discretion it allows, in terms of freedom from supervision, the less will be the satisfaction and vice-versa.

THE COMPARATIVE LEVEL OF WORK SATISFACTION IN LORRY DRIVING

There is some difficulty in persuading interviewees that it is possible to make a clear distinction between the actual job and the work situation and then to elicit an estimate of satisfaction in these distinct spheres. The worker's perspective is that the two spheres are often so closely interconnected that there can be no meaningful distinction. In each of the samples lorry drivers and factory workers, the interviewees were asked two separate questions on the work situation. The firms' sample of lorry drivers were asked to rate how much they liked working for their particular firm, as were the factory workers. The categories here are 'like it a lot'; 'neither like it or dislike it'; and 'dislike it'.[24] Both the lorry drivers in the firms' sample and the factory workers were asked to state what they disliked about working for their firms as were the lorry drivers in the café sample. The indication is clearly that the lorry drivers have a

[24] An index is constructed from the responses to this question with weightings of $+1$, 0, -1. The 3 point index is constructed from the sum of the products of the weights times the numbers in the categories divided by the number in the sample. The question was not put to the drivers in the café sample. The closer the index approaches $+1 \cdot 00$ the higher the level of satisfaction.

higher level of work satisfaction than the textile factory workers. The differences are considerable.[25]

The chief sources of work satisfaction mentioned by the lorry drivers in their conditions of work: in the firms sample 60 mentions of conditions are made by B.R.S. drivers and 5 by drivers in the private firm. The condition of major importance to the B.R.S. driver is his hours and times of work. Such mentions are noticeably lacking amongst the private haulage drivers and B.R.S. drivers remark on this.

> 'I wouldn't leave B.R.S. to go to a private firm due to the excessive hours I would have to work with private enterprise firm. There's no sleep or regular rest. In the private firm we had to cover up for the boss due to his delays, or waiting at the docks.'

> 'About nationalisation—you have your regular hours but in private enterprise you do your ten hours then they ask you to work another ten.'

> 'You have your hours. There's no working all the hours that God created like you do in private firms today.'

Almost the reverse is true when the managements of the two firms are considered as a source of satisfaction. Thirty-four mentions of management are made, 20 of them by private haulage drivers, and 14 by B.R.S. drivers. The private haulage driver likes his management because it allows him discretion in his job, (11 drivers mention this). The B.R.S. drivers, if they favour their management at all, favour it because it obeys the rules which have been laid down for the work situation.

> 'The conditions, the union, everything is above board being a government job, its a much fairer job than on a private firm.'

Compare this with the most frequent type of mention by the private haulage driver about his management.

> 'They don't have the whip out and they don't say do this, do that.'

[25] See Appendix, Table 14. Comparative Work Satisfaction.

'The management leave the job to the particular driver to do his work, and we're not bothered at all, as long as we do the job.'

'The job is more that you are your own boss. Once you get out of here they leave you alone. There's nobody watching you, that's a thing I don't like.'

Pay is mentioned by 15 drivers in the sample and drivers from the private firm are rather more likely to mention pay as being satisfactory than B.R.S. drivers. Mentions of other factors giving work satisfaction total 17, 10 of these being mentions of comradeship in the occupation.[26]

The workers in the textile factory, in contrast to the lorry drivers in the firms' sample,[27] have as their major source of satisfaction their relations with fellow-workers. 30 per cent of the total favourable mentions (71 = 100) were on this topic. Wages and methods of payment constitute 18 per cent of the favourable mentions while management/supervision, and the closeness of the work place to home each make up 14 per cent of the mentions. A comparison of the lorry drivers and the factory workers shows that the lorry driver tends to be satisfied with his work if he has reasonable working hours and a good management, whereas the workers in the textile factory tended to stress relations with fellow workers and money.[28]

THE SOURCES OF WORK DISSATISFACTION IN
LORRY DRIVING AND FACTORY WORK

The factory workers are likely to view management and supervision as a major source of work dissatisfaction. This factor totals 29 per cent of the mentions on factors giving dissatisfaction (52 = 100). Wages and methods of payment and the insecurity of seasonal work respectively accounted for 13 per cent. Complaints about hours of work account for a further 10 per cent of mentions.[29]

[26] See Appendix, Table 15. Factors in Work Satisfaction amongst Lorry Drivers.

[27] See Appendix, Table 16. Factors in Work Satisfaction and Dissatisfaction of the Textile Factory Group.

[28] See Appendix, Table 17. Sources of Work Satisfaction in Lorry Driving and Factory Work Compared.

[29] See Appendix, Table 16.

Amongst the lorry drivers in the firms' sample the factors giving rise to dissatisfaction with the work situation are conditions of work and managements.[30] Forty-two drivers in the sample say that they dislike nothing about working for their firms: 20 out of the sample of 63 B.R.S. drivers and 22 of the 39 private haulage drivers. To this extent the private haulage driver is much less dissatisfied with his organisation than the B.R.S. driver. Twenty-seven of the 33 complaints about conditions come from the B.R.S. drivers, 16 of these being about the rules at the B.R.S. depot.

> 'Some of the stupid things carried on in general; the men at the front desk not knowing their job. The ten hour day when the job could be completed in another half an hour.'

> 'They penalise you for petty things. One driver calls another names and he gets reported; and if you park up in (a named town) and come home then you get a couple of days suspension. I don't think this matters.'

This latter complaint about the management penalising swearing works all the way up as a foreman pointed out.

> 'I wanted two blokes so I called them on the "blower". They didn't come so I went and looked after them. I was going up the stairs and I could see them down in the cab of a lorry. I shot down and dragged them out and I said, "Yow two, you'm rodney idle bastards and I'm tekin' yow to see the gaffer." They said "Aye and we'll see the gaffer about yow usin' bad language on us." I said, "Yow can tell him what the fucking hell yow like." Well I saw the gaffer with them and yow know what he said to me? He said, "A man like you should know better", so I said, "All right gaffer, them blokes is not 'rodney idle bastards', the'em 'rodney idle skunks' ".'

The more general complaints about rules are in the form:

> 'Too much red tape, a weekly sheet and a log sheet.'

Sixteen drivers in the B.R.S. sample complain about the rules while no driver in the private firm does this. The more formal structure of B.R.S. compared with the private firm undoubtedly

---

[30] See Appendix, Table 18. Factors in Work Dissatisfaction amongst Lorry Drivers.

induces the unfavourable attitude to the members of management at B.R.S. who have to enforce these rules.

Drivers at B.R.S. are much more likely to criticise the organisation of the firm and the way in which their work was organised (8 drivers at B.R.S. mention this, compared with one at the private haulage firm) than the drivers in the private firm.

> 'I dislike nationalisation, the bureaucrats in the office are theory men, they're not practical men and as an experienced hand I don't like working to rule; and you get two vehicles sent out on one job, it's inefficiency.'

> 'There are too many governors here.'

A further cluster of complaints about the management and staff are made against the traffic clerks who administer the lorry drivers in that they give them specific directions about the job to be done.

> 'The office staff and the management I dislike, they're not worth a wank; they're crooked, there's class distinction.'

> 'You get buggered about so much. You've got more bosses now under nationalisation than ever you had under private enterprise.'

> 'The only thing I dislike is that there is too much class distinction between the staff and the operatives. It seems that the staff can do no wrong and that the drivers do all the wrongs. I've never known a clerk to be really suspended. Four men down here were suspended because they lost a considerable amount of revenue (the roles of the four men are here named). They were suspended with full pay. It was nothing but a holiday for them. The (a named status), they made him a job and now he's (doing a named job). We've never heard of this one (the new role), it's a new one on us. The (two other named role occupants) were downgraded for a time but have since been regraded back to their own grade. This is only proving to us that the clerical section can do no wrong. We've only got to step out of line and we get three days' suspension.'

This criticism of the traffic clerks (9 drivers mention this at B.R.S. compared with only 2 in the private haulage firm) may be due to the fact that the representatives of management who are not always aware of the difficulties which are inherent in the specialist job of lorry driving are attempting to limit the area of discretion at job level. However, it may also be that there is a status conflict between the clerks and the lorry drivers. The studies by Lockwood[31] and Dale[32] both emphasise the importance of status to the clerk. In this case the clerk takes home rather less pay than the lorry driver who is traditionally his status inferior. Certainly there is adequate ground for a plausible hypothesis of resentment on this basis for the antagonism between the two sets of role occupants. This is only really a component of the general dislike of the organisation. At the B.R.S. depot the drivers dislike the rules which govern their work and in consequence they dislike management which has the job of enforcing such rules.

The further evidence quoted below is also indicative of this point. Almost four times as many drivers in the private haulage firm as at B.R.S. say they like the management because it allows them autonomy at job level.

> 'The job is more that you're your own boss. Once you get out of here they leave you alone. There's nobody watching you all the time, that's a thing I don't like.'

> 'The Management leave the job to the particular driver. We're not bothered at all as long as we do the job.'

> 'As transport firms go its reasonable. As regards red tape there's not too much of it. Some transport firms have rules and regulations but you're free from that here.'

The statements above are from drivers employed in the private haulage firm. Contrast these with the remarks of B.R.S. men on dislikes about their management:

> 'The job is top heavy. Too many administration staff—that's our biggest grumble. In this nationalised industry they treat drivers like children, whereas in the private firms they trust you and you are responsible . . .'

> 'Quite a lot of people are trying to run the B.R.S. and they've no idea—they're just boys out of school. Driving is different to work in the office. Down the office you get boys of 18 and 19 telling you what to do, how to load. Well I've done it for 'x' years and they've

[31] Lockwood, D. *The Black Coated Worker: A Study in Class Consciousness* Allen and Unwin. London, 1958.

[32] Dale, J. R. *The Clerk*. Liverpool University Press. Liverpool, 1962.

not been in it 'x' minutes. Half the stuff wouldn't ride if you took notice of them. I don't. You're responsible for the vehicle and the loads so I don't take any notice of them. That's what I find so annoying.'

'We're always getting fucked about. It's the inefficient way it's run by the office staff, they tell two of us to go to the same place.'

'If I do a job voluntary I do it better. If I do "sheeting" (covering the load with canvas sheets and secure it by means of ropes to the lorry) on my own I make a good job of it. If the foreman told me to do it I'd say fuck him and the wagon. I know my job and I like to be left alone to do it.'

Clearly the B.R.S. driver has less autonomy at job level than the driver from the private haulage firm. As a result the closer organisation at B.R.S. is likely to cause frustration amongst drivers who demand a wide area of discretion at job level.

It is not clear whether there are significant differences in the sources of work dissatisfaction between lorry driving and factory work. The sources are often only vaguely identified. The overall major source of work dissatisfaction amongst the firms' sample of lorry drivers seems at first sight to be their conditions of work, which accounts for 33 out of 67 positive mentions of dissatisfaction in the work situation. The biggest single factor amongst the factory workers, on the other hand, is management and supervision. Fifteen mentions (29 per cent of the total) are made of this factor. A second look shows that amongst lorry drivers the proportion of mentions, management, supervision and very closely allied organisational factors account for 40 per cent of the total. If the rather vague 'too many rules' factor is added then management and supervision become the major source of work dissatisfaction amongst the lorry drivers in an even bigger sense than for the factory workers.

ORGANISATION AS A FACTOR IN WORK SATISFACTION AMONGST LORRY DRIVERS AND FACTORY WORKERS

It has already been noted that organisation (in the sense of being the instrument of mobilisation of fluid resources towards the goal of production achievement) is a major source of dissatisfaction at work for both the lorry driver and the factory worker. What follows is a closer specification of this point. This is to be achieved by an examination of work satisfaction levels in B.R.S. and the private haulage firm; an examination of such factors in the differences; followed by a comparative examination of such different attitudes to management as exist between the two types of road haulage firm and the textile factory.

Work Satisfaction

On work satisfaction the evidence is that drivers from the private haulage firm are more satisfied with their work situation than the B.R.S. drivers.[33] The B.R.S. driver likes his pay, conditions and 'other' aspects (the comradeship, variety, and trade union representation) to a much greater extent than the drivers from the private haulage firms, but the private haulage drivers have a view of management which is considerably more favourable than that of the B.R.S. driver.[34] In fact the position between the two sets of drivers is reversed almost exactly when conditions and management are considered. The conflicting desire for reasonable conditions of work accompanied by freedom from the constraints imposed by organisation is apparent and is best stated by the drivers themselves. All the statements which immediately follow are made by B.R.S. drivers.

'I've nothing against the firm (B.R.S.) but I would prefer to work for my old private enterprise firm. There doesn't seem to be the initiative here as with the old firm. Here they just want more and not a proper job with it.'

'I left the railway because I was between two fences all day. I'm an individualist and railwaymen talk railways and drink with railwaymen. They've a one track mind and they idolise the job. I've no love for nationalisation but, and it's a big but, I don't want to go back to the 26 hours per day and the bad conditions. This is the best job in the world from the point of view of conditions.'

[33] See Appendix, Table 19. Work Satisfaction in Nationalised and Private Firms.

[34] See Appendix, Table 20. Factors in Work Satisfaction in Nationalised and Private Firms (Ratio Method).

'I would prefer to work for my previous private man. There was personal contact there. I'd get back and he'd say "Where the fuck have you been?" I'd say "Where the fuck have you been? Sitting on your fucking arse all day!" He used to lend me money, he lent me fifty quid once. But the private firms now exploit the men too much. They have you working excessive hours for too little money. This makes men unsafe. Here (at B.R.S.) you neither ask for favour nor give them—a good thing.'

'Before this I was on for (a named private haulage firm) and I used to work for 33 hours before a sleep period. There was one time when I was only home 12 days in 14 weeks. Here if blokes have a good vehicle they prefer not to put it in for repairs if it's basically O.K. since they are frightened of losing it. The traffic clerks especially at (a named branch) consider themselves little tin gods. They're under the impression that all they have to do is to issue an order and it's automatically carried out. Yesterday I did two loads and last night they wanted an explanation of why I'd only done two, when the only explanation that they should want is on the "Op. 6" . . .'

Writer 'What's the Op. 6?'

'The daily and weekly running sheet of the vehicle. If the information isn't enough then the dock foreman or the manager will give them any additional information. What they don't realise is that the driver is only human and if it wasn't for the driver they wouldn't be in a job. On (a named private haulage firm) the money was good and there were good vehicles. The money was even good if you worked your legal hours, you could pick up £13 on trunking. I got on champion with the management at (the named private haulage firm). With them the managers and owners are in personal contact with you at all times but the attitude of the management on this job is "if you don't like it you can do the other thing." A friend of mine here missed a load but the rule is that if it's not on the Op. 6 then you don't do it. When this friend got back the manager said "if you don't like tramping the way it is there's no job for you." What I don't like is that a traffic clerk will give you a verbal order and he won't record it on the Op. 6 and if anything goes wrong when you're carrying out the order then it falls entirely on the driver. It's the same with anything on B.R.S. If you're in the wrong they'll "bone" you about it, but if you're proved right they don't want to know you, if they did they'd lose face. Otherwise the job's not too bad.'

Thus although the actual physical working conditions are better at B.R.S. than those in the private firm, the B.R.S. drivers feel a sense of frustration. They are surrounded by rules which separate them from the management and thus are unable to solve the problems arising in the actual job for themselves or in conjunction with management as in the private haulage firms with which they had been previously connected.

Attitude to Management

The attitude to management is investigated from two points of view. Firstly it is desirable to know how the worker in question views the management of the actual firm for which he works. A further insight may be gained if the worker's conception of an 'ideal' management is known.

Sixty per cent of the drivers in the firms' sample have a favourable attitude to the managements of their firms. This figure has, however, limited value in application since the total firms' sample is not homogeneous in terms of management. When the individual firms are investigated, B.R.S. drivers have a less favourable view (56 per cent have a favourable view) than the drivers in private haulage firms, where 64 per cent have a favourable view of their management.[35]

Trampers in both firms have the most favourable view of management of all the categories of driver. This is significant as the tramper has a job which takes him away from his management for most of the time while he is at work and the area of discretion is correspondingly wide. In fact in the private firm trampers even find their own loads which determines where they will go. Part of a tramper's role is thus a managerial expectation. Trunkers on the other hand see their managements on most shifts and there is considerably less discretion in the job as the routes are pre-set and there is a prescribed time in which to do the job.

The largest single reason for the favourable attitudes is the way that management treats drivers in disciplinary terms. Clearly management is seen as having certain prerogatives, and its authority as such is accepted, but within these prerogatives

[35] See Appendix, Table 21. Attitude to Management.

any management action may be viewed as being fair or unfair by the lorry driver.

'The depot manager is fair but he is not a practical man—he's only an office boy. I don't have much to do with them on nights.'

This statement suggests that although a manager may be fair he is not really likely to understand the problems that a lorry driver might encounter. Four other drivers mentioned that their managements allowed them to get on with the job without interference once they were given it. This proportion was higher in the private haulage firm than at B.R.S. although numbers in each firm were the same.

'Nothing. I've never seen them (the management), if you do your work right they never bother you.'

'I think they're quite good, they leave the job to the particular driver.'

On the whole there is less sign of the lorry driver's approval of management on the score that he is left to his own devices in the job in the firms' sample than there was in the café sample. In the café sample however the attitude to management in relation to job control was revealed in a question on the firms in general. The other reasons for a favourable attitude to management are only vaguely, if at all, related to the problem of area of discretion at job level.

The reasons given for an unfavourable attitude to management are more relevant to the problem of autonomy or discretion area at job level. Seven drivers in the sample complain of too much work and four trunkers also mention this reason. The amount of work to be done will limit the freedom which the driver has; not only will it limit the freedom to take time off but also limit his ability to plan a work scheme, and to do the work as a craftsman would do it:

'At the moment not so good in this depot, they wanted 12 to 13 hours work in 10 hours—they expect too much.'

'They like to put a quart into a pint pot, they're all right but nearly all these transport people are the same. There's overloading, they say pick up 17 tons instead of 15 ton 12.'

Management inefficiency is also spoken of by 6 drivers. The

statements below criticise the management in relation to the job of lorry driving as the drivers see it:

> 'The depot superintendent seems to be O.K. Most of the managers were taken over with nationalisation and as far as I'm concerned they're just dead wood. There's not the interest taken.'

> 'Person to person I've never had any quarrels with him but the people in the office give out work which sends the drivers in circles. And they give you stupid things to put on (the vehicle) together. They should have to do six months' manual work.'

These examples are taken from statements made by drivers at B.R.S. There are fewer statements of this kind made by the private haulage drivers and they are less definite about the causes of the problem.

The remainder of the expressed reasons in the unfavourable attitudes constitute a resentment of the bureaucratic nature of the firms, particularly B.R.S. Too many 'bosses', no personal contact with the management, the wrong people in the jobs, and so on, are attitudes which are more likely to be a consequence of lack of knowledge of the jobs of other people in their organisation than due to interference with the occupational specialism. Though of course as organisations get increasingly bureaucratic the roles are increasingly prescribed and this creates problems with specialists. The B.R.S. drivers have a more unfavourable attitude to their management on the whole than have the private haulage drivers. The attitudes at B.R.S. are also more crystallised than at the private haulage firm, as is indicated by the fact that drivers at B.R.S. give fewer favourable and more unfavourable reasons than the drivers in the private haulage firm.

A conversation held with a driver at B.R.S. reveals that management does indeed interfere with the drivers and the way that they do their job. It also reveals a good deal of resentment:

> 'I don't think much of them (the management). There's a lack of co-operation between management and men. You haven't got the feeling that you can go and see them, there's no personal touch.'

Writer 'What sort of a boss do you want?'

> 'You want a man who'll give you a job and tell you to get

on with it—a man who trusts a driver to get on with the job. He'll get twice as much done as the other. We can ruin a boss if we want to you know. We proved that with a man called (a named manager). He messed us about, so that when it came that he wanted us to work "substitution".'

Writer 'What's "substitution"?'

'Well, he wanted us to work on Good Friday and have Easter Tuesday off so we got together and said no—that fucked him up. The division (divisional management) weren't pleased with the cunt. The B.R.S. lost £20,000 over that. They didn't like that. The division took it that he couldn't get on with the drivers and that's no good is it? They've moved him out of the way now to (a named depot). He's a bit better now but you see when it comes down to it he's dependent on the drivers.'

Writer 'How else could you fix him?'

'Well, say we get to the docks first and there are 15 private blokes (drivers from private firms) behind us. Well we let them go first. Maybe only two at each dock say London and Liverpool but it all adds up and he loses the revenue on those lorries for a day.'

This conversation indicates that the lorry driver expects to have an area of discretion at job level. This is not surprising as 72 per cent of the drivers in the sample said they felt they had a responsible job as they were alone in charge of valuable loads and vehicles. Two further statements, both made by B.R.S. drivers, who were not in the sample but from drivers who were met while the writer was on participant observation, make the same point about the driver as a man who knows his job:

'The thing that's wrong with B.R.S. is that they won't let you use your initiative. If you do a job on your own bat they'll call you over the coals for it, yet if you ring them up, they'll tell you to do exactly the same thing. They don't like you to do anything that they don't tell you, they must give the orders—you know what I mean.'

'Drivers spend time messing about the depot—the clerks say, "Oh I haven't got anything for you for a minute, go and have a cup of tea 'drive'." "This when the bloke is from Scotland and you know perfectly well that there's a load at (a named firm) for Scotland.'

The third hypothesis that was made is that the more mechanistic the organisation the less will be the work satisfaction. Mechanistic in this sense means that there is limitation on job discretion by organisation hierarchy. If the hypothesis is applicable to the situation then the factory worker should (as he is organised at the batch production level and therefore has a certain amount of freedom) find management more a source of dissatisfaction than the lorry driver.

There is some evidence to indicate that the factory worker also is a person who has or feels that he has something of importance to say about his job:

'I can't suggest a thing at all—they had a fitter on my mate's machine for nine weeks. I told (a named supervisor) that what they were doing wouldn't work and it didn't. (The named supervisor) said it would but it didn't and the thing had to be scrapped.'

'There is a tendency to ignore the views of a working person, although you have the committee you can't get things done quickly apart from that.'

The remark of a weaver is just as direct:

'He should listen to the operators point of view. He should really know the jobs that people are on in the factory. He may give an order that can't be done—on speed for instance. He may be well qualified but if he doesn't know about the machinery he should, and he should learn as much as possible about the job.'

The factory worker may well criticise the management for its inefficiency just as the lorry driver does.

'I've a sense of frustration owing to the inefficiency of management, I dislike this a heck of a lot.'

'The lack of getting on with the job, the progress, the supervision is bad.'

There is evidence that the factory worker is just as frustrated by management as is the lorry driver but the qualitative importance is not nearly so great amongst the factory workers in general as it is amongst the lorry drivers. The socio-technical system affects the way in which management and supervision can be made of primary importance in organisations. Firstly the socio-technical system may be such that management is very close to the worker, as in a factory, or it may afford freedom from supervision, as in lorry driving. Sixty-nine per cent of drivers in the café sample said that freedom from supervision characterised their work. Any slight attempt, such as would not be noticed in the factory, on the part of road haulage managements to limit job discretion, immediately makes the management factor in the work satisfaction of the lorry driver much more important than it is in the factory. The findings[36] on this point are very much in line with what is written above. In terms of ratios of favourable to total comments on management, private haulage drivers favour their managements much more highly than either the B.R.S. drivers or the factory worker. The figures indicate that the 'mechanistic' nature of B.R.S. produces a view of management which is at about the same level of favourability as that in the factory in spite of the presence of the lorry driving socio-technical system at B.R.S.

The picture of an ideal management is different between the lorry drivers and the factory worker. We have seen that the lorry driver is more likely to see management and supervision as a factor which can cause work dissatisfaction than the factory worker, but given the socio-technical system and comparative autonomy from management, the lorry driver is also much more likely to see his management in a more favourable light than the factory worker.

This attitude difference may be due purely to the socio-technical system itself or it may be due to the differences in 'ideal' managements between the lorry driver and the factory worker. In terms of 'ideal' behaviour pattern the lorry drivers tend to think that their managements should be 'instrumental' while the factory workers have an 'expressive' ideal view of their managements.[37]

The ideal manager for the lorry driver has two main quali-

[36] See Appendix, Table 22. Management/Supervision as a Factor in Work Dissatisfaction.

[37] These terms derived from Bales, R. F. *Interaction Process Analysis.* Addison-Wesley. 1949.

ties. Firstly he needs to have an understanding of the lorry driver's position when he is actually doing the job, and secondly he needs an objective knowledge of the problems of the industry in general. In the firms' sample, 135 out of 142 replies mention one of these two qualities. These two qualities are closely interlinked and may be summed up as meaning that the driver expects management to play its part efficiently while at the same time understanding his problems.[38]

The factory worker's conception of ideal management is different from that of the lorry driver. The ideal manager should above all be approachable:

> 'He needs the ability to get on with all types of men, from the lowest, to the skilled worker.'

Thirty-four of the total of sixty-three mentions of ideal characteristics of a factory manager indicate that he should have an expressive function.[39]

Differing interpretations can be put on the primacy of expressive and instrumental ideal functions of managements in the two contrasted situations. The most applicable interpretation seems to be that the lorry driver expects his management to have the relationship of an expert with him. It would be a relationship between equals. Such a system of organisation would be equivalent to Burns and Stalker's organic system where everyone in the organisation is committed to the organisational goals but leadership and direction takes place on a communicative and advisory basis between experts at different levels.

Management imposes greater constraints on the worker in the factory situation and in the organisation of road haulage at B.R.S. than does the management at the private firm. The extent to which management can restrict the lorry driver in his job is limited by the socio-technical system in lorry driving but the extent to which management tries to restrict the driver will create differences in work satisfaction. The lorry driver's job satisfaction is derived from the autonomy which he has both in the sense of Blauner's first two categories, control over the 'pace of work, time, and physical movement' and also in terms

[38] See Appendix, Table 23. Qualities of the Ideal Transport Manager.
[39] See Appendix, Table 24. Qualities of the Ideal Factory Manager.

of control over the social and technical environment. This chapter indicates that if these 'freedoms' are not accompanied by freedom from supervision then there is a considerable lowering of the level of work satisfaction amongst lorry drivers.

In terms of Tannenbaum's control curve[40] for the analysis of the distribution of control within organisations, the lorry driver demands that the control curve be horizontal. In the overall work situation the expectation of a straight line curve or some close variation is empirically possible. Whilst he is actually away from the depot he has almost complete control whereas in the depot the position is reversed. The two positions would cancel each other out producing the more horizontal curve. It is management's recognition of such a position concerning the ideal control curve which will produce greater work satisfaction amongst lorry drivers.

It is apparent that the level of work satisfaction can be related to the existence of organisational control forms. The level of work satisfaction is found to vary inversely with the presence of prescription of occupational roles. The more clearly hierarchical the organisation seems to be, the less is the level of work satisfaction. It is reasonable to take the existence of hierarchy as an objective indicator of the level of prescription in occupational roles. The factor of technical determinacy is not held constant between the firms in which the investigations are carried out. In spite of this the results may be taken to be even more significant than would otherwise be the case. All the subjective indicators show that the lorry drivers have a considerably higher level of work satisfaction than the factory workers. The B.R.S. drivers have a much lower level than the private haulage drivers, but still higher than the textile workers. The only explanation of this seems to be that which is in line with the earlier theoretical discussion. In spite of the advantage of a relatively open socio-technical system the organisational controls at B.R.S. reduce the level of discretion normally present in such a system.

Figure 5 shows the objective reasons for this. It will be noticed that the complexity of structure is vastly greater at

[40] Tannenbaum, A. S. and Georgopoulos, B. S. 'The Distribution of Control in Formal Organisation.' *Social Forces*. October, 1957. Vol. 36. pp. 44–50.

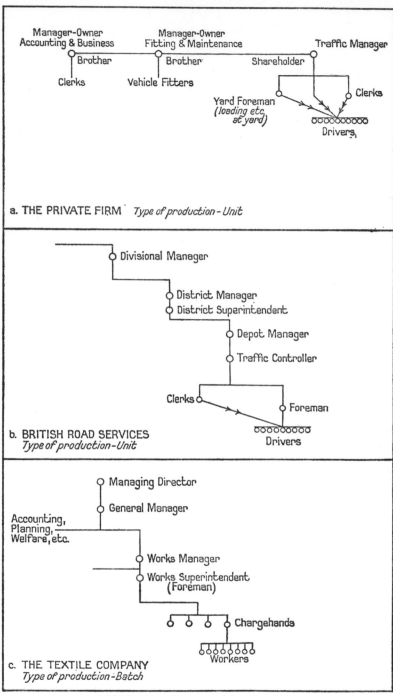

a. THE PRIVATE FIRM *Type of production - Unit*

b. BRITISH ROAD SERVICES
Type of production-Unit

c. THE TEXTILE COMPANY
Type of production-Batch

FIGURE 5. *Structures of the Three Firms*

the B.R.S. general haulage depot than at the private haulage firm. The existence of rules at B.R.S. is the most striking difference between the two firms. At the private firm there seemed to be only one rule and that was that a particular route was not to be taken. British Road Services provide a newly engaged driver with a booklet which says 'Welcome to B.R.S.', and explains the company's size and the functions of various partial structures. More important, the new employee receives another booklet which tells him what he should do in certain situations. It is in this way that the job is highly prescribed in the case of anything going wrong. In normal circumstances the B.R.S. driver is given his job by clerical workers who hand out the envelopes from behind a counter. As this chapter has shown, it is this part of the structure which articulates the conflict between mechanistic organisation and workers in open socio-technical systems. The clerical workers thus control the blue-collared lorry drivers in a very direct way. The lorry drivers claim that these clerks are not able to understand the exigencies of their occupation, a claim not entirely justified, in that some of the clerks had been lorry drivers themselves. Apart from the existence of rules at B.R.S., which in many cases were beneficial to the drivers, the hierarchy looked 'top heavy' and oppressive to them. Most of the drivers at the depot had little to do with the actual depot manager, who had risen from the clerical side, and this reputedly so, except on matters of discipline when they had done 'something wrong'. In the textile factory, the hierarchy, and the relatively closed socio-technical system ensures that work is constantly supervised with the expected social–psychological effects.

In terms of the earlier theoretical discussion as to the degree to which organisations may be considered as socio-technical systems we have to say that many variables in the systems have not been held constant. This is in the nature of this type of research. It is thus impossible to extract the precise effect of not holding constant the type of production.

Following on from Herzberg *et al.* the evidence afforded by the lorry drivers is that satisfaction, even a job which has plenty of 'motivators', can be reduced by a mechanistic type of organisation in which job level discretion is reduced. The evidence is that the lorry driver demands, if he is to have a high level of work satisfaction, a management which allows him a high level of discretion at job level.

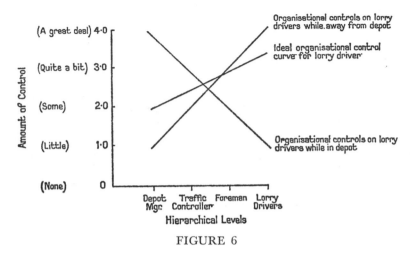

FIGURE 6

*An Estimated Ideal Organisational Control Curve for Lorry Drivers
Derived from Tannenbaum and Georgopoulos (1957)*

Figure 6 indicates a possible level of control for lorry drivers which would produce an involvement towards the problem and organisational ends as a whole, as in the 'organic' form of Burns and Stalker. There could be no possibility of a formal–informal polarisation. At present the evidence is that in terms of 'compliance', the lorry driver's involvement with his occupation is 'moral' and the power orienting him is 'normative'. By contrast he has a calculative or even alienative involvement and a strictly utilitarian compliance with the firm in which he works. These modes of analysis are naturally in terms of tendency rather than actual empirical existence of the pure form. The lorry driver it seems, expects to be given a job and then to be allowed to get on with it. In terms of the 'time span theory of responsibility' the driver's main expectation of management is that he be regarded as an expert, in an organisation which is at that point in time 'organic'. This derives from the fact that until he gets back to the depot no questions are asked about the job. Nevertheless, he does not expect to be left completely alone. In the lorry driver's view an ideal manage-

136

ment is one which knows its job as well as he knows his own job. Thus we describe the ideal curve of control in an organisation as active and polyarchic.

The evidence on the lorry driver's expectations of organisations is a parallel to his expectations about socio-technical systems. The physical freedom and job discretion afforded by the open socio-technical system in lorry driving has to be accompanied by a relative freedom from the constraints of organisation. The physical mobility in a lorry driver's job represents the situation of the ad hoc leadership pattern of Burns and Stalker's 'organic system' or Gouldner's 'natural system' model of organisation. Freedom from organisational constraint which is removed will not be compensated for by improving working conditions and containing them in 'mechanistic' or 'rational system' models of organisation.

VI

OCCUPATION AND FAMILY LIFE

An actor in a social system is involved in a greater or lesser number of status sets. In this chapter we shall consider the relations between two of the many status sets open to actors. An actor has a status or position in regard to his occupation and another position in regard to his family.

In contrast with more traditional societies there is an increasing separation of family and occupational activities in contemporary industrial society.[1] Partly as a direct consequence of the ascendancy of the occupational subsystem and partly as a result of concomitant urbanism the structure of the family has altered during the course of industrialisation. In structural terms family dynamics are away from the extended kinship pattern and towards nuclearity. The modern family is increasingly to be viewed as the family of procreation, the man, his wife, and their young unmarried children. This is not to deny the continued existence of extended family, particularly amongst the working classes, both in the more traditional areas and also on new housing estates. Geographical proximity and separation are a potent force in the survival of the extended kinship arrangement; willingness to participate requires opportunity to participate in order to effect survival.[2]

[1] Parsons, T. and Bales, R. F. *Family Socialisation and Interaction Process.* Routledge & Kegan Paul Ltd. London, 1956. p. 354.

[2] Mogey, J. M. *Family and Neighbourhood.* Oxford University Press, 1956. 60 per cent of the families from both St. Ebbe's and Barton had blood relations in Oxford but 60 per cent of the St. Ebbe's families had 'regular meetings' with their kin as opposed to only 30 per cent of the Barton families. p. 81. Willmott, P. *The Evolution of a Community.* Routledge & Kegan Paul. London, 1963. 'Local extended families, which hold such a

Occupation and Family Life

Any discussion of the effects of occupation on family life involves a consideration of relationships within the family as well as the more external structural aspects. Bott[3] has developed a useful conceptual framework here. Her concepts of 'segregated conjugal role-relationship' and 'joint conjugal role-relationship' define very clearly the types of relationship which are possible between the spouses. The type first referred to indicates a pattern where husband and wife have separate though complementary tasks and many independent activities in leisure. The second type refers to a predominant pattern of supplementary task roles and very few independent leisure activities and interests. Bott found the most marked role segregation amongst manual workers and a tendency for professional people to have more joint conjugal role relationships but this was by no means uniquely so.

A survey[4] of several studies suggests that the more traditional pattern of segregated role relationships within the working class family is changing. Men are now more likely to share in activities traditionally engaged in by their wives. There is now a greater degree of companionship between husband and wife in the working class family.[5]

Although Bott's study involves a small number of families it is quite clear that there are a great many variables involved in the determination of role relationships within any particular family. A further fruitful consideration may be through an examination of the functions of the family. The functions of the family which have not been whittled away are more important than formerly when they were part of a much wider set of functions.[6] The main functions of the family at present

[3] Bott, E. *Family and Social Network*. Tavistock Publications. London, 1957. pp. 53–7.

[4] McGregor, O. R. and Rowntree, G. 'The Family' in *Society Problems and Methods of Study*. Editor A. T. Welford. Routledge & Kegan Paul. London, 1962. p. 415.

[5] See in particular: Young, M. and Willmott, P. *Family and Kinship in East London*. Routledge & Kegan Paul. London, 1955. p. 145.

[6] Fletcher, R. *The Family and Marriage*. Penguin Special. Penguin Books, 1962.

central place in the older districts, have grown up in almost identical form on the estate, . . .' p. 109.

are the 'rearing of children and the "maintenance of individual emotional stability" function in relation to adults',[7] in other words child-rearing and provisions for the emotional stability in the adult members of the family. Dennis[8] suggests that the tendency to companionship between the spouses is importantly linked to an increasingly associational world outside the family.

It is quite clear that the effects of an occupation on family life will be diverse, firstly due to the different forms any particular effect on the family may take in empirical terms, and secondly arising out of the structural and functional diversity existing in families. The inter-relation of family life and occupation of the long distance lorry driver can be analysed with reference to the following continuum:

1. Mutual compatibility of the actor's roles in the two institutional areas.

2. Rationalised compatibility of acceptable mode of adaptation between the two institutional areas.

3. Incompatibility through the actor's conflicting roles in the two institutional areas.

The internal role relationships and functions of the family are aspects which will be more affected by occupation than the wider structural aspect. Lorry driving will have an effect on the companionship and maintenance of emotional stability areas of family life and also on the socialisation function. This is not to say that further structural differentiation within the family of procreation may not take place due to the 'extreme' occupation. The effects of industrialisation on the internal roles and functions of the family are diverse and the evolved characteristics of the contemporary family are outlined by Fletcher.[9] Titmuss has suggested some possible effects of industrialisation on the worker and the consequences for the family. Industrialisation with its persistent rationalisation has an adverse effect on the worker's ability to plan for his family and give it stability

[7] Parsons, T. and Bales, R. F. *op. cit.* p. 354.

[8] Dennis, N. 'Secondary Group Relationships and the Pre-eminence of the Family'. *International Journal of Comparative Sociology.* Vol. III, No. 2. 1962.

[9] Fletcher, R. *op. cit.* p. 128.

and status, while advanced technology may reduce the worker's initiative in the sphere of the family as well as the factory. All this may or may not be a source of mutuality in the marriage relationship.[10] The patterns of the occupational system and kinship have been noted by Parsons to be strongly contrasted, particularly in terms of achievement[11] required of the husband–father.

In short we shall be concerned with the way occupations affect the structure of the family in the sense of any reaching out to the kinship network by either husband or wife. Attention will be directed particularly at the relations of husband and wife and the way in which there are adjustments in roles to fulfil the functions of the family. In particular we shall be concerned with socialisation of the children and pattern maintenance or companionship. For the purpose of illustration, hypotheses and, if possible, some kind of empirical evidence should be presented to provide a clear picture of the actual variants in the analytical framework.

Within the wide 'compatibility—adaptation—incompatibility' framework for the analysis of the relationship between family and occupation there are several useful subdivisions which can be made. Compatibility can be presented in two plausible situations. Firstly where the occupation is carried on inside the home the whole family is involved. Although this situation in the early industrial revolution was very unsatisfactory for family life,[12] it can be assumed that it was acceptable in the normative sense amongst members of the family. A modern parallel occurs in the case of the immigrant family which keeps a shop or café. The docker is to some extent in this situation, since due to the 'causal' nature of his occupation and the closeness of his residence to his workplace, he may be at home at odd times. This gives him a strong family orientation.[13] This patriarchy is changing with decasualisation and

[10] Titmuss, R. M. *Essays on the Welfare State.* Unwin. London, 1963. Chapter 6. Industrialisation and the Family.

[11] Parsons, T. *Essays in Sociological Theory*, Free Press, 1964. Chapter 14. 'Certain Primary Sources and Patterns of Aggression in the Social Structure of the Western World.'

[12] Fletcher, R. *op. cit.* p. 84.

[13] Simey, T. S. (Ed.) *The Dock Worker*, Liverpool University Press, 1954. pp. 48, 54.

overtime but a new kind of structure of equality is emerging in the docker's family through wider social changes.

The second compatibility situation is where the actor, the husband-father, has two distinct roles to play but is able to segregate them in the social and psychological sense almost completely. The postulation is that of a person who has a 'nine to five' job who manages to devote his whole self to that job in that time and then be equally active in his domestic life (task sharing[14] and companionship with his wife) after five o'clock.

Adaptation is in evidence where one of the institutions is adjusted in some way to suit the requirements of the other. Adaptation will essentially involve strain in some sense. It may be hypothesised that this is the most frequent relationship between the two institutions. The family may adapt itself to the exigencies of the occupational role of the husband-father or the husband-father may change his occupational role to enable the family to fulfil its functions.[15]

The first possible effect to show itself would be a change in the task roles of the adult members of the family. The wife-mother would tend to become dominant in the task roles of the household with, as a polar case, the possibility of exclusion of the husband altogether. The husband does not share in the domestic work and also withdraws to some extent his companionship from his wife. This occurs in coalmining communities, and Dennis, Henriques and Slaughter[16] suggest that there is a strong connection between the miner's need for the security of close companionship of his fellows while he is at work; his consequent association with his fellows in his leisure; and an almost complete division of labour in the nuclear family. This division of labour is so strong that the wife and children may almost be considered as a separate structural subsystem with the wife never understanding or even knowing what her husband's job is in any detail.

[14] Herbst, P. G. 'Task Differentiation of Husband and Wife in Family Activities', in Bell, N. W. and Vogel, E. F. *A Modern Introduction to the Family*, Routledge & Kegan Paul, London. 1960.

[15] See article 'Keeping the Married Men Afloat', *The Guardian*, 15th May, 1965, on Merchant Navy Officers.

[16] Dennis, N., Henriques, F. and Slaughter, C. *Coal is Our Life*, Eyre and Spottiswood, London, 1956.

The policeman seems to be rather the opposite in this respect. The necessity of clear segregation of his public and private roles very often means that he is detached from his neighbours, as are also his wife and children. He has a tendency to carry over his occupational role into his family life, which annoys his wife. The social isolation of the policeman and his family probably means that his wife knows a good deal about his job.[17]. The adaptation that the policeman's wife has to make is often considerable especially in country forces. In the country the policeman's wife is almost as tied to the job as is the policeman himself; she must see callers and take messages when her husband is out. The wife of the country policeman apparently accepts this, but in the cities the lack of proper leave and long hours of work produce tension in the policeman's family. The community isolation due to occupation also causes difficulties and a policeman on shiftwork may have difficulty in seeing his children. It is a cumulative effect of these and other factors which may make the policeman change his occupation, but in general the family role is adapted to the requirements of the occupational role.[18]

In both the miners' and policeman's cases described, the family life has to a greater and lesser degree adapted to the occupation. There are some occupations which the wife will not adapt to, in these or any other ways. The husband has to leave his occupation either before his marriage or fairly soon afterwards. Such an occupation would be that of seaman where the husband would be away for long periods, perhaps as much as eighteen months at a time.

It is an example of this kind which provides the basis for the final category of relationship of the actor's roles in his occupation and family. The Hull fisherman's work takes him away from home for three weeks at a time. There is an attempt at compensation for absence to both wife and children by the fisherman. He gives the children lavish presents and does domestic tasks for his wife, 'behaving indeed like the prototype "companion" husband.' In spite of this the fisherman is to a

[17] Banton, M. *The Policeman in the Community*. Tavistock Publications, 1964. pp. 199–209.
[18] Cain, M. Chapter 6. 'The Life of a Policeman and his Family' in Ben Whitaker *The Police*. Penguin Special. Penguin Books. 1964.

great extent a stranger to his children and tensions develop between himself and his wife. The most concrete indicator of the incompatibility of occupational and family roles is the table of comparative divorce rates which Tunstall produces. In ten years fishermen accounted for 5 per cent of the divorces in Hull and the East Riding of Yorkshire while making up about $2\frac{1}{2}$ per cent of the population of working men.[19]

The compatibility, adaptation, and incompatibility between the roles attaching to statuses in the two institutional spheres is discussed. Two possible models are developed for the lorry drivers' occupation and family roles. Before the two models are developed it is necessary to classify the units which form their components.

A unit is a status occupant, such as husband-father, wife-mother, or a child. Interaction within the family unit is the basis of the system which is the conjugal family.[20] It is assumed that the system is an organic one and thus that there is an equilibrium state within it. Equilibrium is where the units of the system are in a constant state relative to each other and where a boundary is maintained in discrimination with the 'non-system' or external system. As will be noted from the earlier discussion, it is difficult to postulate any absolute state in which there can be equilibrium.[21] In talking about inter-action what we are concerned with in manifest terms is inter-action through task activity and companionship in more general terms. The variations in the connectedness of role relationships in the nuclear family are related to the con-nectedness of the external social network in which the husband and wife may be involved. Role segregation in family life is not necessarily correlated with strain and unhappiness in mar-

[19] Tunstall, J. *The Fishermen*, MacGibbon & Kee. London, 1962. pp. 161–3.

[20] This notion is derived from Homans' concept of 'internal system' (Homans, G. C. *The Human Group*) and from Zelditch, M., Jr. 'A Note on the Analysis of Equilibrium Systems' in Parsons, T. and Bales, R. F. 1956. *op. cit.*

[21] 'Occupational roles are specific and easy to describe. Familial roles are diffuse: they cover many different activities, the organisation of which is left to the discretion of the individuals concerned.' Bott, E. 1957. *op. cit.* p. 202.

riage,[22] but Tunstall has suggested that this can be a primary source of strain.[23] Clearly if companionship is reduced below a certain level then, even with strong norms of role segregation and external social activity, the resulting pattern of family life will be different from what is acceptable to family and community norms.

We assume that the conjugal family is a system in equilibrium within some boundary prescribed and maintained by normative and ideological notions of behaviour. Such boundaries, and consequently equilibria, will vary as the norms and ideologies vary with the reference groups from which they are derived. Both models to describe roles in the family make this assumption, at least implicitly.

In Model I the role relations cycle is from companionship to companionship. The hypothetical equilibrium position is that of the conjugal family contained within a system boundary. In this model there is disequilibrium when the husband is away because of his occupation. There is strain and resulting adaptation. The husband 'compensates' his wife by intensive participation in family activities when he is at home. While he is away the wife either has the children for company or seeks out a relation (usually her mother) for companionship. There is adaptation through strain caused by the reduction of companionship, the wife becomes lonely and unless this is countered things will go wrong with the marriage.[24] In the end when the economic needs of the household are fulfilled the pressure of family and community life will pull the driver back into 'local work' thus restoring the companionship equilibrium.

In Model 2 equilibrium is again assumed, as in the first model. The normative processes arising out of the need for maintaining the economy of the household legitimize the husband's absence. The disequilibrium which follows is much more serious in that the strain which results produces an adaptation which takes a different form. The husband does not compensate as the now differentiated sub-system of wife-mother and children has produced an equilibrium position in

[22] Bott, E. 1957. *op. cit.* p. 219.

[23] Tunstall, J. 1962. *op. cit.* p. 161–3.

[24] National Council of Social Service Pamphlet 'Loneliness' Revised 1964 Edition. p. 27.

itsclf.[25] This equilibrium means that compensation is rejected, the husband is considered an outsider, part of the external system and thus someone (or perhaps even *something*) which produces a disturbance in the equilibrium situation. In this situation, the husband, being outside the family in the social psychological sense, has arrived at a position where the rewards of family life in terms of emotional satisfaction are reduced, as also are the corresponding duties to bring such rewards. Secondly, with the release from a conception of duty, he has with his mobile occupation a greater possible chance of wider selection[26] of a suitable female partner as a mistress. At a later stage such disengagement, through the equilibrium process in the partial conjugal subsystem, the man's biological and psychological needs[27] are only to be fulfilled through the

[25] 'By contrast the man whose job demands his absence from home for two days or more at a time is forced to make new social contacts to help him occupy his leisure hours; and even though he may restrict himself entirely to members of his own sex for this purpose, his feeling of participation in family and domestic life is bound to suffer somewhat. Wife and children have to adjust to becoming a self sufficient group, exclusive of the father, for a relatively large proportion of the time, and daily routines must be established which do not include the father, and which may through habit continue to exclude him even on the few days when he is at home.' Newson, J. & E. *Patterns of Infant Care in an Urban Community.* Penguin Books, 1965. p. 216.

The fisherman's wife examples this behaviour. 'Almost all wives seem eager for their husband's next return. But often the same wives say that they can't stand having the man around the place when he's out of a ship.' Tunstall, J. *op. cit.* p. 163.

[26] Mobility may mean two things. The wider number of 'mates' to select from and also a strange community in which mores are irrelevant to the driver. Gibbens describes the occupations of 270 patients at V.D. Clinics: 'There was ample confirmation of the varieties which have often been described before—the mobile professions, the sailors, soldiers, commercial travellers, lorry drivers . . .' Gibbens, T. C. N. *The Clients of Prostitutes.* The Sixth Alison Neilans Memorial Lecture. The Josephine Butler Society. 1962.

[27] Using the notion of Malinowski's functionalism—that institutions are geared to the needs of the humans who compose them (The Scientific Theory of Culture) and the example of the 'outfit'—the travelling break-down gang—provided by Cottrell, this is a very plausible hypothesis. 'Some are married, but their infrequent opportunity to go home plus the absence of female companionship frequently leads the "outfit" man to abandon the family as a means of sex gratification. A great many are only

selection of an 'outside' mate or in other words 'another woman'. This can even reach the state of double structure.

SECRET 'WIFE' OF LES THE LORRYMAN

Lorry driver Leslie Higgs made regular trips between London and Glasgow. And at the end of each 400 mile journey was a wife to welcome him. In London there was his legal wife, Jean, 34 year old mother of his two children. In Glasgow there was Mary McCoun who thought Higgs was single when he 'married' her. From Sunday to Tuesday 34 year old Higgs lived with Jean in London. Then he got in his lorry and drove off to Glasgow and Mary. Yesterday—the fourteenth anniversary of his marriage to Jean—Higgs appeared in Glasgow's Sheriff Court, accused of bigamy.

Daily Mirror, 10th November, 1964

Conversely the wife's perception of her husband's absence and its connection with infidelity can lead to the wife taking up with another man. It may be that lack of companionship and the availability of another man is the basis of a separation. A further possibility is that the wife is very much overworked as, due to her husband's absence, she is carrying most of the housework and organisation. The two major samples of lorry drivers, the café sample, and the firms' sample, throw some light on the two roles of the lorry driver, his role as husband-father and his occupational role.

THE LORRY DRIVER'S TWO ROLES

1. Satisfactory Integration of the two Roles

Earlier we have noted that the lorry driver is described as an individualist in his work role. Any carry-over of this role into the sphere of family life produces the logical extension that one function of the occupational role is to provide an escape from family life. In fact only one driver made a mention of this kind. This driver, married with children, when asked why he had changed to his present job replied.

'For more money and to get around, I can have a dirty night out in 'X' town and no-one knows.'

---

intermittent deserters, but the bulk have completely severed family ties.'
Cottrell, W. F. *The Railroader*, Stanford University, California. 1940.

The lorry driver is generally a family man in many senses of the word. In the café sample 173 drivers were married, 155 of these had children. The firms' sample comprised 92 married men, 87 of whom had children. This does not mean to say that the family position with regard to the occupation is seen as being entirely satisfactory. Nearly all (168) of the married drivers in the café sample said that they were happily married but when it came to giving an indication of the attitudes of their wives, 49 per cent of the married drivers said their wives' attitudes towards the occupation were unfavourable, while 47 per cent said their wives had favourable attitudes. The drivers in the firms' sample indicated that their wives had rather less enthusiasm for their occupation than those in the café sample. Fifty-one per cent of the married drivers had wives whose attitudes were unfavourable while 41 per cent of the wives were favourable to their husbands' occupation.[28] The long distance drivers reported unfavourable attitudes more frequently than did the shunters, with the wives of trunkers showing the least favourable attitudes.

Legitimated Absence. The lorry driver's family pattern overwhelmingly approximates to the movement from companionship to companionship outlined in Model I, as would be expected. The career of the lorry driver is such that he is likely to be a tramper during the early years of his married life, that is between the ages of 25 and about 38. The mean average age of the trampers is 38 but this is not to say that many trampers are not well over this age. The average age of entry into tramping is between 26 and 36 for all these categories of driver with trunkers entering earliest and shunters at the greatest age. The point is that drivers tend to take up long distance work to provide extra money for the family as the pay in local driving is likely to be less. In this sense the behaviour of absenting himself from home and family is legitimated by the wives. It is notable that drivers are much more likely to say that they moved into tramping for financial reasons than with any other type of driving.[29] Money was given as a reason for

[28] See Appendix, Table 25. Wives' attitude to Lorry Driving.

[29] See Chapter III, Table 11. Reasons for Changing Jobs Given in Employment Histories.

moving 29 times, 16 of these were for the movement into tramping.

Legitimation of the driver's absence is likely to take two forms, either the wife will have rationalised her position or she will see the advantages absence brings as compensation. The 41 per cent of married drivers in the firms' sample made 31 mentions of reasons for their wives' favourable attitude. The most frequent mention is firstly that the wife had become accustomed to her lot, and secondly that the money is a compensation.[30] Trampers give their reasons mainly in this pattern. It is the money which the wife will accept as a legitimate reason for absence.

> 'She doesn't like it when I'm away too long but she accepts it because when I'm away I'm earning money for the home.'

> 'At the moment she says nothing because we're saving money but later she wants me to get a job locally.'

> 'My wife's quite happy about it, she gets her good money every week but she's always glad to see me home.'

> 'We both considered it and thought we would have the money first and then come off the road, when we have got what we want.'

> 'She doesn't like me being away so much but I want to earn what I can while I can and she understands that. She's very good—it will be different when we've got things settled (Hire Purchase commitments). I'll probably go local driving when I've filled my stocking.'

> 'It's my job and she doesn't mind at all, she's satisfied with the good money I give her.'

Many of the reasons given for wives' attitudes being favourable are mere rationalisations. It is quite possible that wives will accept absence because they are 'used to it' but statements like:

> 'She's got used to it now, she takes it for granted but when we first got married she didn't like it—but now she's a real lorry driver's wife and she won't have anything said against.'

and:

> 'At first she didn't like it but she's sort of getting over it. I suppose like everything else they get used to it.'

[30] See Appendix, Table 26. Reasons for Wives' Favourable Attitude.

149

can readily be transformed into comments like the following:

'She accepts it—put it that way.'

'I told her I earn the wages and how I do it is my affair and if she didn't like it then we'd have to come to some other arrangement. I don't want to work in a factory from 7 to 5 every day and throw her the wages on Saturday.'

The Compensation Effect. The first model indicates at the second stage a compensation effect. Both the wife and husband adjust to the situation to make it acceptable to them. The wife may rely on her children for company or may turn to her kin. Some drivers even said that their mother-in-laws came round to stay at the house while they were away in the week and there were signs of frequent visits by wives to their mothers and vice-versa.

'As long as she gets the wages that's all she worries about, she's got company with the kids. If she hadn't got the kids I wouldn't go away, I'd get a local job.'

'She's used to it now, she doesn't mind I don't think. I've got a girl 16, she's company for the wife now.'

'She's satisfied now I'm home every night, but when I was tramping it got very boring for her—her mother used to come and sleep at the house.'

The husband on the other hand may attempt to compensate his wife for his absence by a more intensive participation in family affairs at the weekends. Indeed 7 married drivers in the café sample said that their marriage was rather better for their absence and the consequent compensation effect, or perhaps even without this.

'She likes me doing it, she likes to get shut of me for a bit.'

'My wife worries, I think, when I'm away but she doesn't show it, but what she likes about it is that when I've been away for two or three days, it's like a second honeymoon. I don't mean only in the sex sense but just the get together—you know.'

'She's used to it now—it was very different at first, I should imagine. I'm away every day and I think we look forward to seeing each other all the more due to this, instead of being at home all the time, getting on each other's nerves.'

'This job makes you appreciate your home life more since you're away two or three nights of the week. If I went home and went out with the boys I'd expect her to moan, she's alone all the week.'

The compensation by the husband takes the form of intensive interaction with his family at the weekends. In the café sample 43 per cent of leisure activities are home centred as opposed to being outside the home. Further 46 per cent of the activities are family centred rather than being with people outside the lorry driver's nuclear family. The drivers in the firms' sample report a similar leisure pattern with regard to family and home activities. Family centred activities comprised 42 per cent of the total activities, while home centred activities averaged about 49 per cent of the total.

Drivers realise the deficit in home life that their occupation produces and some of them consciously attempt to compensate themselves and their families by home and family centred activities when they are at home. Six trampers and two trunkers in the firms' sample make statements indicating this kind of reinforcement of family life:

'I stay at home. Being out so often, when you do get home you prefer to stay in the home, painting and decorating and gardening.' (Trunker)

'I stay at home in the house, its a change to see it, I don't bother going out much. I get plenty of pints when I'm away.' (Tramper)

'I spend it at home with the wife—I rarely go out. I always like to be home on a Saturday to do the shopping with her and watch the T.V.' (Tramper)

The tramper seems to have an occupationally induced duality in his pattern of leisure behaviour. On the one hand he has the pattern which is relevant when he is away from home, and on the other, that for when he is at home.

'When I'm "up the road" its usually the pictures, and when I'm at home I spend the leisure time with the wife and kids, such as it is.'

'When I'm away I take a walk round town and go to the pictures or the pub. I stay in the house when I'm at home. I'm out enough when I'm away.'

'Probably out with another driver to the pictures or for a drink. When I'm at home I spend the time indoors with the family.'

In some cases the wife has not adjusted to her husband's occupation which means that the husband may have to change his occupation or at least his firm in order to get more family and home life. Fulfilling his wife's expectations is not always easy since there may not be other jobs available or other firms with the same sort of jobs with different (in the sense of improved) working conditions. One driver, a tramper, told the writer of a specific experience where he was able to make such an adjustment.

'She likes the money. She didn't like it when I was on tramping. I'd been away from Sunday to Friday and when I got back she'd gone to the mother-in-law's. She left me a note saying "You think more of your job than me—you can have your married life." So I rang up the boss and I told him I was finishing and then went and fetched her. When you're tramping you never know where you're going and when you're coming back and this makes a big difference to a woman if she knows when you're coming back.'

Predominance of Ties to the Family. There is a period in the lorry driver's career in which the home and family orientation tends to primacy. His absence or disassociation from home is no longer legitimated by his wife. This may occur because the children have grown up and left home and the wife is now left completely on her own, or it may be just that many of the expenses of early married life have been attended to. In Chapter III we have seen that the pull of family and community life is a major factor in the driver's moving out of long distance driving and into a local driving job. The present chapter has indicated that while the drivers' wives are prepared to legitimate absence for financial reasons in early married life, many of them regard this as a temporary legitimation.

It is clear that once the driver has left long distance work the attitude of his wife changes. In the café sample 10 married drivers indicated that their wives held favourable attitudes towards their occupation because they were 'local' drivers, while in the firms' sample two drivers' wives had favourable attitudes for this reason. Sometimes the wife's attitude is one which is mildly in favour of the driver getting a local job.

'She doesn't mind me having the job but anytime I'm fed up she's willing for me to change it. We're away so long that she'd rather me have a job with less money and be local, that's her version, I asked her.'

Other wives may have very severe attitudes.

'As you can understand they get browned off sometimes. It s okay if I get back twice a week but if I've been away a fortnight she says "You can get rid of that job as soon as you like." '

'She says I think more about the lorries than I do of her—I should have married a lorry—that's when I'm going away on a Sunday, of course, she doesn't like that at all.'

Drivers respond to this kind of pressure either by giving up long distance driving or by giving up driving altogether. Very often they are willing to make such a change anyway as they have reached an age where the job is becoming difficult for them. The greater difficulty of the older man meeting the physiological requirements of the job coincides with the reduced need for money with a contracting family and also their wives' need for companionship. Some of the older long distance drivers made statements indicating their probable response to such pressures. Some will leave driving altogether.

'The wife is fed up with me being away so long that's why I'm thinking of getting out of driving.'

'She's on about it (the job). She doesn't like it but she realises that the money is just about as much as I can earn in my position. She doesn't like me being away all the time. She worries about smashes. It's hard for a woman. If she's still on about it in two years' time when the boy finishes his apprenticeship I shall change.'

Others will change the type of driving that they do, from long distance jobs to shunting.

'She accepts it but she would like to have me home every night. When the girls finish school I'll apply for a lighter job. When I'm about 55 I'll get a lighter job.'

The conclusion about the first model of the driver's solution of the relationship between his two statuses is that there is a legitimated absence during early married life but as time goes on and the economic problems become solved, drivers' wives like their husbands' occupation less and less. In later life, towards the end of his career, the driver is subject to severe pressure from his wife to either get a local driving job (shunting) or to leave lorry driving altogether. Some drivers may put off or withstand such pressure until late middle age and health changes create additional pressure for them to leave their particular type of driving or completely leave the occupation.[31] It is this kind of driver who is likely to rationalise his wife's attitude, and possibly to disregard the dangers in doing so.

2. Conflict between the Two Statuses

Our second model shows the risk which the lorry driver runs in his family life if he fails to realise the strain which his occupation places upon it. The first stage of the second model assumes the same equilibrium position as the first model. The interaction position is a hypothetical 'normal' with normal interaction between the driver, his wife and their children. The driver, being young, needs the money to build a home for his family and to this extent his absence is legitimated. In the second

---

[31] Banks, O. 'Continuous Shift Work: The Wives' Point of View.' *Occupational Psychology*, Vol. 30, 1956. In a study of the wives of shift-working steel workers Banks found that wives were more likely to complain about the loss of their social life than of breaks in the domestic routine. Nevertheless 22 per cent said it was more difficult to prepare meals and 11 per cent said it was harder to get washing done. If this example can be extended to the lorry driver then it should be noted that trunkers and shunters do not do shifts as such, but the tramper subjects his family to continuous and irregular shift work. The wives dislike irregularity in the tramper's case but in the case of trunkers it is the wives' dislike of being in the house alone at night which will be a source of pressure on him to leave long distance driving. The evidence on shift work is somewhat conflicting. Zweig F. in his 'Worker in the Affluent Society' says that there is little difference between the proportion of age groups amongst those who find shift work and night work upsetting for reasons of health but almost all those that do find it so have wives with strong negative attitudes to night work. McDonald, J. C. ('The Social and Psychological Aspects of Night Shift Work'. Birmingham Ph.D. Thesis 1958) found that 85 per cent of night workers' wives said they would prefer husbands to work on days. This was for various reasons such as anxiety about being alone at night, being lonely and having to rearrange domestic affairs.

model, however, certain mechanisms operate to produce a state of non-legitimated absence of the driver from his family.

The Genesis of Non-Legitimated Dissociation. The lorry driver's hours and conditions of work leave him very little time for domestic life. This means that his wife will do the tasks which normally would be done by her husband if he were at home more. In the firms' sample more than half the number of reasons for the unfavourable attitude of wives were those of absence from home and family[32] and many of these were from the trampers. Accident worries, night work, and the irregularity of hours of work are the other major sources of wives' unfavourable attitudes. Absence from home means that drivers will not see their children as they normally would as well as not being able to do tasks about the house in the true pattern of the companionship family.

> 'She hates it—it's the kid like. She has the responsibility of the father and also the jobs that need doing at home.'

> 'She did complain about me being away when the family was young.'

> 'She didn't like the night trunk. I used to go away on Sunday night and not get back until Tuesday. Its away from home and the pipes burst in the cold weather and she couldn't fix them.

It is not surprising, if through his occupation the lorry driver is not able to fulfil the normatively determined role of a husband-father in the companionship family, that the wife is likely to develop a certain amount of self-sufficiency, and to regard the husband as something external. This is shown by the fact that drivers say that their wives' domestic routines are actually disturbed by their irregular times of returning home.

> 'It's damnable. I can't tell you what she says. I sit down to my dinner and its burnt when she throws it across to me. I say "That's lovely, love".'

It is perhaps this sort of thing which discourages the driver from going home more often than he does, after a time. The possibility is then that his wife will get lonely and seek other male companionship.

[32] See Appendix, Table 27. Reasons for Wives' Unfavourable Attitude.

As a further check to the proposition that wives have a higher frequency of unfavourable than favourable attitudes to their husbands' job, the drivers in the firms' sample were asked whether they thought lorry drivers should be married or single men. Only 19 (19%) in the sample said that they thought that lorry drivers should be married. This compares with a percentage of 91 per cent of drivers in the sample who are married. Fifty-three drivers in the sample said that the lorry driver should definitely be a single man.[33]

The 19 drivers who said that lorry drivers should be married made mention of various reasons for their opinion.[34] Six drivers said they thought trunking and shunting were normal jobs, and there was mention by 6 drivers that family responsibilities made the driver more responsible in his job. This latter ties in with the views of managements illustrated in Chapter II, when they said they preferred to employ family men. Being 'looked after' when he comes home is another reason why the lorry driver should be married, as is also the necessity of having 'someone to come home to'. Domestic convenience of having a wife is more frequently mentioned than the emotional satisfaction which she provides.

The reasons for the lorry driver being a single man are very crystallised indeed.[35] In the sample 29 drivers mention the fact that the occupation takes them away from home, 18 men specifically mentioning tramping as doing this. The married lorry driver has the worry of a family while he is away from it and his wife can be very lonely and not have 'much of a married life'.

> 'On tramping he should be single, on trunk its immaterial, but tramp definitely single. His wife would be the loneliest person in the world. A tramper is best single with no ties, he'll work on with no worries.'

> 'Single. There's no home life—my baby only sees me two nights a week. I see him on Saturday but otherwise he's usually in bed when I come home and go away.'

[33] See Appendix, Table 28. The Lorry Driver's Attitude to Marriage.

[34] See Appendix, Table 29. Reasons Why a Lorry Driver Should be Married.

[35] See Appendix, Table 30. Reasons Why a Lorry Driver Should be Single.

'For a woman it isn't much life—it's a single man's job on journey work but most of us are married strangely enough.'

Even amongst these remarks some men indicated that they were on long distance work because of the need to finance the home.

'Money comes into it. I can't imagine a lorry driver liking a tramp job except for money so I take it that all lorry drivers are married.'

'If I were single I wouldn't be on this job. I wouldn't be up the road if I were single.'

This last remark is difficult to interpret. We cannot be sure whether the man is away from home in order to earn money to support his family, or whether he wishes to get away from home. The interpretation put on this is that in fact it is the desire to earn money for the home which took that particular tramper away. While only one driver amongst all the drivers interviewed in the study said he himself was using the job to get away from his wife, there were 3 drivers in the firms' sample who said that the occupation could be used as an escape from family life.[36]

'It's what the wife gets used to but being away from home makes it a single man's job. You get no pleasure out of marriage if you're away but some chaps like to get away.'

Non-Legitimised Dissociation. One lorry driver, whom the writer met while hitch-hiking, complained that he was 'having trouble' with a mistress of his who now wanted to be taken home. He said that he had been living with this woman for some years as he had always been on the same route ever since starting with the firm. He was going to 'give her up' as she was now pressing to be taken home presumably to live with the driver, his wife, and their three children. The mobile occupation both reduces the possibility of the family fulfilling its function as a unit within which sexual needs may be satisfied, while at the same time it increases the range of sexual opportun-

[36] While the writer was carrying out participant observation he was told that some trampers, and one in particular, liked to go away on certain routes because of the mistresses they had in places on those routes. One man's wife would ring the office and ask that her husband should not be sent on a certain run. The office usually obliged the wife.

ity in places where the man is not constrained by the mores of his own community.

Certainly there are temptations and problems for lorry drivers when they are away from home. Soloman,[37] in her study of transport cafés describes the lorry drivers' prostitute. She suggests that the welcoming or not of the 'scrubber' or 'smoker' at a café by the owners is a factor which affects the patronage of that café. Many drivers in the firms' sample knew about such cafés, and would not stop at them, but there were other drivers who enjoyed this part of their occupational life, even if only to be entertained by watching the proceedings.

> 'You missed some good entertainment at (a named café) on Friday night. They were all there, shouting and going on about who was going to go with this bloke. Then the police came—you should have seen them all scatter.'

Whether the lorry driver is more likely to have a regular mistress or whether he tends to patronise the scrubber is open to investigation. What is relevant here is that the family as a unit is not fulfilling his needs while there is ample scope for sexual opportunity due to his mobile occupation. Certainly he has this problem and is likely to be tempted.

> 'If you ask me, a married bloke, who has been married for some time, is not going to do without it (sexual intercourse) for the time when he is away on the job.'

> 'I don't think they should be married. There's too many off the right road.'

> 'Single. When lorry drivers are away from home they're going out with different women and picking up these different pick-up girls.'

The second model for relationship between occupation and family roles, as well as suggesting that the lorry driver will have increased sexual opportunity, suggests also that firstly the wife will be lonely and regard her husband as a stranger or at least someone who interrupts her domestic routine. Both these points are adequately illustrated. The final phase with the wife is that the loneliness and burden of running the home while the

[37] Soloman, E. *op. cit.*, 1954.

driver is away tend to make the wife look out for another man. There is such a case in the firms' sample. One driver, a tramper with the private firm, who had four children, had his wife leave him while the study was being made. He was one of the most difficult men to get hold of at the time of interviewing as he was almost never in the depot, but away working up and down the country. Soon after the time of interview his wife left him for another man. There is another source which can cause the woman to leave her husband and this is a perception of her husband's infidelity while he is away from her. Such a perception may well be justified as illustrated by comments from general conversation with drivers in the sample:

'One girl we brought down from (a named town)—a lovely girl, mind—oh yes—all six of us trunkers had her—even (a nickname for an old driver) had her that night. She was lovely, but she said herself she was over-sexed.'

Two drivers indicated that the single man could have considerable sexual opportunity while out on the road:

'Single—you could have a rare time if you were single.'

'Single, then you can pick up all the 'cuife' on the road.'

Another driver reported his wife's awareness of sexual promiscuity by members of her husband's occupational group:

'Be easier to say what she doesn't say. She often wishes I'd pack it up but then if you want the money . . . There's been some plays on T.V. lately about lorry drivers picking up "bits of stuff" and my wife said "Oh, so that's what you get up to is it"?'

The consequences of such awareness are that the wife will not trust her husband and will believe that her husband is being unfaithful to her. The perception of infidelity is possible by both wife:

'Preferably to be a long distance driver a man should be single —there's no doubt about it, it does tend to break up homes but the trouble is that once you get on to it you feel the call of the road and that's it. That's what happened in my case. I've had damned good jobs and I've had to pack them up. Lorry driving can break up homes just as it's done to mine in the last couple of months. It's lonely for the wife—you see they want to be taken

159

out and when he's not there to take her out she says "He's up the road having a good time. Why shouldn't I?" '

and husband:

'I've been thinking about it. There's not much sex life on this job . . . With me I never tell my wife when I'm going to be back because then she won't have anybody in. If she says "When will you be back?" I say "I don't know" or if I say "Tomorrow" and she says "Will you be early or late?" I say "I might be early or I might be late, it all depends." '

Such a belief in the other partner's infidelity, or even the possibility of it, will make a tremendous difference in the conjugal relationship in terms of reciprocity of interaction. The barrier already created by the new equilibrium within the family when the husband is away becomes emphasised as the wife is seen to no longer fulfil her function and her husband is thought to be unfaithful. The final breakage is illustrated by the marriage history of one tramper in the firms' sample. When asked whether he thought lorry drivers should be married or single, he said:

'Single—my marriage broke up because of it.' In response to the question on his wife's attitude to lorry driving he continued:

'I wouldn't like to repeat what she said when I was married, in fact during the war years she followed me down the street and begged me not to go away. The trunk job that I was doing was the cause of my marriage breaking up—my one night home was on a Saturday night. I thought of changing the job but the trouble was that I didn't do it or I might have saved my marriage. I've had eight years to reflect, my ex-wife craved my company and I'm just beginning to realise it. I've two daughters living with me and for their sake I'm carrying on with the job (tramping) now. It provides them with the little pleasures they're entitled to. That's my way of trying to make up for the marriage I was responsible for breaking up. Adultery was the cause, being away from home, the temptation you know. I'm absolutely sure it wouldn't have happened if I hadn't been a lorry driver. I would have led a different life entirely. I shall not marry again. I wouldn't burden another woman. It's a lonely life for them. My ex-wife actually reared my children since I was away from home so much. I would see them going to school as I was coming home,

160

and see them coming home as I was going to work. No, I wouldn't recommend lorry driving. I had a nervous breakdown. I was in a poor state over domestic worries.'

Such a case is a concrete example of the possible effects of the occupation of lorry driving on the driver's married life. The mechanisms and process from companionship to divorce are clearly illustrated. It is important to be clear that such cases are rare in statistical terms, though perhaps not as rare as the number in which the mechanisms can be articulated would suggest.

CONCLUSION

Our information is that the lorry driver's family can adapt itself to his occupation and such an adaptation may take a number of forms. On the other side of the coin the lorry driver may adapt his occupation to the needs of his family life. The position seems to be summarisable as follows:

A family unit may be conceived of as being made up of a number of component relations, each of which in a particular society may be normatively regulated. The component relations are, firstly, the economic relationship, through which the economic well-being of the family is taken care of by the husband–father's obtaining and distributing his earnings. Secondly, there is the political component which includes those relationships involving the way in which the family as a unit is organised and, in particular, who organises it. The social relations component refers to members of the family affording each other companionship, with reference to emotional stability of the members. Lastly there is the sexual relations component.

In a homogeneous community, where the occupations are well defined, the demands of the occupational role may be incorporated into the normative structure. By contrast, in an occupationally heterogeneous community such generalised norms as do exist may be ill fitted to particular cases. Modification of such norms to fit the particular cases may be difficult as where, for example, the wife will not see the occupational necessity as much as her involved husband. Further modification will be difficult to effect due to pressure from the reference groups of spouses.

The lorry driver's occupation requires that his presence in the family unit is more limited and more irregular, than in many other occupations. This conflict between the normatively regulated needs of the family as a unit, and the lorry driver's occupationally induced pattern of behaviour suggests that there will be strain. Since also the lorry driver tends not to live in a community of lorry drivers, the differential demand of the occupation will set up a demand for a strain-reducing adaptation, both in the family and out of it, and an acceptance of modified norms.

There is evidence of both strain and adaptation involving a new normative structure amongst the lorry drivers themselves on each of the types of family relationships outlined above. The models for adaptation which have been previously discussed are thus incorporated into the more general scheme of a discussion of these relationships.

Adaptation in terms of the economic relationship takes the form of the lorry driver entering long distance lorry driving in order to provide for the needs of his family in the early and most costly stages of building a home. At a later stage in the lorry driver's career he will tend to change out of long distance driving into shunting or local driving as the need for money is less great in the later stages of family life when the house payments are less of a burden, and more particularly (as many lorry drivers may in fact rent rather than buy a house) when the children have grown up and left home. In terms of the economic relationship we can say that the primacy of adaptation is of occupation adapted to family needs rather than vice-versa.

By contrast the political relations show a primacy of adaptation by the family. The husband–father is not at home, particularly in the case of the tramper, with sufficient regularity and frequency, to be the mainstay of organisation in the family. It is the wife who has to take on much more of the problem of organisation than would normally be the case. She may even have to do her own repairs in the house.

In both the political relations and the social relations components of the total interactions within the family there is a major adaptive effect which is occupationally induced. The husband attempts to compensate his wife and family for his absence by a more intensive effort to organise and give companionship when he does return home at the weekend. Some drivers took this to extremes by doing the household cleaning and cooking meals but more usually there was a conscious realisation on the part of the driver that the weekends were meant to be spent with his wife and family and very likely to be spent at home.

Sexual relations in the lorry driver's family have to be adapted due to the occupation. The irregularity of the tramper's visits home or the persistent night work of the trunker clearly alters the pattern of sexual relations. This is so much so in the case of the tramper that the overwhelming view of the drivers in the firms' samples is that a lorry driver, and in particular, the tramper, should be a single man.

Most of these adaptations are accepted by the lorry drivers though in some cases the evidence is that some adaptations are only partly acceptable. There seems to be more evidence that the wives do not accept them as fully as do the lorry drivers themselves. In essence the types of relations discussed above are in terms of adaptation which is acceptable on the whole to both partners. This is basically Model 1, the legitimated dissociation adaptation. Model 2 is a demonstration of the consequences of the strain involved in adaptive behaviour with the illustration of behaviour which is clearly maladaptive in normative terms and in terms of the family's continued existence as an entity. The strain of trying to adapt—the formation of internal family equilibrium exclusive of the lorry driver husband—could possibly lead to the setting up of emotional barriers between the lorry driver and the rest of his family. The consequences of this, plus the opportunities for extra-marital sexual relations in a mobile occupation, can conceivably lead to the breakdown of the lorry driver's family life.

In conclusion, it is necessary only to say that adaptation which is made is, on the whole, acceptable to both partners but such acceptance could never imply that adaptation results in the ideal pattern of family behaviour, either in the context of the pattern valued by members of the family themselves, or the pattern idealised by the wider community.

VII

WORK AND NON-WORK
IN LORRY DRIVING

In previous chapters an attempt has been made to examine the work life of the lorry driver and his attitude to this. The last chapter indicates that his occupation has definite consequences for his family life. What follows is an insight into the relationship of the lorry driver's work role to his other roles in the work situation and also to his pattern of leisure activity.

The activities of the lorry driver in the different zones of his life, his work life and his leisure life, produce different types or patterns of interaction. For analytical purposes the lorry driver may be considered to engage in publicly-visible interaction in three zones. These zones comprise his interaction: in his home community; in the performance of his work role; and in his destination community. The major concerns here are the relative importance of the lorry driver's work life compared with his life in the leisure sphere and also the extent to which such zonal behaviour patterns are distinct, or related.

The primary importance of man's work in determining his total behaviour pattern is often emphasised.

> In our society the successive phases of (man's) life tend to be defined in terms of his relations to the world of school and work; pre-school, school, work and retirement . . . There is a certain order in the lives of men in a society . . . The ordering in our society . . . is very much a matter of a man's relation to the world of work.[1]

[1] Hughes, E. C. *Men and Their Work*. Free Press, Glencoe, 1958. See also the abstract of Raymond Mack's article 'Occupational Ideology and the Determinate Role'. *Social Forces*, Vol. 36, No. 1, 1957. p. 37.

Hughes goes on to suggest that as well as being in a central position in the lives of men, work is also highly segregated or distinct from other activities.

> There are a time and place for work; times and places for family life, recreation, religion and politics. The mood and frame of mind of the place of work are supposed to be different from those of the rest of life.[2]

Dubin has suggested that too much emphasis has been placed on the work of men as the determining force in their behaviour, which is of the greatest importance. Dubin's research, involving men working in three plants of which a sample of approximately 500 were questioned, showed that for almost three out of every four workers, work and the work place are not central life interests.[2] The factory worker is not as likely to gain satisfaction from his work as from activities in other spheres. The same applies to the locale of meaningful social relations. In contrast to these findings Dubin[3] has shown that about three out of five workers indicated that the employing industrial company was the most significant organisational form in their lives. The implication here is one of minimal necessary participation of factory workers in their work situation and the really meaningful activity and social interaction taking place outside this sphere. This implication is one of distinctive spheres of activity and interaction. Wilensky[4] discusses two hypotheses about leisure behaviour; the 'spillover leisure hypothesis' and the 'compensatory leisure hypothesis'. The former indicates a carrying over of the type of behaviour involved in the workplace. The illustration is one of the alienated, bored factory worker showing an individuated non-creative leisure pattern. The latter shows the factory worker as making up for his alienation in the workplace during his leisure time. The implication of both hypotheses is that non-work patterns of behaviour are not at all isolated from the work behaviour of the individual, although the two spheres are distinct in physical

---

[2] Dubin, R. 'Industrial Workers' Worlds'. Chapter 13 in Rose, A. M. *Human Behaviour and Social Processes*. Routledge & Kegan Paul, London, 1962.

[3] Dubin, R. 1962. *op. cit.*

[4] Wilensky, H. L. 'Work, Careers and Social Integration', *International Social Science Journal*, No. 4, 1960. p. 554.

terms. The present chapter takes Wilensky's view of leisure, namely that the work role of the lorry driver will affect his behaviour in his leisure activities. This has already been shown to be so in the case of his family life. Lorry drivers then, will be looked at from the point of view of their interaction patterns in three zones, home community, work group, and lastly destination community.

In Chapter II it is shown that the lorry driver, particularly the lorry driver employed by private haulage firms, works a greater number of hours per week than the hours worked in manufacturing industry, and indeed the average shown for all manufacturing industry exclusive of agriculture. The hours worked by lorry drivers in both public and private haulage firms are longer than in the building and construction industry. The private haulage lorry drivers work even longer hours per week than the agricultural worker.[5] The daily working shift is also a long one. In private firms drivers work for eleven hours per day, while the drivers at B.R.S. have a ten hour daily shift. Often these shifts are at irregular times and thus, even when the driver is working at a local job, the effect of actual hours of work and times of work on the leisure pattern will be considerable. In view of such considerations, the risk of repetition of such data seems slight compared with the risk of understating its importance.

The average number of hours worked weekly are estimated at 56·4 for private haulage drivers and 50 for B.R.S. drivers. Both estimates are derived from the firms' sample but in both samples the picture of long hours is confirmed. The drivers in the café sample show a good deal of irregularity in the number of hours worked and in their 'comings and goings'. 23·5 per cent of the 200 drivers in the café sample said that they spent either one or two nights away, while 61 per cent (the remainder) said they spent between three and seven nights away every week.[6] Trampers spent, on average, four nights away,

[5] See Chapter II, Table 4.

[6] See Appendix, Table 31. Number of Weekends Worked (Café Sample).

trunkers three (nights or days), while shunters spent no nights away at all except perhaps very occasionally.

The biggest majority (61·5 per cent) of the drivers had their weekends away from work and so were able to spend them at home in their own community but some drivers reported having only half the weekend free while for some others there is sporadic weekend working. Thirteen per cent of the sample reported working more than one weekend in four but less frequently than one in two. Ten per cent of the café sample said that they worked more frequently at the weekends than one in two.[7] The trampers and shunters are most likely to work at the weekend. The tramper tends to start his week's work on a Sunday morning, while the shunter has to load up vehicles in preparation for the trunkers who will begin work either on Sunday or Monday night.

The drivers in the firms' sample confirmed these findings, based on the café sample, on the hours and periods of work of the lorry driver. The trunkers work at night and sleep in the day, though if they are on a 'changeover' trunk they sleep in their own house in the day time. The trunker is much more likely to be 'at home' than the tramper but during the week it is unlikely that he will have a great deal of leisure other than that which is spent in bed. The writer's experience is that most of the trunkers spend the whole day, or almost the whole of it, in bed. They would get home about eight o'clock in the morning and go to bed round about ten o'clock, get up at six in the evening and start off for work again at about eight. Only seven trunkers, (19 per cent of all trunkers) spent three or more nights/days away from home in the week. Some of the B.R.S. trunkers are on a shift known as 'fortnight about'. They work at shunting for a fortnight and alternate this with a fortnight's trunking. This makes a difference to their leisure pattern as they can then have their 'social life' in the fortnight in which they are shunting.

The trampers on the other hand are much more likely to spend more nights away from home, perhaps three, four, five, or even more than five in a week. The mean average number of nights spent away per week is four in the case of the tramper.

[7] See Appendix, Table 32. The Occupational Categories of Drivers who work more than One Weekend in Four.

It has been shown earlier that it is this loss of home life which makes tramping the least popular form of long distance lorry driving amongst all types of drivers in the firms' sample taken together. Shunters, by contrast, rarely spend nights away from home. Eight shunters (21 per cent) said they spent either one or two nights away from home in the week but the vast majority (76 per cent) said they spent no nights away at all.[8]

The trampers fare worst again in the amount of continuous time that they spend away.[9] Both trunkers and shunters are unlikely to spend more than one night or one day away from home at a stretch, though with non-changeover trunking the pattern is one night, the next day and the following night away for a continuous period. The mean number of continuous days/ nights spent away from home is 1·49 for trunkers, 1·18 for shunters, but it is 4·25 for trampers. A driver employed at B.R.S. is likely to be away from home for a longer continuous period of time than the private haulage driver. B.R.S. drivers spent 2·69 days away at a stretch on average, while the average is 2·36 for those employed by the private haulage firm. Over the whole sample the average is 2·56 days. The figure may be higher at B.R.S. because of the distances involved in the work. This is unlikely to prove an explanation of the difference in its own. What is more plausible is that B.R.S. drivers are less able to 'do a dodgy' (to run through to home regardless of hours worked) than are the private firm's drivers.

The hours and time periods of work can be recognised as being potentially the major variables in the lorry driver's pattern of interaction with people in his own community. Tramping is the worst type of driving job to have from the point of view of being away from home and community. The view of tramping held by many lorry drivers is aptly expressed by one shunter:

> 'Tramping, that's the type of job that's suitable for a single fellow. I'm prevented from it because my wife is not in the best of health.'

[8] See Appendix, Table 33. Nights Away from Home in the Week (Firms' Sample).

[9] See Appendix, Table 34. Length of Continuous Time Away Per Week (Firms' Sample).

However, it is likely that the trunker also, is little able to participate in community activities, as although he is likely to be at home, he will be asleep. It is to be expected that lorry drivers will vary in their patterns of behaviour in the home, or base community, due to the fact that lorry driving is by no means an homogeneous occupation. Trunkers, trampers, and shunters have vastly differing working conditions from each other. The type of driving that is done is thus the major variable in the formation of the lorry drivers' leisure activities and interaction in his home community.

A second important variable is the type of community in which the lorry driver lives. In certain circumstances work and non-work patterns of behaviour are mutually reinforcing.[10] This may be due to the stability of the workplace and the work community as in the old tinplate industry in South West Wales.[11] It may also be due to the fact that although the work place and the residential community are differentially located the work and non-work patterns of behaviour are mutually supportive. Fishing is such an industry. In a study of a community of fishermen on Hull's south west side, Horobin[12] suggests that the values and outlook produced by fishing as an occupation permeates the community as a whole. He says that 'fishermen are a race apart' and the whole community may be considered as a subculture.

> Although fishermen do not form a very high proportion of the population even in this area (about 11 per cent of the male working force), they are the key group in the industry, and the industry dominates the area. Thus practically the whole of the population in this area, including the shopkeepers are geared to the rhythm of fishing.

Other conditions in communities indicate that there is a

[10] Kerr, C. and Siegel, A. 'The Interindustry Propensity to Strike. An International Comparison', in Kornhauser, A., Dubin, R., and Ross, A. M. *Industrial Conflict*. McGraw Hill, London, 1954. Evidence is presented on strike epidemiology. One of the relevant factors is considered to be the mutual reinforcement of occupational groups when a homogeneous 'isolated' community occurs as in mining and dockwork.

[11] Chadwick-Jones, J. 1960, *op. cit.*

[12] Horobin, G. W. 'Community in the Hull Fishing Industry'. *British Journal of Sociology*, 1957.

M

169

considerable degree of accommodation of behaviour patterns where there is disparity between work and non-work patterns. The study of the fishing community mentioned above is a case in point. The problem of the time distribution between work and non-work may be accommodated where there is a pre-dominance of the occupationally induced varied time pattern. The prevailing spirit or ethos and the extent of the occupational content of such a community ethos is all important in determining the extent to which time separated occupational groups and their members are accommodated. In a steel working area such as Sheffield the ethos is that of making steel and all those patterns of behaviour that go with it. This raises the whole question of the function of a community in occupational socialisation. Fishing and mining communities tend to socialise the potential fishermen and miners. Mining communities are a very good example of visible leisure patterns socialising potential miners. Mining communities are pervaded by the occupation and norms originate in the exigencies of work situation. The more or less total division of labour on a sexual basis in the miner's family is due to the need of the miner for company of his own kind. The work situation, with its dangers, involves the necessity of close comradeship through the miner's close dependence on his workmates, and it is a natural carry-over that much leisure time is also spent with workmates. Close bonds created by the exigency of the work situation, once generated, do not end with the end of the shift. It is quite possible that the young man is already half a miner before he even goes down the pit for the first time because he lives in a mining community.[13]

At the other extreme occupation and community may be so far apart that there may be no accommodation unless the prevailing pattern of unresolved strain may be considered as such. McDonald[14] has argued the specific point that night-shift work has the effect of making the people involved feel outsiders in their own community. He says that the group participation of night-shift workers in the community is reduced and that

[13] Dennis, N., Henriques, F. and Slaughter, C. *Coal is Our Life*, Eyre & Spottiswode, London, 1956.
[14] McDonald, J. C. 'The Social and Psychological Consequences of Night Shift Work'. Ph.D. Thesis, University of Birmingham, 1958. p. 204.

there is a 'widespread feeling that as night workers, they are
regarded by the wider community as "social outcasts".' This,
continues McDonald 'appeared to strengthen their solidarity
sentiments'.[15] McDonald's investigation was carried out in
what is usually described as an 'amorphous urban community'
in the English Midlands. Another example of an occupation
which can cut its incumbents off from the community is given
to us by Cottrell.[16] The American railroader's life is dominated
by the 'time dependency' involved in his occupation.

> '. . . the pattern of social relationships set by the occupation
> vitally affects the social life of the railroader . . . Time dependency
> cuts the family off from other groups in the community as well as
> its members from each other. It interferes with community
> activity, preventing the assumption of civic responsibility, and
> denying status so gained.'

The two occupations discussed above, night shift factory work
and working on the railway have the effect of differentiating
the lives of the people involved from those of the remainder of
the community. In terms of community life such people have
an extra-normative pattern of behaviour, which makes work
and non-work quite separate.

In the extreme case of disparity between the community of
residence and occupationally induced behaviour, the occupational incumbent may represent a close parallel to Park's[17]
'marginal man' or Simmel's 'stranger'. A good illustration of
such a polar case is Cottrell's discussion of 'the outfit', the

[15] McDonald, 1958, *op. cit.* See also Lipset, S. M., Trow, M. A., Coleman,
J. W. *Union Democracy: The Internal Politics of the International Typographical
Union'.* Free Press, Glencoe, 1956. The isolation and differentiation through
night work made for solidarity among the printers.

[16] Cottrell, W. F., *The Railroader,* Stanford University Press, 1940.
pp. 76–7.

[17] Park, R. E. 'Culture Conflict and the Marginal Man', Chapter 28 in
Race and Culture, Free Press, 1950, pp. 372–6. 'The marginal man as here
conceived, is one whom fate has condemned to live in two societies, and in
two, not merely different but antagonistic cultures.' Park refers to Simmel's
notion of the 'Stranger' as being 'the one lives in intimate association with
the world about him but never so completely identified with it that he is
unable to look at it without a certain critical detachment'. For a discussion
of what Simmel calls the 'Objectivity' of the stranger, see pp. 402–8 in
Wolff, K. H. *The Sociology of George Simmel.* Free Press, Glencoe, 1950.

travelling repair gang, and their experiences in the communities which they visit during the course of their activities. This notion of the outsider is useful as it serves to highlight both the effects that an occupation may have on the behaviour patterns of its incumbents and also the possible reciprocal behaviour of people in residential communities towards the incumbents of the occupations in question. Fishing and mining produce very definite patterns of behaviour but in a community where fishermen and miners are respectively the major reference groups such behaviour is not deviant. With the travelling breakdown gangs in Cottrell's study there is a definite example of deviance by an occupational group in a community which is not able or willing to accommodate it except under certain circumstances.

The lorry driver is a worker in a relatively new industry, in that, compared with railways, and before them, the canals, the road haulage industry is a consequence of the development of the vehicle manufacturing industry of the twentieth century. The road haulage industry is growing rapidly, which may mean that the stability necessary for tradition to evolve is lacking. A further important condition of the lorry driver's situation is that he does not form an occupational residence group as do steelworkers in Sheffield, railwaymen in Crewe, or fishermen in Hull. Many of the drivers interviewed lived ten to twenty miles away from Welshtown, rather than in the town itself. The hours and working conditions indicate a distinct time-erratic work pattern for the lorry driver, even if he is a shunter, but particularly so if he does long distance work. Thus the lorry driver has the problem of great disparity between his work and non-work life, without an occupational residential community to reinforce his behaviour, or even to accommodate such a behaviour pattern. He is not, however, in as extreme a position as that of Cottrell's breakdown gangs on the railway.

Because of the lorry driver's hours of work, his leisure activities in his own community will be severely limited. The chapter on his family life indicates that the lorry driver's leisure activities are highly linked with his family. When he is at home his activities are as likely to be home or family-centred as not. This is in line with the changes in the stratification process generally taking place in the wider society.[18] Life styles are tending to merge but there is considerable argument as to how far this process has developed.[19]

In the café sample, drivers were asked three questions on their use of leisure. Firstly, they were asked what they usually did with their leisure; secondly, what they did with it immediately prior to being interviewed; and thirdly, what they most liked doing with their leisure time. The responses to these questions indicate a range of from 43 to 52 per cent of the total of activities mentioned, to be home centred. From 36 per cent to 46 per cent of responses over the three questions indicate family-centred leisure behaviour.

The responses of the drivers in the firms' sample shows a similar level of home and family-centred activity. The total number of activities given in answer to a single question on leisure activities, 'What do you usually do in your free time? Who accompanies you?' was 210.[20] Forty-five per cent are home centred and 30 per cent are family centred. Trunkers mentioned the least number of activities (1·81 per person) while trampers mentioned the most (2·29). All types of driver tend to have a high proportion of individual activities.

Trampers have the biggest percentage of family-centred activities and the smallest percentage of home-centred activities. The family life of the lorry driver indicates that the tramper has an occupationally induced dual leisure pattern. Suffice to say here (the other side of the pattern is discussed later) that while he is at home, the tramper's leisure activities are to a great degree family centred. This is partly due to his sheer absence from home and partly due to his attempt to positively and consciously compensate his family for his absence during the week. Many drivers would say that when they were at home at the weekend they would either stay at home or take their wives and families out for a run to the seaside in their cars. This is the most frequent family-centred leisure pattern of the lorry driver (in particular the tramper)

[18] Abrams, M. 'The Home Centred Society', *The Listener*, 26th November, 1959.

[19] Goldthorpe, J. H. and Lockwood, D. 'Affluence and the British Class Structure', *Sociological Review*, July 1963.

[20] See Appendix, Table 35. Lorry Drivers' Activities in Leisure Time.

while he is at home. All sorts of other activities were mentioned but family- and home-centred activities, plus 'messing about with the car' and gardening, seem to predominate.

> 'At nights when I'm away, I go drinking, or to the pictures or playing billiards and snooker. When I'm at home I like to take the wife out but most of the time I'm happy just to stop in with her.'

In the sense of leisure in general, rather than a distribution of activities between two institutional areas, the trunker can suffer deprivation as much as the tramper. The trunkers report the least number of leisure activities and from their work times it is obvious that their activities will be reduced and that they will be in relative social isolation. One trunker told the writer that he wanted to return to tramping for the following reason:

> 'I'll go from here now and I won't see anybody, you know what it's like on the "—— run" and then I'll get back tomorrow and go to bed and the next night I won't see anybody either.'

This man, normally of quiet disposition and easy going, became extremely agitated when the foreman said the change had still to be discussed by management and he said:

> 'Right, I've asked twice, you can tell them this. If I'm not posted for tramping by Friday dinner-time they can fucking wrap 'em up (i.e. his cards) for Friday night. They can please themselves.'

In addition to a general question on leisure activities in the samples a question on participation in associational groupings was also put to the drivers. Associational groupings refers to those groups, such as club activities, where purposes and activities, though multiple, are defined, and formal membership is required. It also refers to groups which are less definite but still regular, such as the public house kind. The question was worded in the form, 'Do you belong to any political, social or religious groups, or to a trade union?'

Amongst the responses of the drivers in the café sample there were considerable signs of reduction in participation in such associations directly due to the occupation. The biggest area of associational membership amongst lorry drivers in the café sample is club membership. Most of these clubs are drinking clubs, although they are called works social clubs or conservative, labour, or liberal clubs. Fifty-one mentions of club membership are made altogether.

The extent of the participation is not high. Only 76 (36 per cent) 'participations' were made less than one month prior to date of interview. Just over half (53 per cent) of the total were made less than three months prior to the interview date. Forty-seven drivers said that they had participated in some group (the great majority in this case referred to the trade union) over six months before the interview. Forty-four drivers said they were members of groupings (again mostly references to the trade union) but that they never went along to meetings. Thirty-nine drivers (19·5 per cent of the sample) reported no group membership at all.

As well as the low participation rate implicit in these figures there is some direct evidence of reduction in participation. Thirty drivers in all made remarks indicative of such a reduction.

(Trade Union) 'I went a month ago. It's very awkward if you are up the road. No there's nothing else. I never know when I'm going to be home.' (Tramper)

'I used to play football but I can't guarantee it now because I was always late home from work on Saturday and they put me on the Reserves.' (Tramper)

'I like a game of darts but you never know when you're going to be home—you can't belong to a team.' (Tramper)

'No doubt I would have joined a club but this job doesn't sort of cater for it.' (Trunker)

'What free time! Most of it I spend in bed. At weekends I'm with the family.' (Tramper)

The firms' sample also shows indication of the lorry driver's reduced participation. Participation is analysed in more detail.[21] The instances of participation in five areas of associational grouping are shown. These are social and drinking clubs; sports and other specific interest groupings; religious associations; trade unions; and political affiliations. The most frequent participation is in social and drinking club activities, and, a

[21] See Appendix, Table 36. Associational Group Participation (Firms' Sample).

close second, trade unions. Lorry drivers appear to be only infrequently members of interest groupings, religious groups, and seem rarely to have political affiliations. Most drivers are likely to have participated in some kind of associational grouping between a week and a month prior to being interviewed and few drivers appear to have gone as much as a month without participation.

An index system[22] is used to hold the time factor constant when the various occupational categories are placed under investigation. The indices[23] show that B.R.S. drivers, on the whole, have a higher participation rate than their private haulage colleagues, with one exception, the shunters. The biggest difference in the rate between firms occurs between the B.R.S. trampers and the trampers in the private firm. This ties in with the differing conditions in the types of firm which are noted earlier. As the hours of work and conditions would denote, it is the tramper in both types of firm who has less chance to use his leisure within his own residential community. In the firms' sample it is quite definitely the tramper, and not the trunker who participates least. The trampers' participation index is about half the value of that of the shunters while the trunkers' participations and memberships produce an index in between the ones for trampers and shunters. The participation index varies inversely with the hours of work in the type of driving job. The long distance drivers spend less time, and have less to spend, in their own communities than the short distance shunters. The tramper may be away for as much as a fortnight at a time, and if he is a 'private' tramper he may work as long as work is available. Although the trunker is a long distance driver and a night worker he is for the most part able to organise his leisure life as he has regular runs. He is not as able to do this as is the shunter who has the greatest rate of participation in associational groupings. Thus it seems reasonable that the

[22] The index is constructed by weighting numbers in each participating category. The index formula is $\frac{fxw}{N}$: that is, the sum of the frequencies multiplied by the weights and divided by the category under investigation. For the weights see Appendix, Table 37. Associational Group Participation.

[23] See Appendix, Table 38. Participation by Occupational Category in Each Firm.

evidence on the participation differences between the types of driver is significant.

On the face of things lorry drivers may have a lower participation rate than workers who have static jobs within their own residential community. Further it may also be true that the trampers' family centredness is only what might be expected in view of a general trend towards family centred behaviour. Young and Willmot[24] find a decrease in voluntary association outside the family with the movement of families from traditional working class residential areas to new council estates. The shunters in the firms' sample have the highest average age of the three types of driver. It may be that the shunters tend to be less family centred in their leisure purely because they were socialised in a different era. On the other hand it may be that because the shunter is home at night he need not concentrate on family centred leisure to the extent that the tramper does.

A comparison of the participation[25] amongst lorry drivers with that of non-lorry driving groups, suggests that there is at least something in the hypothesis that a mobile occupation will reduce its amount. Between long and local distance drivers it is the long distance driver who is the lowest participator, and the tramper in particular. When firms are compared, it is the B.R.S. driver with his shorter hours and more regular work and better conditions in general, who can and does participate more than his private haulage colleague. In short, participation is very much a matter of hours and working conditions. The words of a driver in the category least likely to participate, the private haulage tramper, sum up the situation much more dramatically than statistics:

'I sleep, I've no hobbies.'

Compared with other non-lorry driver groups, the lorry drivers have a lower participation rate. Out of the 21 survey groups reported on, the lorry driver groups come in the bottom half of the list in participation terms with the exception of the shunters, who have the fourth highest participation rate of all

---

[24] Young, M. and Willmot, P. *Family and Kinship in East London*, Routledge & Kegan Paul, London, 1954.

[25] See Appendix, Table 39. Comparative Indices of Social Participation.

the survey groups. The trunkers in the firms' sample are also above the average firms' sample rate but as would be expected there is a considerable gap between them and the shunters. The trampers show the lowest rate of any category in the firms' sample with a higher index than only one group, the café sample of lorry drivers.

The indication is that the occupation severely affects the lorry driver's leisure activities in his own community, in that his absence prevents him from participation in associational groupings. Where the evidence is not so conclusive however, is in the area of family and home centred leisure behaviour. Certainly the tramper is highly family centred in his leisure behaviour within his own community. However he is not significantly any more home centred than the reports of Young and Willmot on the inhabitants of the newer London council estates. Bohan also reports such a finding in his study of life in Newtown, which is in fact an old part of Welshtown. Both studies emphasise home-centred behaviour, even if it is only 'watching tele'.[26]

INTERACTION IN THE PERFORMANCE OF THE WORK ROLE

The socio-technical systems described earlier indicate either actual or possible patterns of interaction during the course of the worker's performance of his job. The assembly line allows for less freedom of interaction than does the technical organisation in the tinplate work group. The lorry driver, if he obeys the work rules, would conceivably not interact with anyone while he is doing his actual job of driving. His cab and his moving work situation preclude a great deal of interaction which would be possible and natural in a static work group.[27] There is a paradox here, the paradox of the collectivity amongst lorry drivers in spite of the existence of conditions for individualism.

The paradox is easily explained, in fact there is a good deal of interaction in the course of the performance of the work role. There are, at the same time, considerable indications of isola-

[26] Fr. H. Bohan, 'A Social Survey of Newtown' Cardiff. Department of Industrial Relations, 1964. Cyclostyled. See in particular Table 25 in Appendices.

[27] T. Lupton, 1963, *op. cit.* for an example of such interaction.

tion. The firms' sample of drivers were asked if they thought their job was a lonely one, and if so, if there were any compensations for this. Nearly two thirds of the sample say they find their job a lonely one. There is little difference between the categories of driver on this point. Considerably greater difference does occur between the drivers of the two types of firm. B.R.S. drivers are rather less likely to report loneliness than the private haulage man. Again this is consistent with the differences in conditions between the two firms.[28] The reasons given for the feelings of loneliness are as would be expected.[29] Drivers say that they are alone in their cabs or that long distance runs are lonely.

> 'It is lonely in a sense, you're in the cab on your own but you get used to it. Myself I've always been a lone wolf. I keep my own company and I'm able to please myself what I do and how I do it.'

> 'You adapt yourself to it. It's lonely when you're driving but you call in a café and mix with people, but even on driving you can meditate and work out dozens of problems.'

The last driver quoted indicated loneliness in his job but there is a more general evidence of compensation to be found in the cafés along the route. The socio-technical system shows the possibility of such interaction when the driver stops for a break. This is in fact a major item in the lorry driver's autonomy. Other remarks show the existence of regular interaction.

> 'It can be lonely, especially if you are on a long run. You're on your own in the cab and there's nobody to talk to, only when you stop in the cafés and meet some of your friends.'

The drivers who say that their job is not lonely give reasons such as the possibility of meeting other drivers and a variety of different people.[30] Other drivers say that the conditions of the road do not allow feelings of loneliness to arise.

> 'No, we mix with each other in cafés and you know each other on the road and you stop and help each other; if you're in trouble about six drivers will stop. It's very rare one won't stop.'

[28] See Appendix, Table 40. Loneliness in a Lorry Driver's Job.
[29] See Appendix, Table 41. Reasons for Reporting Loneliness.
[30] See Appendix, Table 42. Reasons for Reporting Not Lonely.

'No, a lorry driver gets to meet people that he wouldn't meet in another job. He meets different people in different towns.'

'No, not so much these days because there's so much traffic on the roads that you haven't time to be lonely. There's a café every two or three miles now, there used not to be years ago.'

The compensations for the loneliness that almost two in three drivers experience are mainly social. Drivers meet fellow drivers in cafés or meet different people during the course of their work, or pick up people wanting lifts. There are other types of compensation which are not social however, and these indicate the individualism mentioned earlier. Five drivers say that being their 'own boss' is adequate compensation.

'Yes, it's a lonely job, but you are independent'.

An earlier quotation indicates individualism amongst lorry drivers in an extreme form but several drivers mentioned the feeling of liking the fact that in isolation they have time to 'meditate' and 'work things out'.

'No, there's plenty to do. There's so much on your mind. You think about driving and other things.'

It seems that although the lorry driver's work situation produces the conditions of isolation making for loneliness, very few lorry drivers are totally uncompensated for this. Only 14 (14 per cent of the sample) say that there is not any compensation for their loneliness, while the other 48 of the 62 'lonely' lorry drivers indicate some form of compensation or other.[31]

In fact there is a high level of contact between lorry drivers while they are at work in spite of the spatial isolation. This is because they control the technology of the job and can thus make sure of social contact. Nine out of every ten drivers report that they have contacts with other lorry drivers.[32] The figure is higher for B.R.S. men than for the private firm's drivers. Contact is higher amongst trampers than other types of driver, and shunters have the least amount. The difference is due to the fact that the tramper stays away from home for a much longer period than the trunker, while the shunter is a

[31] See Appendix, Table 43. Loneliness and Compensation.
[32] See Appendix, Table 44. Contact amongst Lorry Drivers.

purely local driver. The contacts at destinations will be discussed later as it is convenient to illustrate the tramper's leisure pattern when he is away from home, at that stage. The trunker makes fewest contacts probably because his work situation is becoming so (relatively) restricted by his schedule (perhaps as much as 350 miles per night may be demanded of him). This reduces the comradeship amongst lorry drivers which is said to have existed formerly.

> 'No, I don't really bother, only with the drivers I know on this particular route, it's getting more than a job, it's a feat of endurance. There's not really enough room on the roads for all of us. Lorry drivers aren't so mixy nowadays since there are so many of them. Also the schedule is so tight that a driver has to keep to it, whether on B.R.S. or private enterprise.'

Ted Murphy,[33] a lorry driver who has written his autobiography, hints at a decline in comradeship amongst lorry drivers. A journalist, Strachan,[34] in a series in the Aberdeen *Press and Journal* also suggests that the old spirit of comradeship is no longer there. The findings in both café and firms samples of lorry drivers support such a view. Nevertheless there is a good deal of interaction amongst lorry drivers. The fact reported earlier, that lorry drivers tend to be at loggerheads with the people who load and unload them or at least to resent the power such people have and the inconvenience they cause, tends to increase the drivers' interaction amongst themselves. This is not to say that many lorry drivers do not have pleasant social relationships with people they meet in factories and elsewhere. Indeed frequently such relationships are highly meaningful to drivers. Drivers who said they preferred tramping frequently said this was because they had made friends 'all over the country'. The place the lorry driver is most likely to make contact with other lorry drivers is in cafés and at other places on his route.[35] The signs here are that as well as stable interaction patterns between drivers there is a good deal of less stable, and in fact, transient interaction. Interaction is in many cases so sporadic that you might or might not see 'that

[33] Murphy, E. *The Big Load*, T. Poulis, London, 1963.
[34] Strachan, E. 'The Long Haul'. A series of twelve articles in *The Press and Journal*, Aberdeen. 26th August–10th September, 1963.
[35] See Appendix, Table 45. Places of Contact with Other Drivers.

driver on for (a named firm) who is selling nylons'. Drivers may be on the same run yet not see each other for as much as two or three weeks. The transience of the situation is evident where drivers are not on a regular route, as in tramping.

> 'Yes, we generally have a conversation when we stop for a meal. We generally talk about the wagons and exchange views.'

> 'Yes, when you go in the café and start talking to another lorry driver. You've never seen him before and you'll probably never see him again, but you talk about loads and where you are going.'

The more regularly a driver makes a particular run the more likely he is to have a stable interaction pattern with other drivers but the numbers of different drivers contacted are fewer than would be the case in tramping. Many trunkers travel in groups, stopping at cafés with other drivers from their firm. Some drivers have calls that they make with such regularity that as soon as they enter a café they are acknowledged by many others already eating there. One trunker the writer travelled with, knew a considerable amount about his surroundings. The light was on in that house because 'she's feeding the new baby' or that rail signal was up for such and such a train, and so on. This driver had for a number of years spent his tea breaks with railway signalmen as their boxes were close to the road, or taken them alone in the rest room of a large factory. Interactions of this kind were not perhaps as usual as the group interaction patterns shown below.

Example 1

Four drivers were on the same run but two of the drivers were not on this particular run regularly. The two 'new' drivers asked one of the regular drivers what he should do once the change-over point had been reached. Times that certain places should be reached were given, and the amount of time which could comfortably be spent in the café was also communicated.

Example 2

Some drivers were and are in the habit of having a 'cat-nap' at some point on route. If the driver was known to another driver and his schedule was also known then this driver would wake him up. One older driver would leave the changeover point last and would usually draw up alongside all the drivers in his group and press his horn two or three times until a waving limb appeared from under the customary large coat covering the driver. The waking up of drivers does not only take place amongst drivers of the immediate group but may take place between drivers of different depots or firms. Sometimes this 'waking up' was used as a joke, though this was rare as the driver who was woken up would have to be a good friend to take that kind of joke.

> 'You want to give your mate a bit of a shaking up. What you do is to spot him "sleeping up" and go quietly by him and turn your wagon round. Draw up to him as close as you can facing him and switch your lights on. Then hold your hand on the horn. He grabs hold of the wheel and turns it in all directions! He's got to be able to take that kind of joke mind, otherwise he gets out of the cab and docs a bit of work on your face.'

Example 3

One driver remarked that he had marked the number of a car on the roof of his cab. The driver of this car had reported a lorry driver from his firm for dangerous driving. If the car is seen again then any driver from that firm will try to 'ditch' the car until the driver has learned his lesson.

Example 4

The drivers on a certain run were supposed to be at a certain place at a fixed time to deliver the loads. One driver, a fast driver, always got in first and unloaded and went back to the transport yard with his empty lorry. This was disliked by the other drivers since he was exceeding the norm of output. Many things were said amongst the drivers in the yard with regard to this and the word got around that this driver was 'carving the job up' (taking less time than the time allowed for the job). Eventually this driver's vehicle was reported faulty and the management alleged it had no alternative but to take the driver off the particular run and put him on to tramping instead of trunking. The driver protested to the union but none of the other drivers would support a 'stoppage'.

Example 5

Drivers can tell whether a hitch-hiker is a lorry driver or not by the fact that when wanting a lift he will jerk his thumb in a certain way; or will display the appropriate group symbols such as a small case, which trampers carry when they are going to stop away overnight, or log sheets.

Example 6

Drivers at the B.R.S. depot were refused work on a Sunday night. Checks were made at the office on Sunday and again on Monday. As a result there was a meeting at a convenient point on the route (one that is always used to check loads, tyres and to discuss problems with drivers from other firms) between the drivers from two B.R.S. depots. The men at one depot had had an uneven share in Sunday shifts. These facts were collected and presented to the manager at one of the depots, and this practice was stopped.

Example 7

Soloman[36] reports that codes were used by lorry drivers to communicate with one another. She says 'Hours of lonely driving through the night are relieved and acknowledged by flashes of headlamps and messages exchanged in passing, by this medium.' In the café sample a driver mentioned this system.

> 'It's not lonely since someone flashes you and you don't feel lonely.'

Participant observation showed some instances of this code. On the first night of the participant observation a driver of a trunk vehicle from another firm passed the lorry which the writer was in, and there was a whining noise as it did so. The driver flashed his lights continuously and the other lorry pulled

[36] Soloman, E. 1954. *op. cit.*

into a lay-by. The two drivers discussed the problem in the lay-by and checked the tyres of the vehicle. Then the other driver said thanks and continued his journey.

The light signals as given to the writer by this driver were:

1. one flash to call a driver *out* to overtake;
2. one flash to call a driver *in* after he has overtaken;
3. continuous flashing if there is danger of some kind or presence of a police patrol car.

These light signals are not universal however, and as such they may cause some danger to other drivers. If there is any kind of misinterpretation at speed then there could easily be an accident. One of the writer's drivers on participant observation agreed that the light flashing system could be dangerous.

> 'I had a bit of an argument with X, who said I was following this bloke and I flashed him up but he didn't call me on, so I dropped back and then I got up a bit of speed and went up to him again and flashed him again but he didn't call me on. So I could see that the road was clear and I overtook and the fellow was waving me on. So I said, Well X, he was using the proper signal, you weren't. And for me I never take any notice of car drivers who flash me.'

Some of the flashing signals are quite makeshift and may mean various things to different people. A light flash in the day time, with a thumbs down sign, or a wave of a log sheet, may mean that there is a police or Ministry check further along the road. On seeing these signals drivers will stop and fill in their log sheets. Again these same signals may be used to warn of an accident further along the road. The non-universality of such signalling is shown by a statement of Martin Redmayne, Parliamentary Secretary to the Treasury which is quoted in *Roadway*, the journal of the Road Haulage Association for November 1962.

FLASH OF INSPIRATION

I always thought two dips and a blink by a commercial vehicle driver with his headlights meant: 'If I can catch you up I'll do you.' But it isn't so. The other day I stopped at a café and asked a lorry driver about this signal. 'No, guv.,' he said 'you've got it all wrong. It means there's a nice little bit at Joe's caff and I'm stopping off for a couple of hours.

The light flashing system is universal enough to provide considerable protection from the police and Ministry officials. The practice of one driver waking others up enables drivers to 'have half an hour' without the worry of whether they will be late getting back to the depot. This was especially useful to the trunkers who did other jobs in the day time or, as with one man, who had a day-time mistress. Mostly the 'sleepers up' were drivers who had difficulty in getting to sleep in the day for domestic reasons.

> 'She decides to clean the house about 11 o'clock. She doesn't come into the room but she seems to need to bang my door with the hoover about a dozen times to get the carpet brushed.'

These patterns of interaction are applicable to the trunker. In general, interaction during the performance of the work role is irregular and sporadic except where there are groups of men travelling on the same route who are from one particular firm. Nevertheless there is evidence of a generalised interaction system amongst lorry drivers indicating a collectivity which, as a consequence of their conditions of work, produces patterns of behaviour which are distinctive. Further illustration of such patterns is given in the discussion of interaction amongst the trampers at destinations.

INTERACTION IN THE DESTINATION COMMUNITY

The picture of interaction is so far mainly that of the trunker on a regular route interacting with a small number of other drivers with regularity and perhaps with a few other people who are not lorry drivers. This is due to the schedules which have to be met and a generally low possibility of meeting other people at night anyway. The shunter, in the writer's experience tends to interact more with the people at the factories and docks, where he loads and unloads his lorry. Several shunters had a joke swapping relationship with the clerks at various factories. On the other hand, the tramper is likely to interact sporadically with large numbers of different people, drivers and non-drivers in an irregular and unstable fashion. It is the tramper who has most contact with other lorry drivers. It is when he is away from home and in lodgings that the tramper makes his contact with other trampers.

186

'Yes, I meet them at nights in the digs. I generally get talking to the chaps at night. I go to the pictures or for a drink with them. You may never see them again but they are a very friendly bunch once they get in those digs.'

Another driver told the writer how during his tramping days he had always met the same bunch of trampers where he was staying in London every week. He recalled that one night they had arrived at the 'digs' late and their customary parking space had been taken.

'We just towed the other blokes' lorries out of the park. There was a bit of a dust up like, but we never had any trouble with them again, as a matter of fact after that we would all go drinking together.'

This kind of pattern seems to be general. Once in his transport digs, the tramper would wash, change, have his meal and then go for a night out with 'the boys'. This is essentially the other side of the picture in the dual leisure pattern of the tramper. His evenings out while he is away contrasts with his home and family-centred pattern of leisure while he is actually at home.

The dual life of the tramper fits the pattern of what has been described, in Chapter VI as the legitimated dissociation pattern. The opposite of this is of course where his absence is not legitimated by his wife. It is important to recognise that though the behaviour pattern of the 'night out with the boys' is not always the case, it is far more often so than not. The public image of the lorry driver may often be that of a man flitting from town to town, sleeping with one man's wife or another, or whoring from sleazy cafés. For the most part this picture is extremely inaccurate, yet for some cases it is entirely true. Three trampers met by the writer, had mistresses at that time whom they were seeing regularly. This was also the case with one of the trunkers. There can be little doubt that a good deal of such behaviour does in fact go on amongst lorry drivers, though it is difficult to say whether it is more prevalent amongst them than workers in static jobs. Gibbens' evidence on V.D. clinic users is certainly a pointer that the mobile 'professions' are much in evidence.[37]

[37] Gibbens, T. C. N., 1962. *op. cit.*

It is quite clear that the tramper has considerable inter-action with a wide variety of people while he is away from home in his destination community. In a sense he has two distinct lives, one at home and another which is quite definitely a product of his absence from home. It will be remembered that tramping is taken up at a time when a major part of the occupational socialisation can take place. It is reasonable to assume that the period spent tramping is the crowning part of the socialisation process. During this period he learns how to rope and sheet; where to go for loads; and how to negotiate his way about the country. He also learns a way of life which is different from that of the 'static' worker. When there is nobody in a café that he knows he is silent. Yet when a group of drivers get together they swap stories of loads, journeys and places. These stops while they may be seen as being against the interests of the employing organisation are an essential part of the tramper's socialisation process. Undoubtedly much of the conversation is idle gossip and jokes, but much will be conversation about difficulties in loading some kinds of material and the problems of driving certain types of lorry. More important as far as the free enterprise tramper is concerned is the knowledge of the industrial areas of the country and the places where loads may be obtained. It is in the interaction with other drivers that the tramper learns his 'code' words for getting on with the people in the factories, docks and warehouses where he goes for his loads. He may exchange the funniest, filthiest, sickest jokes with these people. To some extent he is forced to play the role of the fornicator boasting of his wild times with women up and down the country, if only because the people in the factories seem to like this. In consequence, the driver who has lived up to the stereotype gets his load off or on, all the more quickly.

One of the consequences of such interaction amongst lorry drivers is that of producing a common sentiment and value orientation. The sentiment is expressed through a language with which the occupational group is more or less familiar whereas the outsider is not. This section indicates the 'chummy' semi-personalised interaction in cafés and 'digs' between trampers. The interaction between trunkers is more regular and more personalised. Trunkers tend to have regular stopping places and the subjects under discussion are more likely to be the state of affairs with regard to wives and children, the garden, or 'the driver who was on for . . . who used to come in here . . .', and of course the work itself.

The writer's experience of conversation in cafés during breaks was clearly that the talk was mainly of loads, lorries, hills, etc. Sometimes these conversations were highly esoteric.

> 'You know (a certain hill) . . . well you know how you have to drop down to second by the ruin with the (a named make of lorry). Well last Wednesday I picked a load of "flats" . . . etc. . . .'

The eventual outcome of such a description is usually that the driver indicates exactly how he was delayed on a particular journey. Ted Murphy in his autobiography confirms the existence of such sentiment on the basis of a common knowledge of the job.[38]

> 'We nattered a little about friends absent, then as usual the conversation turned to shop proper. I don't suppose there is another body of men like us for discussing their work. Eighty-five per cent at least of drivers' talk is various aspects of the job. Though to be fair much of it is of interest and its nature is varied and always changing. New types of wagon, always a firm favourite. Roads up, Roads down, speed traps, sections presided over by unusually tough cops, loads, return loads, firms, governors, foremen, sometimes even wives. Yes! you must admit we have lots of scope.'

Further evidence of such sentiment can be gleaned from the samples. A driver in the firms' sample remarked:

> 'You should hear the drivers on Saturday dinner time at [a named public house]. They move more loads and change more wheels in two hours in there than they do in two weeks on the road.'

In spite of the transience in the social situation the lorry driver has a superb communication system. By virtue of the long distance mobility, news about drivers and events involving them, may be known from one end of the country to the other by morning.

> 'We have as you might say "a grape vine". If a driver has an accident at the other end of the country at night, then we'll all know about it almost as quick as the firm he works for knows.'

[38] Murphy, C. E. *The Big Load*, T. Foulis, London, 1963.

The general conclusion is that in spite of spatial separation, lorry drivers are very much together as a group. A rather striking, though fictional illustration of this is to be found in one of Bill Naughton's short stories *Late Night on Watling Street*. There are two relevant passages which are worth quoting at some length. The first illustration concerns group reaction to a lorry driver who has been caught speeding by the police.

> 'I wouldn't rob you Jackson,' he said, 'You might need it. I see old Babyface did you again back up the road there on the Long Hill.' As soon as Clive said that, the atmosphere changed. 'Bloody hard luck, Jackson', said Ned. 'I hope they don't scrub your licence', said Taff. I gave him a look. A lot had happened to him since that. 'He must have nailed you just after he left us' said Walter. He took out his fags, handed them round, hesitated then held the packet out to Jackson. Jackson thought it over for a moment and then took one. The matey feeling came up them, the feeling of all being drivers and the law always after you.[39]

The second illustration is one of group sanctions amongst lorry drivers. The sanction is functional because although lorry drivers have some kind of a competition with the police, this is limited by a framework of norms. Clearly both the police and the lorry driver have to exist together and as a result there is a certain amount of leeway allowed in law enforcement. The driver described above is 'at war' with the police, and as far as he is concerned competition is conflict in that he eliminates two policemen altogether. He kills the two policemen by deliberately pulling up suddenly when they were following close behind him in their car. He goes into the cafe after the accident and after telling an older driver about it.

> 'Jackson', I said, 'what's the idea of telling me all this?' He smiled softly and then he said, 'A bloke don't want to walk around with a basinful of that on his mind. I know I'm safe with an old driver.'
> I went in after him. There were half a dozen drivers in. Walter and Willie, young Clive, a driver and his mate from Glasgow, and an old driver from Hull. They all gave nods and waves to me. But as for Jackson, not a word was spoken. Not a sign was made. You felt everything going dead quiet. Lew was wiping the tables and he kept right away from where Jackson sat. Ethel was behind

[39] Naughton, W. *Late Night on Watling Street*. MacGibbon and Rees, London. 1959.

the counter and she never gave him so much as a glance. She looked across to me and waved her hand. Jackson looked at her, but she didn't seem to see him. I knew then that the word had gone round. It doesn't take long. He might have got one across the law but he hadn't got one across Watling Street. Nobody would split, but already North and South, they were putting the poison in for him. Within a week he'd be lucky to get a civil cup of tea anywhere along the A.5. And I could see by the look on Jackson's face, he knew one thing at least, no matter what the police found or didn't find, he'd never get anywhere with Ethel now, and his driving days on Watling Street were over.

The passage above is fiction in the sense of being written to entertain rather than to reveal truths. However a social process is clearly illustrated here. If the sanction had not taken place then the existing behaviour patterns of the whole group would have been threatened, in that the police would have tightened up their enforcement of some of the rules.

The differential nature of subculture is presented in its most pronounced form through a language common to members of the subcultural group and highly esoteric. Lorry drivers are no exception to this formulation.

'Douse the glim'	*meaning*	lower the headlights or put them out
'Coasting downhill'		an easy task
'Cowboy'		a reckless driver
'Cement mixer'		a lorry with a noisy engine
'Kidney buster'		a hard-seated lorry
'Bull hauler'		driver of a cattle lorry
'Screech the brakes'		punctual, on time
'Haulage holes'		driving an empty lorry
'Having a bash'		completing a journey without regard for regulation speed and hours
'Red flagger'		an old lorry ready for the scrap heap
'Cackle crate'		a poultry lorry
'Bare back'		a lorry without a trailer
'Rag top'		a lorry with tarpaulin cover
'Balloon load'		a light but bulky load
'Reefer'		a refrigerated meat lorry
'Barnacle'		an old driver
'Jive jumper'		bad gear changing

'Scorching the road'	*meaning*	quick braking
'Skins'		tyres
'Tailgating'		running too close to the vehicle ahead
'Gallopers'		vehicles exceeding the speed limit
'Armstrong started'		hand cranked
'Crash'		any kind of misfortune
'A nut down'⎫ 'A lay-by' ⎭		resting in a quiet spot on the road
'Trunker' ⎫ 'Fly by night'⎬ 'Night hawk' ⎭		night driver
'Shunter'		day driver working locally
'Tramper'		long distance driver
'Pirate'		owner of an illegally operated lorry
'Scrubber'		woman, road prostitute
'Gypsy'		a particularly dirty specimen of scrubber

The above are some of the examples of occupational terminology quoted by Soloman.[40] The writer did not hear many of these words during the course of his investigations so it must be presumed that there is a certain regionalism about the terms. Some of them of course were heard, and below follows a short list of additional terms that the writer heard.

'Rigid'	*meaning*	a fixed framed vehicle
'Artic'		an articulated vehicle made up of a powered 'unit' and 'trailer'
'A slave wagon'		an articulated vehicle enabling a quick turn round
'Clogging it' ⎫ 'Clog happy'⎭		fast driving
'Cogging' ⎫ 'Running out of stick'⎭		coasting along out of gear
'Flogging a log'		falsifying log sheets
'Scrubber' ⎫ 'Queenie' ⎬ 'Smoker' ⎭		woman prostitute of the roads

[40] Soloman, E. 1954. *op. cit.*

'On a dodgy'   *meaning*   running illegally for own benefit
'Head down'   having a sleep in the cab
'Having a go'   running illegally for firm's benefit

CONCLUSION

The interaction patterns of the lorry driver are directly affected by his occupation. His leisure pattern is affected by his occupation in that his job is one characterised by long and irregular hours of work. The amount of interaction which the lorry driver has when he is away from work is limited by his hours and times of work, even if he is a shunter. It is the tramper's leisure pattern which is most affected. He has less time to spend in his own community than the other types of driver. The tramper's leisure pattern is a dual one. When he is at home his interaction is centred on home and family. When they are away the trampers generally have a night out together, although some use the mobile nature of their occupation as a convenient method of having a mistress. There is some evidence that the trunker suffers perhaps as much as his tramper colleague in reduced leisure, but the main body of evidence is suggestive of reduced leisure for the tramper.

It is easy to see how the tramper is so involved in his occupation. He spends so much time connected with it and he has a considerably greater occupational group life than either of the other two types of driver. It is not really possible to make any definitive statement about the distinctiveness between the publicly visible zones of interaction. It is clear that in the case of both the trunker and tramper, the long-distance drivers, the permeation or 'spillover' of the occupation into leisure is considerable. Thus although the types of interaction between the spheres or zones may be different, and distinct in one sense, interaction in the leisure sphere, is certainly relatable to the demands of the occupation. This would be true whether we are considering the driver's interaction pattern in his home community, or his destination community, particularly as his community circumstances are such that there is little or no accommodation in the community for the exigencies of his occupation, as there is in Hessle or 'Ashton'.

The demands of the lorry driver's occupation and its mobile nature, create an interaction pattern or patterns which are publicly visible. Such patterns have consequences for the status of the occupational group as a whole, and naturally enough for the status of individual lorry drivers. This may impel even less contact or interaction in the home community, apart from that within the family, and throw the lorry driver still more heavily back on to his job. These consequences are discussed in the chapter which follows.

VIII

OCCUPATIONAL STATUS

The importance of a person's occupation in determining his social status is increasing in modern industrial society, with its 'aggregation, differentiation, and rationalisation', compared with the more traditional status determinants of family and residence.[1] The individual wishing to increase his social standing will change his occupation to one which ranks more highly in the social scale or adopt the alternative of attempting to raise the status of the occupation as a whole while still remaining in it. The motivation for raising status in the case of both individual and group is that society tends to allocate greater economic rewards to high prestige occupations.[2] Status involves the rights accruing to a social position while role is the set of expectations of an incumbent of that position: the obligations.[3] Raising or lowering the status of an occupational group therefore involves an increase or decrease in the rights of the incumbents. Hughes has produced a framework for the analysis of the rights that are claimed successfully by members of an occupation.

An occupation consists, in part, of a successful claim of some people to licence to carry out certain activities which others may not, and to do so in exchange for money, goods or services. Those who have such licence will, if they have any sense of self consciousness or solidarity, also claim a mandate to define what is

[1] Caplow, T. *The Sociology of Work*, Oxford Univ. Press, 1962. p. 30.

[2] Wootton, B. *The Social Foundations of Wages Policy*, Norton, New York, 1955. p. 68.

[3] Johnson, H. M. *Sociology*, Routledge and Kegan Paul, London, 1961. p. 16.

proper conduct of others towards the matters concerned with their work.[4]

This chapter will present the lorry driver as an incumbent of a status with a pure type of role which lays claim to licence and also to some extent a mandate, and by contrast, as an average type where licence and mandate claims have been either more or less successful. In this sense of the claim for licence and mandate, prestige may be a considerable factor in job satisfaction. Blauner found that job satisfaction and the status of occupations were highly correlated in that high levels of job satisfaction accompanied high occupational status and vice versa. The basic factor in job satisfaction is however, control. The people in occupations with more prestige have more control over their work.[5] These are the occupations where licence and perhaps even a mandate has been successfully claimed.

LORRY DRIVER'S ROLE AS A PURE TYPE

The construction of the pure type will involve an emphasis on the self concept of the role. It will be an extension of the behaviour as it would take place if the lorry driver's definition of his situation was untrammelled by structurally given demands.

The lorry driver emerges as an industrial worker who has grown up in or deliberately chosen a socio-technical system which is relatively open rather than closed. The physically mobile nature of the occupation offers a freedom from the constraints of the 'static' work situation within factory walls. The data indicates that perhaps a third of the lorry drivers in the random sample have been socialised by starting their working life in jobs of a mobile or quasi-mobile kind, such as lorry drivers' mates, errand boys, seamen, telegram boys and so on. A significant proportion of the remainder of the drivers in the samples appear to have rejected the socio-technical system of

[4] Hughes, E. C. *Men and Their Work*, Free Press, 1958. p. 78.

[5] Blauner, R. 'Work Satisfaction and Industrial Trends in Modern Society', in Galenson, W. and Lipset, S. M. *Labour and Trade Unionism*, John Wiley & Sons, New York, 1962.

the factory. About two thirds of the drivers indicated that lorry driving was to be preferred to factory work. Those drivers who had worked in a factory were much more likely to give lorry driving a more favourable comparison than those who had not. The main reasons given for disliking factory work are that it is 'indoor work' which is generally of a routine and monotonous nature, and that it is in one fixed place. The dislike of factory work is very uniform amongst lorry drivers. Over half of them in the firms' sample could not think of anything at all that they would like about it. Amongst the reasons given for comparing lorry driving favourably with the factory, the main ones emphasise the relatively open socio-technical system in the occupation.

To an outsider, the job of driving about the country day after day would seem to have the possibility of becoming routine. As the lorry driver sees it, the job is not just driving around. He is on his own and is solely responsible for his load and vehicle at that particular point in time. Consequently he sees himself as someone who can, and does, make decisions to counter 'on the spot' exigencies. Well over half the lorry drivers in the samples see their job as being a skilled one. This is largely on account of the weight and size of the vehicles driven, the road conditions, and the types of load. Perhaps the most interesting aspect of his view of himself as a skilled worker is that he thinks that he has to be skilled because other road users are so unskilled.

The pure type of lorry driver role seems to produce or attract the sort of man who is more at ease in the open socio-technical system. The physical mobility of this system is in contrast to the 'static' enclosed work situation of the factory shop floor. The indication that the lorry driver's expectations of a job are fulfilled by the occupation is that he tends to make it his career. Freedom, the basis of his job satisfaction, derives from his physical mobility. The second way in which we consider the pure type of lorry driving role is by looking at the place of his role in an organisation structure. It will become apparent as this question is discussed that his organisational role, or at least his conception of it, is very much related to the freedom afforded by the open socio-technical system.

The types of organisational status and role to be considered are those of the bureaucrat, specialist, and professional, in order of ascending autonomy from the organisation and ranging from the supposed full organisational orientation of the bureaucrat to the supposed full occupational orientation of the professional person. Viewed in diagrammatic terms the relationship of the three types of occupational roles in terms of the two axes would look like the diagram below.

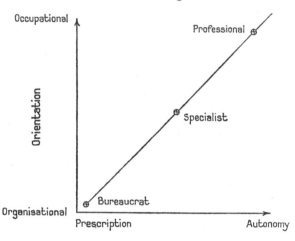

FIGURE 7. *Types of Organisational Man*

The bureaucrat has complete prescription in his occupational role according to the Weberian ideal type, and Burns and Stalker's 'mechanistic model', which is developed on the basis of Weber's model of an ideal type of bureaucratic organisation.[6] Rules, a systematic division of labour, and a hierarchy of authority, ensure that the bureaucrat has an occupational role which is prescribed. The incumbent of a bureaucratic status is powerless to do anything which the organisation would not wish as he is subject to the sanction of exclusion, but even before entering the organisation he has usually agreed to obey the rules. The restriction on behaviour imposed by a bureau-cratic role is such that, outside that which is legal, there is no existence of positive behaviour by the individual. In skill terms

[6] Burns, T. and Stalker, G. M. *The Management of Innovation.* Tavistock Publications, 1961.

the bureaucrat has only expertise which is useful within the organisation. To use Gouldner's terms it is localistic expertise rather than cosmopolitan, and Burns and Stalker[7] make this important distinction. Further points are that the bureaucrat is an appointee and also he can have a life career within the organisation. In order to ensure this life career the bureaucrat will conform as closely as possible to the demands of the task role. All these characteristics of bureaucratic organisations lead to an extreme of prescription of role for the bureaucrat thus making him low on the 'autonomy' axis and on the organisational pole of the 'orientation' axis.

The specialist may have a dual orientation in that his outlook may be both towards the organisation and also towards his occupation. He does not have a specified amount of autonomy in the universal sense and the degree of autonomy which he has will vary with the organisation. Burns and Stalker's 'organic model' of organisation based on data from the British electronics industry shows that autonomy varies in temporal terms even to the extent of an 'ad hoc' leadership pattern. The essential issue here is that the individual depends on the organisation for his occupational existence since his technique is too specific to allow individual practice. In time the occupation becomes more and more bound up with the organisation as conditions become stable and task subdivision can occur. This is probably the case in technology as the techniques either become more and more a synthesis of many disciplines or they become an applied specialism of a main discipline. Nevertheless several studies have indicated that the specialist demands and in fact has a considerable degree of freedom within the organisation. Moore,[8] and also Schneider,[9] both stress the demand for structural autonomy by the specialist. Organisation charts presented in the works of both authors suggest the autonomy of the specialist but there is something of a dilemma. Moore admits to the difficulty of locating the specialist in an organisational structure. He makes the point that the division

---

[7] Burns, T. and Stalker, G. M. 1961. *op. cit.* Chapter 6.

[8] Moore, W. E. *Industrial Relations and the Social Order.* Macmillan Co. N.Y. Revised Edition. 1951.

[9] Schneider, E. V. *Industrial Sociology*, McGraw-Hill, 1957.

of labour typical in 'large industrial organisations makes almost every member of the organisation a specialist'. Moore differentiates the genuine specialist from the position of the skilled workman by suggesting that the role of the skilled workman is largely passive but a specialist acts either in an advisory or less usually a supervisory category. Specialists have also wider training than skilled workmen and are likely to have received this from outside the organisation, whereas the skilled worker may do his apprenticeship within the organisation within which he is eventually employed.[10]

Schneider tackles the problem of explanation of autonomy in the specialist's role through indicating the sources of strain between the specialist and the line structure. The specialist role is contrasted with line roles in terms of role pattern variables. The specialist has a primacy of universalistic and affectively neutral values governing his ego expectations of his role while the line man is much more bound up with the values of the organisation. Schneider's view is that the specialist is eventually subordinated to the organisational demands even if not at first.[11]

In both views of the specialist there is presented a picture of the strain between him and the organisation due to the demand for autonomy. Field[12] in a study of the Soviet physician presents such strain in its sharpest form through the needs and dictates of medical science tending to become subordinate to a developing country's economic needs. The general picture is one of an indeterminate location on the 'control'/'orientation' graph for the specialist. There are several variables which could be considered as making his position more or less determinate. A major variable seems to be the market, while another variable, technology, also seems to assume great importance. The picture that Burns and Stalker[13] give is that stability of

[10] Moore, W. E. *op. cit.* pp. 132–3.

[11] Schneider, E. V. *op. cit.* pp. 125–30.

[12] Field, M. G. 'Structured Strain in the Role of the Soviet Physician'. *American Journal of Sociology*, 1952–60, pp. 493–502. It is important to note that the discussion by Field concerns a 'professional' rather than a 'specialist' role.

[13] See Burns and Stalker, 1961. *op. cit.* pp. 191–2, on the demands for independence by the industrial scientist.

technology is of paramount importance in the determination of the role of incumbents in organisations. In stable market conditions the 'mechanistic' form of organisation is more appropriate, while innovation makes an organic system more suitable since comparative autonomy of the statuses in such a system means by definition that the organisation is more adaptable to change.

Other studies indicate that the specialist expects as a right to be given as much autonomy as is compatible with eventual goal attainment or effectiveness of the organisation. Raudsepp[14] suggests that the creative ability in scientists and engineers is something which is easily inhibited by an aggressive line structure. The supervision of such individuals has to be carried out with great care lest the creative ability is smothered. A study of chemists[15] engaged in research and development revealed that slightly more than a third of the mentions of sources of dissatisfaction by chemists could be classified under the heading of organisation and control. Inadequate policy, 'red tape', pressure for results, and insufficient responsibility and autonomy were among the more prominently disliked features of organisation. Barnes[16] found that 'open' systems' in organisation (i.e. systems where there is relatively high autonomy amongst members, relatively high opportunity for interaction, and relatively high mutual influence between status levels) produced higher levels of satisfaction than 'closed systems'.

To summarise; the specialist is in a status in an organisation which may be more or less organisationally orientated and which is accorded more or less autonomy within the organisation. He will tend to demand autonomy almost as a linear function of his degree of occupational orientation. The specialist will have a greater occupational orientation than the bureaucrat and less of an organisational orientation.

The sociological position on professional roles and the

[14] Raudsepp, E. *Managing Creative Scientists and Engineers*. Macmillan, London, 1963.

[15] Pym, D. 'A Manpower Study: The Chemist in Research and Development'. *Occupational Psychology*, Vol. 38, No. 1, Jan. 1964.

[16] Barnes, L. B. *Organisational Systems and Engineering Groups*'. Harvard Business School, Boston, 1960.

professions in general is in a state of flux. Wilensky argues that professionalisation of occupations is not as widespread as popular generalisation suggests.[17] He quotes the traditional definition of professionalism with its basis of technique and knowledge, exclusive jurisdiction, and standards of performance and prescribed training. Also incumbents of statuses with professional roles have to convince the public that their 'services are uniquely trustworthy'. People with professional roles have a systematic knowledge which they apply impartially and also a set of standards which are involved in the notion of a 'service ideal'. The professional status is accorded high autonomy based on the techniques and acquired knowledge of its incumbent. In this sense, bureaucracy and professionalism are opposed and to a considerable extent mutually exclusive. Wilensky[18] has suggested that there will be an adaptation which results in a mixed organisational form of administration and professionalism, but this is rather difficult to conceive of, at least in any detail. On the other side of the picture, writers emphasise the difference between the two forms of organisation.[19] What is very clear is that the more traditional professional statuses have a greater autonomy than the newer specialist occupations possess or indeed are ever likely to possess. They will thus be high in autonomy on the control axis and close to the occupational pole on the orientation axis.

We have now considered the three main ways in which actors may be related to their occupations and the organisations in which these occupations are contained. The status, or sets of rights which accrue to a bureaucratic position are very much more organisational than those which accrue to a specialist or professional position. The obligations which the incumbents of such positions are expected to fulfil are increasingly more occupationally orientated as the statuses under consideration range from the bureaucratic to the professional pole on the continuum.

[17] Wilensky, H. L. 'The Professionalisation of Everyone'. *American Journal of Sociology*, 1964.

[18] Wilensky, H. L. 1964, *op. cit.* pp. 156–7.

[19] Notably Merton, R. K. in 'The Intellectual in a Public Bureaucracy' in *Social Theory and Social Structure*'. Free Press, 1957. (1964 Printing). pp. 222–4, and Etzioni, A. *Modern Organisations*. Chapter 8. Prentice Hall. Foundations of Modern Sociology Series, 1964.

A fourth possible categorisation of an occupational status is that which is accompanied by what we can term an individualistic role. Such a role is one in which constraints or expectations of all kinds, not just organisational, are reduced to a minimum. There is virtually no occupation which is free from constraint to this extent. Even artists have to take the market into account in order to eat.

The question which now has to be answered is that of where the lorry driver is to be located on the 'control'/'orientation' graph. We shall attempt to find his location through a consideration of the extent to which the lorry driver's occupational status and role is similar to any of those discussed above. The criteria for locating him are: the techniques involved in his occupation; the exigencies and his ideals of his occupation; and, most important of all, his relationship to the occupation within which he works as indicated by the level and sources of his work satisfaction and his relations with his managements.

The evidence is that the lorry driver demands, if he is to have a high level of work satisfaction, a management which allows him discretion at job level. Involvement would be towards the problem and firm as a whole, as in the 'organic' model of Burns and Stalker. He seeks recognition as an expert.

In terms of the orientation and control axes which were discussed earlier the lorry driver has a tendency to appear rather like the specialist. He is occupationally orientated but not as much so as the professional and he also insists for both job and work satisfaction that control over his technology is accompanied by freedom from supervision.

'They (the management) don't ask where you've been. They let you work as if you're on your own. They don't tell you to do something they ask you to do it.'

'They know that once I'm on the road their worries are finished. The responsibility is on me.'

'The boss is good. We're our own boss with this bloke.'

Many drivers in the samples thought of the lorry driver as a man who had responsibility and a considerable skill. There are difficulties and dangers in the job and the management has to recognise that the lorry driver may have trouble while he is away from the depot. From the point of view of the driver as a specialist in the system the qualities expected in management such as: 'should have been a lorry driver', 'knowing the driver's side of the job', 'how to understand men', 'knowing the road conditions', and to some extent, 'knowing the industry and the job' are particularly relevant. Mentions of these qualities constitute 120 out of 142 positive replies to the ideal management question. The remarks entered below indicate the position in attitudinal terms of the autonomy of the specialist and the equality expected between experts in an organic system:

> 'He should have had the experience of being a lorry driver. He should have worked his way up from being a lorry driver. He'd know what it was all about then.'

> 'He should have a sound knowledge of the actual job of driving itself from the driver's point of view.'

> 'He's got to understand the driver's point of view, to give and take and to understand that snags do crop up and to understand this.'

> 'He must know exactly the job that's being done and he must know the time to get from A to B and that you can't fly along with a heavy load at 90 miles an hour.'

> 'He has to know his job and he shouldn't mess the men about too much. They know their job and they can do it or at least the majority of them can.'

This evidence and other findings quoted earlier on the lorry driver's attitude to management, particularly a management of the mechanistic sort can be used as supportive evidence to the contention that the pure type of lorry driver's role is, by virtue of the socio-technical system and his consequent demands in organisational terms, that of a specialist in his own right. The lorry driver has not the autonomy and training to make him a professional worker. This is as clear cut as is the fact that he is not such an individualist (as an artist might possibly be) in his work situation as to have no constraints on him whatsoever.

What then are the factors which produce a workman who is not the ordinary kind of bureaucratised worker? There is a clear difference between the lorry driver and the factory worker in this sense, just as Gouldner can point to a clear difference between the miner in the gypsum mine and the shop floor worker in the gypsum board factory.[20] The factors seem to be the lorry driver's socio-technical system in particular and his total work situation in general. The comparatively long cycle time, the control over the work pace and the technology in the working environment, and consequent alienative relationship with the rule system of the more bureaucratic road transport firm, notably B.R.S.; all these factors produce a different kind of workman from the factory worker, whose relationship with his job is more or less determined in the spatial-technical sense. The consequences seem to be manifested in terms of a different relationship to the authority system. The lorry driver has autonomy in the greater part of his working shift and thus values this discretion more than the factory worker. Further, any encroachment on the discretion in the actual job of the lorry driver will be met with severe resistance. This resistance would not be met with from workers in more bureaucratic situations. The source of the resistance again seems to stem from the work situation but this time it is the extent of the lorry driver's experience, the responsibility, and the skill which he sees himself as having. It will be remembered that the findings on the lorry driver's career indicated that there is considerable opportunity for socialisation into the occupation as the lorry driver passes through a very definite career cycle. During this lifetime of lorry driving in various types of driving job the lorry driver gains experiences which give him his skill. At the end of his career the driver has learned to a considerable extent the exigencies of his occupation and has developed the corresponding skills to counter them. It is basically these skills, which counter the exigencies in his actual job, which are the basis of the claim to specialist knowledge. Such exigencies, with their corresponding skills make the rules imposed by management seem irrelevant to the lorry driver.

The lorry driver's concept of himself as a specialist who is under only the 'remote control' of his management would seem to be a major influence on his political outlook. Although no actual direct question was asked on this subject there seems to be a tendency for lorry drivers to be right of centre in their

[20] Gouldner, A. W. *Patterns of Industrial Bureaucracy.* Free Press, 1954.

political attitude. This is particularly the case amongst the drivers in private haulage firms. In the private firm sample some drivers asked the investigator if he thought nationalisation of the road haulage industry would be a good or bad thing. When the investigator replied that there were arguments both for and against these drivers emphasised their position. They made the point that if they ever wanted to change their job with a particular firm under the present system they could do so. If the Labour Party were to nationalise road haulage then this would not be the case. Amongst these drivers and many others the investigator met there seemed to be a fear of the return of the Labour Party to power. The evidence is that the drivers in the samples are likely to change their firm at any time and for almost any reason but usually because of disagreement with management.

> 'Aye, I have a change about once a year I suppose. With us see its no insult, no crime to change your firm. You meet another driver and he'll say, "Where you doing it now then?", and this is no insult.'

> 'Well one time when I was on for [a private firm] I was going about the right distance in a day and having to fill up every morning. The boss must have seen me once or twice like, so one morning he comes over while I'm at the pump. "Aye, aye, where are you selling it today?", meaning the fuel see. I don't know why but I didn't like that. I threw the nozzle on the ground. I says "Well, you can sell it your fucking self today", and walked off. It was a good job but I never went back there though I could have.'

Headlight, the lorry drivers' magazine, reflects this right wing attitude. A frequent contributor is a Conservative Member of Parliament but he seems to reflect rather than create the political attitude of the occupational group. In fairness to *Headlight* it also provides a space for a Labour M.P. to put the other view.

In the course of his work the lorry driver interacts with any number of people with various roles. These people constitute his role set. Part of the apparatus which group members use to manage their interaction with their role set is what is termed the occupational ideology. An occupational ideology is in its essentials the view of itself that the group would like others to have. Whether the group's image of itself will in fact be reflected back at it by others depends on a number of factors.[21] Our immediate concern here is to identify the ideology of the lorry driver rather than to examine its successful diffusion.

The lorry driver's ideology is that his role is an essential one in the economy. His isolation through his socio-technical system induces the notion that he has to be skilled to do his job and that a major part of his time is used in continuous decision making. A third aspect of the ideology is the lorry driver's conception that he is a professional, a 'Knight of the Road'. He knows the exigencies of driving and is himself courteous to others who use the roads.

There is firstly, his claim that his role is essential to the economy. One driver expressed his feelings on the subject in this way:

'They [the public] don't think a lot about them but in winter they rely on them to get the food through.'

The investigation was carried out in a particularly hard winter, and in consequence fuel was scarce because there were difficulties in its transportation. Coal had frozen into railway trucks and the roads were an alternative.

'They [the public] appreciate what we are doing for the community such as this coal fetching.'

These views on the economic importance of the lorry driver are borne out by statistics for transport in 1962, the year in which this study was begun.[22] In that year 1,541 million tons of goods were transported and 81 per cent went by road. In terms of tons carried, over five times as many goods went by road as by rail. The ton mileage of goods on the roads was twice that of the railways.

Earlier chapters present evidence on the nature of the skills involved in lorry driving. In driving itself there is continuous decision making and in general the work involves the applica-

[21] Dibble, V. K. 'Occupations and Ideologies', *American Journal of Sociology*, Vol. 68, 1962–3. pp. 229–41.

[22] Savage, C. I. *An Economic History of Transport*, Hutchinson, London, 1966. p. 181.

tion of skills learnt in the early career. Such skills as loading the lorry so that it will be safe are crucial, while the tramper in particular must know his way around the country and have mastered the complexities of innumerable factories, warehouses and dock systems. This aspect of the ideology, which the lorry driver attempts to disseminate to his management has been discussed earlier in this chapter. His self concept is that of the specialist and as such his relationship with management should be that of an expert amongst experts. As John Darker, who has had 15 years experience with B.R.S., sees it:

> The operational and administrative difficulties involved in the remote control supervision of drivers away from their base for long periods, when the loss of a spare wheel, or a tarpaulin, or some pallets belonging to customers, can cause much trouble and expense, cannot be shrugged off. [23]

The third assertion of the lorry driver's ideology is that he is a professional driver in contrast to the car driver. As a professional he expects courtesy on the road, and he expects to have to be courteous to other drivers. The driver of the heavy goods vehicle sees himself as a 'Knight of the Road'. The *News of the World* Sunday newspaper has a 'Knight of the Road' award which it makes to people who help others on the road. The 'Knight of the Road' ideology is expressed by some of the lorry drivers in answer to a question on the public image of their group.

> 'They are more polite and have more courtesy than car drivers. They are recommended throughout the country for their courtesy.'

> 'The biggest majority have a high opinion of them for their courtesy and road sense.'

This assertion is partly a claim on behalf of the group and partly an expression of the lorry driver's expectations of other road users. In his job he requires courtesies from other drivers and road users as he has a large and heavy vehicle to manoeuvre and control. This is especially the case when he is entering a main road from a factory roadway. He has a schedule to keep and this is a further reason for him to expect 'courtesies'.

[23] Darker, J. *Long Distance Road Haulage*, Fabian Research Series, 249. 1965. p. 21.

The attempt at differentiation of his driving skill from that of the car driver is also apparent in some of the statements.

'Lorry drivers are superior in driving skill to a car driver.'

'People in general think we are pretty good on the road.'

A Lorry Driver of the Year competition exists, in which the winner will have demonstrated considerable driving skill but a lorry driver does not have to hold a special licence to drive his vehicle. There is an age restriction and some insurance problems for lorry drivers between 21 and 25 years of age, but this is all. Legally the man in the street with a driving licence for a car could do the job. This was not formerly the case. The Road Traffic Act, 1934 (Section 31) made provision for the introduction of special licences for drivers of heavy goods vehicles. This scheme was suspended at the beginning of the Second World War under the Defence Regulations, 1939.[24]

Although other road users form a considerable proportion of his role set, the lorry driver also interacts with people at factories, docks and warehouses. The previous chapter has suggested that in the course of such interaction the lorry driver lives up to the reputation that these people have of him. He jokes and talks with them and gives the impression that his occupation offers many opportunities, mostly sexual, and that he takes full advantage of these. He thus gets his load off or on all the more quickly and if there are favours to be granted, he will get them. The 'bit of a lad' feature may thus be an essential component for the successful lorry driver.

Assertions of the kind described above represent the definition of the situation which the lorry driver has of his role set. It is emphasised that this is the way he likes to be viewed by his role set. With regard to his status set, the accommodation of the roles attaching to his various statuses may be described in terms of a pure type. Generally the status of the lorry driver as an occupational being predominates over all his other statuses. This is due to the occupation providing the economic base for these other positions which he holds. Nevertheless the lorry driver's career pattern can be viewed not only as a progression through time in an occupation but also as an interrelation of activities in at least three institutional spheres.

[24] Personal communication from the Ministry of Transport.

The lorry driver sees himself as a family man and he certainly is so. More than three quarters of the drivers in each sample are married men with children. As such, the way in which he plays his occupational role is inevitably affected by his family position. The typical lorry driver will progress to long distance work more or less as a parallel to getting married and needing the money to make a home for himself and his family. The requirements for the lorry driver's behaviour as between the two institutional spheres are not entirely compatible even at this early stage and it is here that the process of accommodation is most vital. The tramper leads a distinctly dual existence in which he has 'a night out with the boys' while away from home, and compensates his wife and family for his absence by a family centred leisure when he is at home. In this way, some degree of compatibility is achieved and it is usually sufficient for the man to play the separate roles adequately enough to retain his status in the two institutional spheres.

As a citizen, or at least as an actor in his community of residence, the long distance lorry driver is not likely to be able to put in an appearance regularly enough to achieve any status. It is this aspect of his life which is most diminished by his occupation. His participation in his home community will vary according to the type of driving job he holds and the type of firm that employs him. If he becomes a shunter he will have a relatively active life in his home community, while if he is a tramper, especially in a private haulage firm, he has little time to spare for community activities.

LORRY DRIVER'S ROLE AS AN AVERAGE TYPE

In the discussion of the role of the lorry driver as a pure type emphasis has been given to the self concept, in other words the lorry driver's own view of his role. The average type emphasises structurally given demands in that the self concept is toned down by them. A final picture of the role must be the result of the interplay of these two forces.

The pure type of lorry driver's role is seen to be largely the product of the open nature of the socio-technical system of the occupation. As we have stated earlier it is not precisely clear whether the occupation attracts people of a particular personality structure or whether it is the socialisation process that is of first importance. The evidence would suggest that socialisation is a greater factor than the initial personality of the incumbents. What is abundantly clear is that the lorry driver rejects the closed socio-technical system of the factory. The expectations of being afforded a good deal of freedom due to the low level of technical constraint in the mobile occupation are largely borne out. The objective situation in which these expectations can be met is not uniform for all lorry drivers. The tramper has the greatest freedom and the shunter the least. Job satisfaction is reflected accordingly.

The freedom, due to the technology, is not likely to remain a constant feature of the occupation. Even at the present time it is under attack from changes taking place within the industry. While the state of rapid expansion in road haulage continues there is every reason to assume that the tramper will survive. The fierce competition will also continue but due to overall expansion rationalisation need not be the necessary outcome. When the expansion phase stops or even if the rate of expansion decreases it seems a reasonable assumption that most work will be allocated on a more regular basis. This will enable firms to run more trunk services. In consequence the clearing house system may decline and this again reduces the economic viability of tramping. Even at the time of the investigation it was not entirely true to assume that the tramper was free from control to the extent that he could stop where he liked and for the length of time he wanted. Tramping was sometimes the only type of driving job in some of the smaller private firms and the tramper would be pushed to his limits. Work in some areas is difficult to obtain. The haulier may run his business precariously on the basis of one contract which necessarily has to be supplemented by work from other sources. The writer met drivers from this type of firm who were being paid by the trip or on the basis of the 'flat rate' of pay regardless of the hours that the job demanded. These men explained that they saw no point in going to the union as their managements would merely sack them. Under these circumstances the tramper had, and still has, to work all hours to make his pay adequate. Experience of these men was rare, for as one driver put it, 'if you ask one of them to answer your questions for a quarter of an hour its like asking them for five bob'. The reason for this state of affairs is the intense competition in an industry where the rate of failure is high.[25]

Factors making for a future increase in technical constraints are: the new motorways, which when completed will form a national network; containerisation; increased use of the articulated vehicle; and the raising of the speed limit for goods vehicles to 40 miles per hour. In firms which are unionised the speed limit is generally 30 m.p.h. with an average schedule of about 22 m.p.h.[26] There is every possibility that the unions will agree to raise the limit to 40 m.p.h. in practice when the standard of vehicle maintenance is increased. These events will effect an increase in the technical determinacy in the socio-technical system. The implication of the phrase 'turn that vehicle round' is that the lorry drivers socio-technical system will be increasingly more closed.

The technical basis of relief from constraint is, even in an occupation like lorry driving, being whittled away. At the same time the lorry driver's claim to be a specialist is challenged by the management of his firm and is even more likely to be so in the future. The trend is from organic to mechanistic structure in organisation. B.R.S., which since 1963 has been part of the Transport Holding Company, is likely to expand by buying up other haulage businesses.[27] B.R.S. constitutes our example of a mechanistic organisation where the management is most likely to challenge the driver's conception of himself as a specialist. The data show that where this happens work satisfaction is lowered to a level almost equal to that in a factory where the employees have no advantage of technically derived freedom. The role is prescribed at B.R.S. and has little discretion com-

---

[25] Report of the Committee on Carrier's Licensing. Ministry of Transport, H.M.S.O., London, 1965, paras. 3.27–3.32, pp. 29–31. The report points out that bankruptcy is high amongst the smaller firms with 'Contract A' licences. Larger haulage firms fail much less.

[26] Road Haulage Rates. Report No. 1 (Interim). National Board for Prices and Incomes. Cmnd. 2695. H.M.S.O. London, 1965, para. 47, p. 12. The schedule generally recognised by shop stewards at B.R.S. was 22·6 m.p.h.

[27] Report and Accounts of the Transport Holding Company, 1965. Para. 2.43, p. 20.

pared with the private haulage firm. On the private haulage
side of the industry relations between the management and
men may have been artibrary and authoritarian but in many
cases the structure was organic. The solution of a particular
problem was often obtained by a discussion between the owner
and driver. This discussion, though not one between equals, as
between two experts, appeared to be this way to many of the
drivers. Drivers were able to put their problems and objections
personally to the owner and a mutual agreement obtained.
With B.R.S. this practice has disappeared and the driver's
complaint is that he can never see the manager of the depot
except on matters of discipline. Instead he has to approach any
number of intermediaries, of whom few know what his job as
a driver involves, and what is worse, as the lorry driver's
assertion continues, few of whom know even their own jobs.
This, and many other management activities at B.R.S. are all
part of a lessening of the discretion of the lorry driver and are
consequently an attack on his conception of himself as a
specialist.

The claim that he has a specialist or expert role within an
organisation will succeed only if it is accompanied by some
specialist qualification. Status of specialists in organisations
rests upon the attainment of certification of competence. The
lorry driver is unsuccessful in claiming the status of a specialist
because the only qualification he legally requires is to be over
21 years of age and have an ordinary driving licence. The
'Geddes' Report recognises the need for the special licence:

> A heavy lorry can be a particularly menacing vehicle if not well
> driven. More is called for than the skills and attitudes of the
> ordinary motorist . . .

Referring to the plans of the Ministry of Transport to re-
introduce the special licence for the drivers of heavy goods
vehicles the report continues:

> The existence of such a licence, apart from its other considerable
> merits, would make it possible to apply to drivers guilty of
> safety offences a discipline similar to that which revocation,
> suspension or curtailment of a carrier's permit would provide in
> respect of his employer. In this way the fringe of drivers whose
> behaviour does not match their responsibilities could be cut off,

to the advantage of the good reputation of the heavy lorry driver as well as to the benefit of the public at large.[28]

The re-introduction of the special licence is provided for in the Road Safety Bill going through Parliament during 1966. Driving tests designed for potential heavy goods vehicle drivers are an integral part of the scheme.

John Darker suggests that there should be a 'Master Driver's Diploma' which would be a 'senior qualification' and one which would be 'open to all drivers in the industry'. This diploma would be gained by 'the passing of stringent tests of driving skill, and operating "know how" . . . supplemented by some years of actual operating experience'.[29] It seems that this suggestion could have two main results if it were implemented. Firstly in itself it would enhance the lorry driver's claim to have a specialist role within his firm. Secondly it would provide a bridging of the gap between the man's career as a driver and his progression within the organisation that employs him. Such a qualification, as well as being 'economically beneficial' would thus provide him with a knowledge of the symbols required to rise into the management ranks. This would advance particular drivers on the status ladder. More important, it would mean that those drivers left on the shop floor or, to phrase it more appropriately, at the clutch pedal, would be able to deal with representatives of management who knew the problems of a lorry driver.

At the present time the lorry driver fails in his claim to the type of sociological licensing of his occupation which he requires of his management. He is not treated as an expert among experts. This was found to be less true of the more organically structured private haulage firm but almost completely true in the case of the more mechanistic B.R.S. depot. The failure to meet such a structural challenge is by degree small when compared with the lorry driver's lack of success with other members of his role set. While the newer type of management structure only grudgingly allows him a licence of a sort, though not the kind he seeks, others in his role set do not want him to carry on at all. The motorist in his private car

[28] Carrier's Licensing Report, 1965, *op. cit.* para. 6.53, p. p 54–55.

[29] Darker, J., 1965, *op. cit.* p. 21.

is the main challenger here. The lorry driver sees himself as the expert driver on the road and he sees the car driver as just the very opposite of that.

In the café sample 27·5 per cent of the drivers gave the behaviour of other road users as a source of dissatisfaction in their job. The figure for the firms' sample is 23 per cent. Of the mentions of factors given for job dissatisfaction, in the café and firms' samples,[30] 26 and 23 per cent respectively, of the total, are made of this reason.

> 'Private motor car drivers—they park in the most awkward places and they never think of anybody.'

> 'Our biggest bugbear for heavy vehicles is the private motorist because they just come down the road and they think they have the right of the roads. We have to think for them.'

Perhaps the best comment to support this illustration of the car driver through lorry drivers' eyes, is the implicit comment from the two drivers in the *Punch* 'cartoon' below. The best estimate that can be made is that the comment would be concerned with the amateur habits of the car driver.[31]

This conflict will continue. The road building programme in Britain just has not been sufficient to prevent it. Between 1950 and 1964 the total mileage of roads increased by approximately 16,000 whereas the number of vehicles in use rose by nearly 8 million. The 2.3 million cars in use in 1950 had more than trebled by 1964. Needless to say, a considerable increase in vehicles in use, particularly cars, has been projected for the 1980s.[32]

Conflict between lorry driver and private motorist arises because the motorist does not meet the lorry driver's expectations. How then does the ideology of the 'Knight of the Road' fare? Is it accepted as legitimate and is the lorry driver's expert judgement of the amateur motorists accepted by them? The answer is very definitely that it is not. We have already seen that the lorry driver's sociological licence is precarious, and

[30] See Appendix, Table 46. Sources of Job Dissatisfaction in Lorry Driving (Firms' Sample).

[31] *Punch*, 5th February, 1964. p. 187.

[32] Savage, C. I. 1966, *op. cit.* pp. 178, 205.

that his expectations are not reflected back at him by his role set. It would follow quite logically that his mandate—to come back to Hughes' term—is non-existent, and he is only too well aware of this. Lorry drivers in both major samples were asked to state what they thought was the view of 'people in general' of themselves and their job.

© *Punch*—reproduced by permission.

Fig. 8. "Salt of the earth, these long-distance chaps."

The café sample of drivers clearly indicated that they feel their status as an occupational group is not high. Only 24·5 per cent say the public has an overall favourable view of them, while 41 per cent assume that people in general have an unfavourable attitude towards them. Where the drivers give indication of a favourable public image the main reason is the courtesy of lorry drivers on the road towards other road users and the fact that the lorry driver is often a help to other motorists when they are in trouble. Other important reasons for a favourable image are the actual experience of contact with other people by the driver, and also the possibility that the public sees the driver as doing a difficult job of work.

The unfavourable image predominates and the reasons are

illustrated in order of descending importance—the low prestige of lorry driving as an occupation:

'A driver is just a glorified labourer.'

'Not very highly, a lorry driver has no status like a clerk.'

—improper behaviour by lorry drivers:

'They've got a funny idea about drivers, they think we're all crooks and layabouts.'

'They've got the wrong impression. They think you're not clean because you're a lorry driver, in a lot of places they don't want to know you.'

'They think that lorry drivers are the scum of the earth because we live rough and stop in towns with women.'

'They think they're a rough tough lot.'

Many of the statements in this category can be subsumed under two headings of types of improper behaviour, firstly sexual behaviour, and secondly stealing and pilfering. We have already seen that for a lorry driver to 'be off the right road' in terms of sexual behaviour is not all that uncommon. The public hears of this sort of thing through the press. Headings in the Sunday press such as 'After Kisses in the Café' do not help the lorry driver's reputation, even though the driver in this particular case was acquitted of indecent assault of an under 16 year old girl. Less dramatic but possibly more damaging are reports in the press such as the following. The heading is 'Teenage Sex Can Aid Marriage', but the lorry driver is also in the picture.

'The opening of the M.6,' said Dr. Silver (a consultant venereologist) 'has helped to reduce venereal disease at Bolton. We don't get as many lorry girls', he explained. 'They by-pass the district and travel on routes where lorry drivers stop more often for a meal.'[33]

Another major cause of the damaged reputation is the mobile nature of the job.

'Years ago we were thought to be hobos, the scum of the earth.'

'We're classified as tramps by the general public.'

[33] *Western Mail*, 17th July, 1965. p. 9.

'Glorified gypsies they class us as. In a lot of these factories a driver is classed as a dago who travels about the country.'

Other reasons given for an unfavourable view are people's criticism of the driving of lorry drivers and the attitudes to them which drivers experience at loading and unloading points. Although there is a great deal of ambivalence and neutrality amongst the responses to this question, drivers in the café sample feel overwhelmingly that their status is not high.

The drivers in the firms' sample confirm the café sample lorry drivers' view of a low prestige of the occupational group. More drivers in the firms' sample say they think the public has a favourable image (31 per cent) but a slightly higher proportion (43 per cent) indicate an unfavourable image.[34]

Very much the same sort of basis is used for supposing a favourable picture in the firms' sample, as is given by the drivers in the café sample. Courtesy, helpfulness, lorry drivers' driving ability, the difficulties of the job and the experience of others attitude are all mentioned.[35] As a set of reasons for an unfavourable attitude by the public, the drivers in the firms' sample indicate much the same things as do their colleagues in the café sample.[36] The most frequent mentions are of status problems of the occupation and improper behaviour by lorry drivers.

In view of the fact that lorry driving has a status in the Registrar General's terms, which is equivalent to workers who have skill in a more formal sense, it seems something of a mystery at first sight, that the lorry driver should feel that his occupation places him in such a lowly position in the eyes of the public. It is however a clear cut case of an image which he projects which is not reflected back at him. After this happens once or twice the lorry driver is likely to know his social position well enough. The same industry, firms, and physically mobile situation that affords him freedom from technical constraint, produces an occupation which has a low prestige.

Firstly the lorry driver is seen as a potential and actual

[34] See Appendix, Table 47. The Public View of the Lorry Driver.

[35] See Appendix, Table 48. Reasons for a Favourable View by the Public.

[36] See Appendix, Table 49. Reasons for an Unfavourable View by the Public.

danger to other road users. In spite of the fact that the statistics quoted earlier (*see* Chapter II) indicate that he is safer than most, in fact all other categories of vehicle user on the road, when he does have an accident the damage caused is usually of dramatic proportions. Lorries careering down hills in town centres, entering front parlours, and even in one case a bank, causing widespread havoc and death, are regularly headlined in the provincial and national press.[37] The Ministry of Transport's increasing checks on the condition of lorries and the findings of officials are also given prominence in the press. Increasingly the public learns that the lorry driver is someone who drives vehicles which are a menace to others on the road.

As well as being a menace to other road users in the sense of being a danger to life and limb the lorry driver also inconveniences the car driver. The car driver complains of being held up, particularly on hills, behind great fume-belching, slow-moving 'juggernauts'. Many car drivers object to his very presence on the road on this basis.[38] The biggest source of job dissatisfaction was shown to come from adverse contacts with car drivers. In their frustration car drivers do things in order to pass lorries which involve an abnormal risk to them. The lorry driver views such driving as being completely amateur, while the car driver sees him as making the road more hazardous by his presence than is really necessary. The lorry drivers are well aware of the views of the motorists and their representatives.

'If you read *Headlight* you'll have heard that there's been a lot of muck-throwing lately.'

'They've got a bad opinion of us, at the moment the write-ups in the papers say that lorries are in the way.'

'It used to be a good name but lately there's been a lot of mud slung at us. The motoring correspondents are slinging mud.'

[37] Many such incidents are illustrated in full in Chapter II. Illustrations of particular interest in this sphere are to be found in the *South Wales Echo*, 16th October, 1963. See also the *Daily Mail*, 31st May, 1965, in which the details of some recent lorry accidents are summarised, and an article in the *Western Mail*, 17th July, 1965, 'Heavy Vehicles can be Killers'.

[38] *The Observer*, 1st September, 1963. A letter to the editor from a salesman complains that lorries cost him time and therefore money, and thus they should not be on the road at all.

A third unfavourable aspect of the lorry driver induced by his mobile work situation is that he is visibly different from the static residents in particular communities which have to act as host to him on his journeys. As Soloman has indicated in her study, the transport café is a place where things of ill repute go on. In fact though the lorry driver may be respectable, his 'role set' in the café where he has his break may not be. He may be seen as part of a configuration in which deviant behaviour is the outstanding characteristic, thus producing a stereotype. The lorry driver can be a nuisance in direct ways to people living in roadside communities.

> 'We don't change over there anymore. We have to go up to the cafe, people complained about the noise, you know—blokes banging trailers about and shouting and swearing in the middle of the night.' (Private Haulage Trunker)

In the above illustration the lorry driver's language, which has in-group acceptability is 'visible' or rather 'audible' to outsiders. Such language contained in factory walls would be acceptable to the people within them but it gives the group a low image amongst outsiders. The sort of language that is permitted inside the group may be quite alien to middle class residential communities. In the case quoted below the lorry driver is clearly within the law but the effect on the occupational image must have been quite damaging. The case arose out of a conflict with a motorist.

WHAT THE LORRY DRIVER SAID

A lorry driver said at Oxfordshire Quarter Sessions last night that he told a woman motorist she was 'bloody potty' and added: 'A police officer came up when I was going to smack her under the kisser'. The woman, Miss Peter Honorine Ady (48) a fellow and tutor at an Oxford College, has pleaded not guilty to dangerous driving on the A40 on June 26. Mr. P. W. Meed, prosecuting, said Miss Ady, who was driving a Morris Minor tourer, had deliberately inconvenienced the lorry driver, Mr. Charles Parnell, because she was annoyed about lorry drivers driving too close to each other.

The Guardian, 2nd January 1963

This sort of statement easily gives rise to a public image rather like the lorry driver quoted below suggests.

'There's an old saying "a common lorry driver". I don't think they (people in general) think a lot of them. When you say you're a lorry driver they think you're the scum of the earth.'

The improper behaviour mentioned by the drivers in both samples including offences against the sexual mores of the wider society has already been discussed.[39] Improper behaviour also includes criminal behaviour such as stealing. One of the dangers of lorry driving is that someone may have his eye on a valuable load which is being carried. There is always the chance that the lorry driver will have colluded with the 'hijackers' in return for a proportion of the proceeds. One widely publicised case indicated that a whole group of lorry drivers were involved in defrauding a large petrol company over a long period of time.[40] Some of the drivers met during the course of field work, both in the samples and outside them, said they had been involved in some way in such activities. Here are some true confessions.

'I'm not saying this with an inferiority complex but a lot of people in the industry think we're thieves, rogues and cut-throats, and some people in the trade are lending themselves that way.'

During the period of interviewing and participant observation the writer heard of many commodities offered for sale. These included tins of coffee, sweets, nylons, and frozen chickens. One driver told of how his problems were once solved by thieving.

'I was on for (a named firm) with a trailer which was empty and too light to ride, so I "barred" (used a crow bar to lever) some stones from this fella's wall. It was funny because he came out and said "there's some bigger ones in the path". So I said "Aye, I need something heavy, have you got any top blocks?" I was cheeky when I was younger see. Well, he got annoyed then and went all red in the face and said "You put them back", and he took the name of the firm and my name. Anyway I got away from him and stopped to ring up the boss. He just said "Come on in". Mind you, he had to pay for the stones and to have the wall rebuilt.'

[39] See the earlier reference to T. C. N. Gibbon, *The Clients of Prostitutes.*
[40] *South Wales Echo*, 31st January, 1964. Ten of the men sentenced in a case of 'wholesale thieving and receiving' were lorry drivers.

Many lorry drivers may make a 'bit on the side' by having an 'arrangement' about fuel with the garages they call at but some of the opportunities which present themselves offer much greater rewards.

> 'I had two offers today. A bloke just offered me a shed worth £65 for a fiver, and a bloke at (a named firm) offered me £50 just to go in and load up and drive a couple of miles down the road. I didn't do it this time because I wasn't sure how things were there, but I think its alright and next week I'll be there.'

Thus coupled with the licence society affords the lorry driver to be entirely responsible for valuable loads and vehicles there is the persistent pressure on him to be dishonest. From what some of the drivers in the firms' sample say, there is a feeling amongst these drivers that the licence is only grudgingly given. Both the lorry drivers and the public know, from what they read in the press, that the reticent attitude of people towards the lorry driver is sometimes justified. The night time activities of some lorry drivers at transport cafés and other places do much to reinforce this attitude.

We have seen that the lorry driver's role set by and large does not reflect his expectations. This is true of his management as it is true of the public, in particular the motoring public. It is also true of the clients of his firm. The employees of these clients control him completely once he arrives at his destination to pick up or release a load. His presence means more work for these people and they make him feel he is a 'dago' or 'gypsy' by their attitude towards him. Our 'Knight of the Road' is often kept waiting for considerable lengths of time and even the joking ability of the best lorry driver may not get round this.

> 'There are lots of ins and outs on this job. When you get to a place they leave you outside and keep you waiting and then they snatch the paper from you. Dockers are the world's worst for this. They think you're scum—"wait here"—"go there"—that kind of attitude.'

All this delay reflects upon his ability as an expert or specialist to perform his role accordingly with consequences for the conception of himself which he presents to his management.

In addition to his role set failing to reflect his image the average type of lorry driver will be faced with considerable problems of accommodation in his status set. Our prime example, the family situation, suggests this state of affairs and it is clear that while such accommodation works it does not produce the ideal family pattern. Wives often know that his mobile occupation furnishes too many sexual opportunities for some trace of suspicion never to cross their minds. Husbands may also be suspicious and they may not state when they expect to arrive home quite deliberately. While this may be designed to make their wives reticent about having lovers in most cases all it will do is to upset the domestic routine still more. It is the wife who may pull the lorry driver away from his occupation altogether in later years when the children have left home and the family has largely paid for its possessions.

The ability to participate in his local community is reduced in the average type role as it is in the pure type. The average type may well try to increase this participation or get time at home by 'doing a dodgy' and taking a risk with his employment. A good deal of this does go on. Lorry drivers may start away very early in the morning to make up for the mileage they have failed to put in the night previously. If the load has to be there on time then the slightest mistake, such as over-sleeping or a miscalculation of the peak traffic times in towns en route will land him in trouble in his occupational status. It would seem that attempts at accommodation in the status set may only serve to lessen his claim for licence still more.

The British stratification system is often noted for its very numerous idiosyncratic characteristics. Symbols and what may be considered slight traits of behaviour, such as an accent, are used to categorise people. The fact that some years ago lorry drivers were elected the worst dressed men in Britain may not in itself be of any importance. What is represented here however is of crucial significance in the lorry driver's claim for a mandate. The main reason that the lorry driver is unable to claim such a mandate is that a group of such low prestige would never be given one. No occupational group would be able to get a definition of a proper conduct of others towards its work accepted by the public if its general prestige were as low as that of the lorry driver. Some motorists would not admit him licence let alone a mandate. This is due to actual physical inconvenience they suffer through the presence of his lorry on the road rather than any reputational effect. It would seem that he is never to be an expert driver except in his own ideology.

We have demonstrated the sources of his low prestige. What remains is to view the mechanisms or agencies that lorry drivers as a group possess to counter their lack of prestige. The first possibility is the trade union.

An effect of the structure of the road haulage industry, with its many small firms and fierce competition, is the lack of trade union organisation which prevails amongst lorry drivers in general. B.R.S. drivers are 100 per cent organised but the private firms are only scantily so. The larger firm in private haulage tends to have unionised employees more often than the smaller one. In the private haulage firm from which a sample was taken only about half the drivers were union men. This state of affairs seems pretty general.[41] In the towns and industrial areas firms will pay above the negotiated wage rate for a good tramper, or indeed any other type of lorry driver, thus making trade union membership seem irrelevant. In the rural areas firms may be so small and running close to the financial break even point that union organisation seems of little use to the lorry driver. A further factor here is the very personalised relationship between the management and the drivers in small private firms. The most fundamental factor underlying the lack of union organisation would seem to be a perception by the lorry driver that if he can only get the capital he can buy his own lorry and set up in business for himself. The 'tradition of opportunity' still seems very much a reality for a few lorry drivers. It is nurtured by the knowledge of others who have bought their own 'wagons' and have 'made a go of it', in some cases their own managements are examples of this. Although individualism and the tradition of opportunity are all pervasive in the ethos, we have to say that when asked direct questions on the subject the lorry driver is in two cases out of three not expectant of ever changing his occupation. Perhaps the difficulties of making money last out for a week traps the driver into a realisation of the difficulties of raising capital. The lorry driver is more aspiring for his children

---

[41] Where a union card is necessary, such as on the docks, two drivers in a firm may belong. The subscription in such a case is paid by the firm.

than for himself. He is very committed to his occupation in the sense that he feels that, given his circumstances of alienation from factory work, lorry driving will give him the freedom he requires while he is at work.

The fact that he intends staying in the occupation does not seem to impress on the lorry driver the need to organise. A consideration of trade unions as a mechanism to raise prestige shows that the lorry driver does not get much help here. The giant Transport and General Workers is too diversified for this function, though it does considerable work in representing lorry drivers who have run foul of one legal regulation or another. The other two unions are too small to really be of much help in this way.

The second mechanism for ideological dissemination is the occupational journal. In spite of the unorganised nature of the industry the lorry driver is lucky enough to have such a journal. *Headlight*, the 'lorry driver's trade paper' does attempt to support an ideology for lorry drivers and to raise their status and conditions. *Headlight* tries to lay down some definition of what is a reasonable standard of behaviour for lorry drivers, not only with regard to their driving but in their wider role while at work. An editorial in the January issue of 1963 is a particularly good example of the efforts of the magazine on the lorry drivers' behalf.[42]

> It's true that from time to time we nag here about the misdeeds of some drivers. But if we do, it's only because we are so concerned about the public opinion of all lorry drivers, which is not helped by the minority who don't play the game. It is still our belief that, as a body of men, lorry drivers—and especially those who are interested enough in their job are second to none . . . the world's best.

Talking of New Year resolutions and wishes *Headlight* says:

> And we can't do better than wish for more comfort and status for the lorry driver when doing his job.

and later continues:

> Another wish we would make is that it might be possible to persuade people to stop treating the lorry driver as if he were an

[42] *Headlight*, January 1963. p. 9.

unskilled labourer. What, of course, also implies (is) that un-skilled labourers should stop posing as lorry drivers and blacken-ing the reputation of the professional in the eyes of other road users.

Amongst the lorry drivers themselves this ideology is barely developed, as evidenced by the samples. It can only be pre-sumed that the fluidity of the work situation and the derived individualistic ethos prevents a proper formulation of an ideology, as does the lack of public differentiation between the skill required to drive a car and that required to be a lorry driver.

We have to conclude that the mechanisms by which an adequate ideology can be formulated and diffused, are in-capable of meeting the challenges that are made on the lorry driver's conception of his occupational role by his role set. The structure of the industry is such that there is not even a great deal of consensus amongst lorry drivers generally about their role. The pure type of lorry driver role is accompanied by an ideology. The average type has little ideological consensus and there is no really adequate mechanism for ideological dissemina-tion. This being the case the lorry driver will never achieve the mandate which the more developed self concept claims.

CONCLUSION

The contention at the outset of this study is that actors are alienated by structural constraints. Alienation is viewed as a subjective concept involving the state of mind of the actor. A discussion of alienation of necessity must involve the things from which the actor is alienated. Separation or estrangement is perhaps the most all embracing meaning of the term. Powerlessness and meaninglessness, the definitions of alienation thought to be most relevant in the first chapter, may be subsumed under the heading of separation. They are the two major elements giving rise to such estrangement. This study is an illustration of alienation considered as the separation of man from what is meaningful to him and his inability to alter this state of affairs. It is the story of the way in which a group of actors feel they are cheated of their 'rightful' role. This loss of proper role has detrimental effects on their particular occupational status. In terms of our definition of status and role, this means that the actor has to face differing expectations from those he would like, and in consequence his status is not accorded the rights or deference he thinks it should have. Others do not meet their obligations to the status in the way the incumbents would like.

The lorry driver, as an occupational status, has been looked at in two ways. We have considered it where it is accompanied by a pure type of role. This pure type is a construction of what is 'lorry drivery' about lorry drivers. The pure type of role as such represents the self concept of the role. It shows clearly his values as manifested in his occupational ideology and is the unmitigated extension of the role as the lorry driver would like it to be. The average type of lorry driver role is the one which is brought about by the interplay of the self concept with structural demands. Actual performance is a result of the interplay of the orientation of the lorry drivers (self concept) and the structural demands made by technical facilities, organisation structures, the other parts of their role set, and status sets. Alienation is produced through there being a difference between the pure and average type roles. This difference occurs through the structural constraints mentioned. These constraints prevent the self concept becoming a reality. They prevent an emergence of the real occupational self by cheating the lorry driver of any chance of performing his role according to his set of rules.

In the final analysis it must be said that the lorry driver is a retreatist from a supposed alienation of one kind but is caught in alienative forms of another sort. His value of his freedom is maintained by the tools and all the aspects of the technical system with which he performs his role. The claim that he is an expert is recognised by some of the managements, notably in the smaller private firms, when they term him an 'individualist'. The more mechanistically structured firms, which tend to be those which employ the greatest number of lorry drivers, do not recognise him as a specialist or expert. The way he would like to play his role is most seriously challenged by the private motorist who constitutes a major part of his role set. The private motorist regards him as a nuisance rather than a professional driver who is a 'Knight of the Road'. Lastly' although the lorry driver's technical system affords him the freedom he values, and affords him an escape from the confines of factory work, he is in full view of the public. Such visibility is the source of his inability to claim a mandate. His occupational activities are sometimes in contrast with the values of society as a whole. In consequence he has a lower prestige than would otherwise attach to an occupation in that particular category of the Registrar General. His family life, and his life as a citizen participating in a community, are sometimes not in accordance with what society considers it ought to be. Accommodation, to reduce the strain in family life and to bring it closer to society's ideal, may well involve him in lessening or even losing his occupational status.

Paradoxically it is his desire for freedom which alienates the lorry driver. His technical system gives him his freedom and allows him to retain control even though he has a management which will not allow his claim that he is an expert. This freedom has led to a lack of *formal* recognition that he and his kind are a collectivity. He is only weakly unionised and the other existing mechanism for the dissemination of his ideology is, as yet, weak in its effect. The gross society has many competing claims for legitimacy of occupational behaviour before it. It is able to judge these claims fairly only if there are facts available on all aspects of the occupation. Occupational groups which do not possess the agencies to disseminate their ideologies are unlikely to even enter the competition for mandate and may be allowed only a precarious licence. This precarious licence is the source of the lorry driver's greatest alienation. It means that he is separated from the wider society because that society does not recognise the importance of his role. The claim as to the economic importance of his role is unchallengeable, but in his desire for freedom he has not created the agencies through which his claim may be presented.

APPENDIX

TABLE 1

First Jobs of Drivers

Name of First Job		Trunkers	Trampers	Shunters	Total Sample
Lorry or Van Driver's Mate	M	10	4	8	17
Errand Boy	M	4	3	5	10
Unskilled Factory Worker		3	7	1	10
Agricultural Workers		2	4	4	9
Garage Hand		1	3	2	6
Collier's Boy		1	2	1	3
Building Worker		1	2	–	3
Shop Assistant		1	1	1	2
Warehouseman		1	1	1	2
Stable Boy and Horse Driver	M	2	–	1	2
Fireman (Railways)	M	1	2	–	2
Bargehand	M	1	1	–	2
Telegram Boy	M	–	1	1	2
Porter (Railways)	M	–	1	1	2
Fitter's Mate		–	1	1	2
Ragman and Dealer's Assistant	M	1	1	–	2
Seaman	M	1	1	–	2
Carpenter's Apprenticeship		1	1	–	2
Baker's Apprenticeship		2	–	–	1
Paper Making Apprenticeship		1	–	–	1
Electrician's Mate		–	–	1	1
Capstan Operator on Docks		–	1	–	1
Sawyer		–	1	–	1
Apprentice Fitter		–	1	–	1
Apprentice Miller		–	1	–	1
Gardener		–	1	–	1
Apprentice Motor Fitter		–	1	–	1
Baker's Roundsman	M	1	–	–	–
Bakery Worker		–	1	–	1
Tricycle (Ice Cream) Salesman	M	–	–	1	1
Apprentice Welder		–	–	1	1
Kilnworker	M	–	–	1	1
Bus Conductor		–	–	1	1
House Painter		–	–	1	1
Apprentice Electrician		–	–	1	1
Professional Sportsman		–	–	1	1
Cycle Repairer		–	–	1	1
Barman and Waiter		1	–	–	–
Laundry Hand		1	–	–	–
Not Known		–	1	2	3
TOTAL		37	44	38	101

M—Occupation Classified as Mobile

229

Appendix: Tables

TABLE 2

Aspects of Lorry Drivers' Careers

Aspect	Aspects of Career		Trunkers	Trampers	Shunters
1	Age now	Mean	43·86	38·10	45·71
		Median	43·0	37·0	46·0
		Mode (Estimation)	41·28	34·8	46·58
		Standard Deviation	8·433	10·150	12·45
2	Age starting in Lorry Driving	Mean	21·24	23·16	22·92
		Median	19·0	20·0	22·0
		Mode	17·0	19·0	17·0
		Standard Deviation	6·67	6·99	5·85
3	Total no. of years away from Lorry Driving after entry		52·0	104·0	45·5
4	Average no. of years away from Lorry Driving after entry		1·40	2·36	1·18
5	No. of years away from Lorry Driving after entry as % of total career		5·918	9·98	3·97
6	Percentage of career after first entry into Lorry Driving, spent in L.D. (100=no. of years away from L.D.) (after entry as % of total career)		94·08	90·02	96·03
7	Average no. of years in Lorry Driving		21·054	12·32	21·08
8	No. of years in Lorry Driving as % of total career		70·03	51·45	63·47
9a	*Trunkers*. No. who have been		37	29	28
	Percentage no. who have been		100	78	76
	Average age on first entry into categories of Trunking, Tramping, Shunting		33·48	26·62	21·46
9b	*Trampers*. No. who have been		8	44	36
	Percentage No. who have been		18	100	82
	Average age on first entry into categories of Trunking, Tramping, Shunting		34·75	30·50	23·03
9c	*Shunters*. No. who have been		13	22	38
	Percentage No. who have been		34	58	100
	Average age on first entry into categories of Trunking, Tramping, Shunting		40·69	35·73	23·71

TABLE 3

The Best Type of Driving Job

Best Driving Job	Trunkers		Trampers		Shunters		B.R.S.		P.H.		Sample	
	R.T.	%	R.T.	%	R.T.	%	R.T.	%	R.T.	%	R.T.	%
Trunking	25	67	14	32	16	42	19	31	22	56	41	40
Tramping	4	11	23	52	–	–	19	31	6	15	25	25
Shunting	8	22	7	16	22	58	24	40	11	28	35	35
Total	37	100	44	100	38	100	62	110	39	100	101	100
							(102)		(99)		(101)	

TABLE 4

Aspiration and Type of Driving Job Held

Present Occupational Category	Present Occ. Cat. Preferred		Aspiration to other Occ. Cat.		Ratio of Present Occ. Cat. Preferred to Total
	R.T.	%	R.T.	%	
Trunkers	25	68	12	32	0·67
Trampers	23	52	21	48	0·52
Shunters	22	58	16	42	0·58
Shunters, 40 years and under	6	40	9	60	0·40
Shunters, 41 and over	16	70	7	30	0·69

TABLE 5

Shunters, Age and Aspiration Pattern

Shunters who have been	40 years and under		41 years and over	
	Present Occupation Preferred	Other Occupation Preferred	Present Occupation Preferred	Other Occupation Preferred
Shunters only	5	6	2	–
Shunters and Trampers	1	1	7	3
Shunters and Trunkers	–	1	1	1
Shunters, Trunkers and Trampers	–	1	5	3
Total	6	9	16	7

TABLE 6
The Sources of Job Satisfaction in Lorry Driving

Things most Liked	B.R.S. Sample	P.H. Sample	Total Sample
Autonomy	27	13	40
Variety of places	18	21	39
The job itself	16	7	23
Variety of people	12	6	18
Health, open air job	8	4	12
Money	7	4	11
Familiarity	4	1	5
Responsibility	5	–	5
Fellow workers	2	1	3
Security	–	1	1
Looking for 'Smokers'	–	1	1
Total Mentions	99	59	158
Nothing Liked No. of Drivers	1	2	3

TABLE 7
The Sources of Job Satisfaction in Lorry Driving and Factory Work Compared

Lorry Drivers Firms' Sample	No. Mentions		Factory Worker Sample	No. Mentions	
Factors giving satisfaction	*R.T.*	*%*	*Factors giving satisfaction*	*R.T.*	*%*
Autonomy	40	25	Interest	12	22
Variety of places	39	55	Variety	9	17
The job itself	23	14	The job itself	7	13
Variety of people	18	11	Familiarity of job	6	11
Health, open air job	12	8	Relations with fellow workers	6	11
Money	11	7	Wages and methods of pay	6	11
Total on 1st Six Factors	143	90	Total on 1st Six Factors	46	85
Total mentions All factors	158	100	Total mentions All factors	56	100

TABLE 8

Reasons for Liking Factory Work

Reason for finding factory work attractive	B.R.S.		P.H.		Total	
	Sample	Trunkers	Sample	Trunkers	Sample	Trunkers
Out of the weather	14	7	3	2	17	9
Regularity of times and meals	4	3	5	1	9	4
Interesting work	6	2	1	0	7	2
Home life	5	3	1	0	6	3
Conditions and amenities	2	2	1	0	3	2
Short hours	2	2	1	0	3	2
Money	1	3	2	1	3	4
Opportunity for advancement	2	–	–	–	2	–
Security	1		1	–	2	–
Depends on type of factory	–	2	–	–	–	2
Depends on type of job	–	–	1	–	1	–
Not so much responsibility	–	1	–	–	–	1
Factory jobs safer	–	–	1	–	1	–
Lighter work	1	–	–	–	1	–
Better Union	–	–	1	1	1	1
Female workers	–	1	–	–	–	1
Total Positive Reasons	38	26	18	5	56	31
Nothing attractive	31	8	23	5	54	13
Don't Know	1	–	–	–	1	–

TABLE 9

Reasons for disliking Factory Work

Reasons for disliking Factory Work	B.R.S.		P.H.		Total	
	Sample	Trunkers	Sample	Trunkers	Sample	Trunkers
Indoor work	40	18	25	6	65	24
Routine & Monotony	11	1	5	–	16	1
In one place	9	3	3	1	12	4
Supervision	5	4	2	–	7	4
Fumes	2	–	2	1	4	1
Noise	2	1	–	–	2	1
Dust	–	1	1	–	1	1
Clocking in/out	–	–	2	–	2	–
Bad pay	1	1	–	–	1	1
Temperature	–	1	–	–	–	1
Too many people	1	1	–	–	1	1
Shift work	–	–	1	–	1	–
Unfamiliarity	1	–	–	–	1	–
Cannot meet people	1	1	–	–	1	1
Regularity of hours	–	–	1	–	1	–
Strikes	–	–	1	–	1	–
Total	73	32	43	8	116	40
Nothing unattractive	2	1	–	–	2	1
Don't know	1	–	1	2	2	2

TABLE 10A

Comparison of Lorry Driving with Factory Work by Firms

Lorry Driving compares with Factory Work:	B.R.S.		P.H.		Total	
	R.T.	%	R.T.	%	R.T.	%
Favourably	44	71	24	61	68	67
Unfavourably	11	18	7	18	18	18
About the same	6	10	7	18	13	13
Don't know	1	2	1	3	2	2
Total	62	100	39	100	101	100

TABLE 10B

*Comparison of Lorry Driving with Factory Work
by Occupational Category*

Lorry Driving compares with Factory Work:	Trunkers		Trampers		Shunters	
	R.T.	%	R.T.	%	R.T.	%
Favourably	26	70	33	75	23	60
Unfavourably	4	11	6	14	9	24
About the same	6	16	5	11	5	13
Don't know	1	3	—	—	1	3
Total	37	100	44	100	38	100

TABLE 11

Reasons for Favourable Comparison

Reason for Favourable	Trunkers		Trampers		Shunters		B.R.S.		P.H.		Total	
	R.T.	%	R.T.	%	R.T.	%	R.T.	%	R.T.	%	R.T.	%
Autonomy	12	32	15	34	7	8	17	27	12	31	29	29
Outdoor work	5	13	12	27	8	21	15	24	7	18	22	22
Variety of places	2	5	2	5	6	16	6	10	4	10	10	10
Variety of work	3	8	2	5	1	3	5	8	—	—	5	5
Health	2	5	2	5	2	5	2	3	2	5	4	4
Responsibility	3	8	1	2	1	3	3	5	—	—	3	3
Interest	2	5	—	—	1	3	3	5	—	—	3	3
Meeting people	2	5	—	—	1	3	1	2	3	2	2	2
Comradeship	—	—	1	2	1	3	1	2	1	3	2	2
Experience	—	—	1	2	1	3	—	—	2	5	2	2
Can vary work times	—	—	2	5	—	—	—	—	2	5	2	2
Alertness required	1	3	—	—	—	—	—	—	—	—	—	—
Money	—	—	—	—	1	3	1	2	—	—	1	1
Other unspecified	—	—	3	7	—	—	3	5	—	—	3	3
Total	32	—	41	—	30	—	54	—	31	—	85	—

Appendix: Tables

TABLE 12
Reasons for Unfavourable Comparison

Reason for Unfavourable Comparison	Trunkers	Trampers	Shunters	B.R.S.	P.H.	Total
The weather	1	2	4	5	1	6
Conditions in Factories	1	3	2	3	3	6
Money	1	3	1	–	5	5
Dirtier work	1	–	1	1	1	2
Factory Work easier	1	–	–	–	–	–
Factory Work less responsible	–	–	1	1	–	1
Heavier work	1	–	–	1	–	1
No regular meals	–	–	1	1	–	1
Regular hours in Factory Work	–	1	–	–	1	1
Age	1	–	–	–	–	–
Total	7	9	10	12	11	23

TABLE 13
Comparison of Lorry Driving and Factory Work in Relation to Employment Experience in Factories

L/D compares with Factory Experience	With Factory Experience		No Factory Experience	
	R.T.	%	R.T.	%
Favourably	28	82	37	58
Unfavourably	2	6	16	25
About Equal	3	9	10	16
Don't know	1	3	1	2
Total	34	100	64	100

TABLE 14
Comparative Work Satisfaction

Work Satisfaction	Lorry Drivers Café Sample	Lorry Drivers Firms' sample	Factory Workers Sample
Index 3 point	—	0·64	0·54
Ratio Favourable to	212/294	126/193	71/123
Total Comments	0·72	0·65	0·58
Percentage	—	73	67

TABLE 15

Factors in Work Satisfaction amongst Lorry Drivers

Things Liked	B.R.S.	P.H.	Total
PAY	7	8	15
FRINGE BENEFITS	1	—	1
CONDITIONS	55	5	60
Hours and times of work	35	2	37
Types of work, load or lorry	—	3	3
Good well maintained vehicles	7	—	7
Security	4	—	4
Return loads found	3	—	3
Accommodation	2	—	2
Condition unspecified	1	—	1
Other specific conditions	2	—	3
MANAGEMENT	14	20	34
Allows autonomy	3	11	14
Personal factor	—	—	—
Method of discipline	2	1	3
'Approachable'	—	3	3
'One of us'	—	2	2
Obeys the rules	7	—	7
Relations with T.U.	1	—	1
Individual treatment	—	3	3
Other management	1	—	1
OTHER LIKE MENTIONS	10	7	17
Variety	—	2	2
Comradeship	6	4	10
Familiarity	—	—	—
Good T.U. representatives	2	—	2
Unclassifiable positive	2	1	3
Total positive	87	40	127
Nothing liked	1	4	5
Don't know, not mentioned	1	—	1

TABLE 16

Factors in Work Satisfaction and Dissatisfaction of the Textile Factory Group

Factors in Work Satisfaction	Favourable		Unfavourable	
	R.T.	%	R.T.	%
Management/Supervision	10	14	15	29
Relations with fellow workers	21	30	–	–
Security/insecurity	3	4	3	6
Advancement prospects	–	–	1	2
Wages and methods of payment	13	18	7	13
Hours of work	–	–	5	10
Travelling	10	14	3	6
Canteen	1	1	–	–
Seasonal work	–	–	7	13
Temperature	–	–	3	6
Others on work	3	4	3	6
Total on Work	**61**	**86**	**47**	**90**
Interest/boredom of the job	3	4	–	–
Variety/monotony of the job	1	1	2	4
Lightness/heaviness in the job	–	–	1	2
Responsibility in the job	1	1	–	–
Others on the job	5	7	2	4
Total on the Job	**10**	**14**	**5**	**10**
Total on both	**71**	**100**	**52**	**100**

TABLE 17

Sources of Work Satisfaction in Lorry Driving and Factory Work Compared

Lorry Drivers Firms' Sample Satisfaction Factors	No. Mentions		Factory Worker Sample Satisfaction Factors	No. Mentions	
	R.T.	%		R.T.	%
Hours of work	37	29	Fellow workers†	21	30
Management	34	27	Money	13	18
Money	15	12	Management/supervision	10	14
Fellow Workers†	10	8	Travelling	10	14
Total on 1st four factors	**96**	**76**	**Total on 1st four factors**	**54**	**76**
Total mentions all factors	**127**	**100**	**Total mentions all factors**	**71**	**100**

† Relations with Fellow Workers $X^2 = 16.70$. Significant at the one per cent level with 1 D.F.

Appendix: Tables

TABLE 18

Factors in Work Dissatisfaction amongst Lorry Drivers

Things Disliked	B.R.S. Sample	P.H. Sample	Total
PAY	1	4	5
FRINGE BENEFITS	–	–	–
CONDITIONS	27	6	33
Hours and times of work	1	1	2
Loading and unloading	2	2	4
Bad vehicles and maintenance	2	–	2
'Too much to do'	1	1	2
Insecurity	1	–	1
Too many rules	16	–	16
Paper work	3	–	3
Other conditions	1	2	3
MANAGEMENT	20	7	27
Policy: organisation of firm and work	8	1	9
Personal factor	–	2	2
The office staff	9	2	11
Supervision	1	–	1
Unspecified management	–	1	1
Other management	2	1	3
OTHER DISLIKES	1	1	2
Fellow workers	1	1	2
Total Positive	49	18	67
Nothing disliked	20	22	42
Don't know, not mentioned	–	1	1

TABLE 19

Work Satisfaction in Nationalised and Private Firms

Satisfaction Method	B.R.S. Sample	P.H. Sample	Total Sample
'Subjective' 3 point Index	0·63	0·66	0·64
'Objective' Ratio Favourable to Total Comments	0·64	0·69	0·65

TABLE 20

Factors in Work Satisfaction in Nationalised and Private Firms (Ratio Method)

Mention Category	B.R.S.	P.H.	Total
Pay	0·87	0·66	0·75
Fringe benefits	1·00	—	1·00
Conditions	0·67	0·40	0·64
Management	0·41	0·74	0·55
Other	0·91	0·87	0·89
Total	0·64	0·69	0·65

TABLE 21

Attitude to Management

Attitude	B.R.S.		P.H.		Total
	R.T.	%	R.T.	%	
Favourable	35	56	25	64	60
Unfavourable	17	27	9	23	26
Ambivalent	3	5	4	10	7
Don't know	7	11	1	3	8
Total	62	100 (99)	39	100	101

TABLE 22

Management/Supervision as a Factor in Work Dissatisfaction

Firm	Unfavourable Mentions on Management/ Supervision	Total Unfavourable Mentions (All Factors)	Unfavourable Management as % of Total Unfavourable Mentions	Ratio Favourable to Total Comments on Management
B.R.S.	20	49	41	0·41
Private Haulage	7	18	39	0·74
Potex Factory	15	52	29	0·40

TABLE 23
Qualities of the Ideal Transport Manager

Qualities that a Good Manager should Have	B.R.S. Sample	P.H. Sample	Total Sample
Have been a lorry driver	21	9	30
Know the industry and job	19	15	34
Know how to understand men	18	12	30
Know the Driver's side of the job	9	6	15
Be approachable	11	2	13
Know the road conditions	4	7	11
Know the customers	1	–	1
Have consistency and fairness	2	1	3
Have initiative	1	–	1
Have business sense	1	–	1
Be quick thinking	–	1	1
Be patient	1	–	1
Accept the Union Rulings			
Know everything	–	1	1
Don't know	–	2	2
No mention	1	1	2
Total Positives	88	54	142

TABLE 24
Qualities of the Ideal Factory Manager

Qualities of the Ideal Manager	No. Mentions
He should be approachable	20
He should have knowledge of his job and the jobs in the factory	14
He should have ability to get respect and to keep discipline	9
He should know his men	9
He should have ability to deal with men	5
Fairness	5
Education	1
Total	63

TABLE 25
Wives' Attitude to Lorry Driving

Wife's Attitude	Trunkers		Trampers		Shunters		B.R.S.		P.H.		Total	
	R.T.	%	R.T.	%	R.T.	%	R.T.	%	R.T.	%	R.T.	%
Favourable	7	19	15	38	19	56	28	49	10	29	38	41
Unfavourable	25	69	21	53	13	38	27	47	20	57	47	51
Ambivalent	3	8	3	7	–	–	1	2	2	6	3	3
Neutral	1	3	1	2	2	6	1	2	3	9	4	4
Don't know	–	–	–	–	–	–	–	–	–	–	–	–
Total	36	100	40	100	34	100	57	100	35	100	92	100
		(99)								(101)		(99)

TABLE 26
Reasons for Wives' Favourable Attitude

Reasons for Favourable	Trunkers	Trampers	Shunters	B.R.S.	P.H.	Total
Wife used to it	6	8	4	12	3	15
Money	5	5	4	5	5	10
Job is local	–	–	2	2	–	2
'So long as I like it'	–	2	2	2	2	4
Total	11	15	12	21	10	31

TABLE 27
Reasons for Wives' Unfavourable Attitude

Reasons for Unfavourable	Trunkers	Trampers	Shunters	B.R.S.	P.H.	Total
Away from home and family	10	16	6	12	13	25
Accident worries	3	–	6	6	1	7
Night work	9	–	–	5	–	5
Irregularity of hours	–	2	1	–	3	3
Hours worked	3	–	1	2	–	2
Opportunity for sexual licence	–	2	–	–	2	2
Alternative occupations	–	9	–	1	–	1
Age	–	–	1	1	–	1
Leisure & social life interrupted	1	–	–	–	–	–
Total	26	21	15	27	19	46

TABLE 28
The Lorry Driver's Attitude to Marriage

Attitude to Marriage	Trunkers		Trampers		Shunters		B.R.S.		P.H.		Total	
	R.T.	%	R.T.	%	R.T.	%	R.T.	%	R.T.	%	R.T.	%
Married	3	21	8	18	9	24	16	26	3	8½	19	19
Single	17	46	27	61	17	45	30	48	23	59	53	52
Ambivalent	11	30	7	16	4	10	12	20	7	18	19	19
Neutral	1	3	–	–	7	18	2	3	5	13	7	7
Don't know	–	–	2	5	1	3	2	3	1	2	3	3
Total	37	100	44	100	38	100	62	100	39	100	101	100

Question: 'Should Lorry Drivers be married or single?'

TABLE 29
Reasons Why a Lorry Driver Should be Married

Reason for Lorry Drivers Marrying	Trunkers	Trampers	Shunters	B.R.S.	P.H.	Total
Makes Drivers more responsible	3	4	1	4	2	6
Trunk and Shunt are normal jobs	4	1	2	5	1	6
Someone to come home to	–	2	1	2	1	3
Need to be looked after	1	–	2	3	–	3
Wife the reason for lorry driving	1	–	2	3	–	3
No effects on my marriage	1	–	2	2	–	2
Personal preference	1	1	–	–	1	1
Night work	–	–	1	1	–	1
Age	–	–	1	1	–	1
Total	11	8	12	21	5	26

TABLE 30

Reasons Why a Lorry Driver should be Single

Reasons for Lorry Drivers being single	Trunkers	Trampers	Shunters	B.R.S.	P.H.	Total
Tramping away from home	6	7	8	13	5	18
Away from home	5	5	3	1	10	11
No worries at home	4	5	5	8	4	12
Wives suffer	3	5	3	8	3	11
Not much of a married life	—	1	2	2	1	3
Could have a good time	2	1	—	1	2	3
Lorry Driving like being a seaman	2	—	1	3	—	3
Moral pitfalls in Lorry Driving	1	—	1	1	—	1
A Trunker's job	—	—	1	—	1	1
Total	23	24	24	37	26	63

TABLE 31

Number of Weekends Worked (Café Sample)

Weekend Category	R.T.	%
Weekends free	123	61·5
Half weekend free (one day off)	12	6·0
Work 1 in 4 weekends or less	17	8·5
Work more than 1 in 4–1 in 2 weekends	26	13·0
More than 1 in 2 weekends worked–weekends worked	21	10·5
Unanswered	1	0·5
Total	200	100·0

TABLE 32

The Occupational Categories of Drivers who work more than One Weekend in Four (Café Sample)

Occupational Category	Raw Total	Per Cent	Per Cent of Occ. Cat.
Trunker	7	15	11
Tramper	25	53	33
Shunter	9	19	28
Other	6	13	20
Total	47	100	23·5

TABLE 33

Number of Nights Away from Home in the Week (Firms' Sample)

Nights per week away from home	Trunkers R.T.	%	Trampers R.T.	%	Shunters R.T.	%	B.R.S. R.T.	%	P.H. R.T.	%	Sample R.T.	%
Every night, home daily	15	41	–	–	–	–	6	10	–	–	6	6
Every night, home one day in two	9	24	–	–	–	–	–	–	5	13	5	5
Fortnight about	6	16	–	–	1	3	6	10	–	–	6	6
One night	–	–	–	–	2	5	1	2	1	3	2	2
Two nights	–	–	1	2	6	16	1	2	6	15	7	7
Three nights	5	14	8	18	–	–	6	10	4	10	10	10
Four nights	–	–	21	48	–	–	9	14	12	31	21	21
Five nights	2	5	10	23	–	–	8	13	3	8	11	11
Over five nights	–	–	4	9	–	–	4	6	–	–	4	4
No nights away	–	–	–	–	29	76	21	34	8	20	29	29
Total	37	100	44	100	38	100	62	100 (101)	39	100	101	100 (101)

TABLE 34

Length of Continuous Time Away Per Week (Firms' Sample)

Length of time at a stretch spent away	Trunkers R.T.	%	Trampers R.T.	%	Shunters R.T.	%	B.R.S. R.T.	%	P.H. R.T.	%	Total R.T.	%
1 night or 1 day only	20	54	1	2	31	82	32	52	11	27	43	42
1 night 1 day 1 night	16	43	–	–	7	18	6	10	9	23	15	15
2 nights/days	–	–	2	5	–	–	–	–	2	5	2	2
3 nights/days	1	3	13	30	–	–	3	5	10	26	13	13
4 nights/days	–	–	10	23	–	–	4	6	6	15	10	10
5 nights/days	–	–	9	20	–	–	8	13	1	3	9	9
6 nights/days	–	–	5	11	–	–	5	8	–	–	5	5
7 nights/days	–	–	4	9	–	–	4	6	–	–	4	4
Total	37	100	44	100	38	100	62	100	39	100 (99)	101	100

TABLE 35
Lorry Drivers' Activities in Leisure Time

Type of Activity	Trunkers		Trampers		Shunters		B.R.S.		P.H.		Total	
	(1)	(2)	(1)	(2)	(1)	(2)	(1)	(2)	(1)	(2)	(1)	(2)
Individual (need not but may involve family	23	8	17	3	27	4	43	7	16	4	59	11
Family (necessarily involving family)	8	14	20	17	7	9	21	20	9	12	30	32
Activities linked with friends (a) Fam. Mems. present	–	4	–	4	–	7	–	5	–	8	–	13
(b) Fam. Mems. absent	–	10	–	36	–	21	–	36	–	34	–	60
Work or connected activity	–	–	–	–	1	–	1	–	–	–	1	–
Other	–	–	4	–	–	–	1	–	3	–	4	–
Total activities	31	36	41	60	35	41	66	68	28	48	94	116
Av. number activities	1·81		2·29		2·00		2·16		1·95		2·08	
Per cent of family-centred activities	32·8		36·6		21·0		30·5		27·6		29·5	
Per cent of home-centred activities	46·2		40·6		46·0		49·2		36·8		44·7	

(1) Home centred   (2) Not home centred

Associational Group Participation (Firms' Sample)

Association	Category of Driver	Sample / Census	When Last Attended											
			1 week ago but less than 1 month		1 month and less than 3 months		3 months and less than 6 months		6 months and Over		Members but never attend		Total	
			B.R.S.	P.H.	B.R.S.	P.H.	B.R.S.	P.H.	B.R.S.	P.H.	B.R.S.	P.H.	B.R.S.	P.H.
A. Social and Drinking Clubs	Trunkers	Sample	5	3	—	2	—	—	1	—	—	—	6	5
	Trampers	Census	9	—	—	—	—	—	—	—	—	—	9	—
	Shunters		8	2	—	—	—	—	—	—	—	—	8	2
			17	12	3	—	—	2	—	—	—	1	20	15
B. Sports and Other Interest Clubs	Trunkers	Sample	—	—	—	—	1	1	—	—	—	—	1	1
	Trampers	Census	—	1	—	—	1	—	—	—	—	—	1	1
	Shunters		3	3	—	—	—	—	—	—	—	—	3	3
			3	6	—	—	—	—	—	—	—	—	4	6
C. Religious Associations	Trunkers	Sample	—	1	—	1	—	—	—	—	—	—	2	2
	Trampers	Census	—	—	—	1	—	—	—	—	—	—	1	1
	Shunters		1	2	—	—	—	—	2	—	—	—	3	2
D. Trade Union	Trunkers	Sample	4	—	5	—	2	—	2	4	1	1	14	5
	Trampers	Census	4	—	5	—	1	—	2	—	1	—	13	—
	Shunters		2	—	6	—	3	—	6	6	8	5	25	11
			1	—	8	—	2	—	10	4	2	6	23	10
E. Political Affiliation	Trunkers	Sample	—	1	—	—	—	—	—	—	—	—	—	1
	Trampers	Census	—	3	—	—	—	—	—	—	—	—	—	3
	Shunters		1	—	—	—	—	—	—	—	—	2	1	2
All Association Participation	Firms' Sample		44	33	23	2	8	3	22	14	11	15	108	67

TABLE 37

Associational Group Participation

Driver Group	When Last Attended					
	1 week ago-less than 1 month	*1 month and less than 3 months*	*3 months and less than 6 months*	*6 months and over*	*Member but nevver attend*	*Total Participation*
B.R.S. sample	44	23	8	22	11	108
P.H. sample	33	2	3	14	15	67
Firms' sample	77	25	11	36	26	175
TRUNKERS						
B.R.S.	22	10	5	5	2	44
P.H.	6	2	1	8	2	19
All Trunkers	28	12	6	13	4	63
TRAMPERS						
B.R.S.	13	6	3	6	8	36
P.H.	9	0	0	6	5	20
All Trampers	22	6	3	12	13	56
SHUNTERS						
B.R.S.	22	12	2	13	2	51
P.H.	20	0	2	4	9	35
All Shunters	42	12	4	17	11	86
Weights	+5	+4	+3	+2	+1	–

TABLE 38

Participation by Occupational Category in Each Firm

Occupational Category	B.R.S. Index	P.H. Index	Firms' Sample Index
Trunkers	6·555	5·900	6·378
Trampers	4·917	3·100	4·090
Shunters	8·000	8·786	8·289
Firms' Sample	6·306	5·769	6·099

The Index $=\dfrac{[\text{fxw}}{\text{N}}$ which is the sum of the products of frequencies times weights divided by the number in the category. Thus the 27 B.R.S. Trunkers have 44 participations and memberships.

Last Attendance Category (x)	Participations (f)	Weight (w)	Product
1 week—less than 1 month	22	+5	110
1 month—less than 3 months	10	+4	40
3 months—less than 6 months	5	+3	15
Over 6 months	5	+2	10
Member but never attend	2	+1	2
Total [fxw	44	—	177

Thus $\dfrac{[\text{fxw}}{\text{N}} = \dfrac{177}{27}$

$= 6\cdot555$

Appendix: Tables

TABLE 39

Comparative Indices of Social Participation

Survey Group	Instances of Participation	Indices of Participation
Aberavon	114	243
Sandfields Estate	103	234
Kidwelly	75	208
Lorry Drivers' Firms' Sample. Shunters	75	197
Port Talbot Steelworkers	122	194
Port Talbot Shiftworkers	133	190
Baglan Community	79	188
Port Talbot	254	183
Morriston	117	170
Baglan Congregation	45	161
Lorry Drivers' Firms' Sample. All Trunkers	59	159
B.R.S. Lorry Drivers' Sample	97	156
Lorry Drivers' Firms' Sample	149	147
Blaenavon	88	138
Port Talbot: Other Workers	76	133
Private Haulage Firm Sample	52	133
Port Talbot: Non Shift Workers	65	130
Newtown Cardiff, 1964	141	129
West Pontnewydd, 1955	28	103
Lorry Drivers Firms' Sample. Trampers	43	98
Lorry Drivers' Café Sample	177	88

Index—the number of participations (not memberships) in an unweighted aggregate form divided by the number in the category and multiplied by 100.

Sources. All survey groups except the Lorry Drivers groups and the Newtown Survey are quoted from Thomason G. F. 'The Effects of Industrial Changes on Selected Communities in S. Wales'. University of Wales Ph.D. Thesis. Cardiff, 1963.
The Newtown Survey was carried out by Father Harry Bohan as part of work for an M.A. Thesis in the Department of Industrial Relations. University College, Cardiff.

TABLE 40
Loneliness in a Lorry Driver's Job

	Trunkers		Trampers		Shunters		B.R.S.		P.H.		Total	
	R.T.	%	R.T.	%	R.T.	%	R.T.	%	R.T.	%	R.T.	%
Lonely	23	62	27	61	23	60	35	56	27	69	62	61
Not lonely	14	38	17	39	15	39	27	43	12	31	39	39
Total	37	100	44	100	38	100 (99)	62	100 (99)	39	100	101	100

TABLE 41
Reasons given For Reporting Loneliness

Reasons for Loneliness	Trunkers	Trampers	Shunters	B.R.S.	P.H.	Total
Alone in the cab	3	3	8	8	4	12
On long distance work	–	2	8	8	2	10
Night work	3	–	–	1	1	2
Compared with previous job	1	–	–	1	–	1
Some parts of country lonely	1	–	–	–	–	–
Personal	–	1	1	–	2	2
Total	8	6	17	18	9	27

TABLE 42
Reasons Given for Reporting Not Lonely

Reasons for not being Lonely	Trunkers	Trampers	Shunters	B.R.S.	P.H.	Total
Meeting other drivers	8	8	6	12	6	18
Meeting different people	–	3	7	9	1	10
Must watch the road	1	1	2	3	–	3
Get used to it	2	2	–	2	1	3
Compared with previous job	–	1	–	1	–	1
Short distances	–	1	–	1	–	1
Seeing places and things	–	–	1	–	1	1
Picking up people	–	1	–	–	1	1
Other drivers at the firm	1	–	–	–	–	–
Total	12	17	16	28	10	38

TABLE 43

Loneliness and Compensation

Loneliness and Compensation	Trunkers	Trampers	Shunters	B.R.S.	P.H.	Total
Total admitting lonely	23	27	23	35	27	62
Total lonely, no compensations	6	7	3	8	6	14
Total lonely, but compensations	17	20	20	27	21	48
Meeting drivers in cafés/digs	5	11	7	11	10	21
Meeting different people	5	3	1	5	–	5
Autonomy	2	2	2	3	2	5
Seeing different places	–	2	2	–	4	4
Having own thoughts	–	2	1	3	–	3
Meet drivers at destinations	1	–	1	1	1	2
Personal preference	–	–	2	–	2	2
Can pick up people	1	2	–	–	2	2
Other drivers in firm	1	1	–	2	–	2
A good living	2	–	–	1	–	1
Carry radios in the cab	–	–	1	1	–	1
Can go to the cinema	–	1	–	–	1	1

TABLE 44

Contact amongst Lorry Drivers

Much Contact	Trunkers		Trampers		Shunters		B.R.S.		P.H.		Total	
	R.T.	%	R.T.	%	R.T.	%	R.T.	%	R.T.	%	R.T.	%
Yes	32	86	41	93	32	84	57	92	33	85	90	89
No	4	11	3	7	6	16	5	8	6	15	11	11
Not mentioned	1	3	–	–	–	–	–	–	–	–	–	–
Total	37	100	44	100	38	100	62	100	39	100	101	100

TABLE 45
Places of Contact with Other Drivers

Place	Trunkers	Trampers	Shunters	B.R.S.	P.H.	Total
Cafés and places on route	29	37	24	46	31	77
Lodgings	7	27	2	22	10	32
Destinations	5	11	16	17	12	29
Depots	2	3	7	9	2	11
Socially outside work	2	1	2	3	1	4
Other	–	–	1	1	–	1
Total	45	79	52	98	56	154

Destinations include loading/unloading points, changeover points, etc.

TABLE 46
The Sources of Job Dissatisfaction in Lorry Driving
(Firms' Sample)

Things most disliked	B.R.S.	P.H.	Total
Other drivers (car)	12	11	23
Weather	13	4	17
Problems of loading/unloading	9	7	16
Road conditions	11	3	14
Away from home	5	1	6
Bad vehicles, breakdowns	–	4	4
Management	4	–	4
Waiting around	3	–	3
Pay, subsistence	1	2	3
Accommodation	–	3	3
Monotony	2	–	2
Too much responsibility	1	1	2
Long hours	–	2	2
Problems of age, security and promotion	1	–	1
'Smokers' in cafés	–	1	1
Rules, Ministry, Police, etc.	–	1	1
Total Positive	62	40	102
No Dislikes	13	7	20

TABLE 47

The Public View of The Lorry Driver

Public View of Lorry Driver and Job	Trunkers		Trampers		Shunters		Total Sample	
	R.T.	%	R.T.	%	R.T.	%	R.T.	%
Favourable	11	30	13	30	13	34	31	31
Unfavourable	20	54	18	41	16	42	43	43
Neutral	1	3	2	5	4	11	7	7
Ambivalent	4	11	9	20	5	13	18	18
Don't know	1	3	2	5	—	—	2	2
Total	37	100	44	100	38	100	101	100
		(101)		(101)				(101)

TABLE 48

Reasons for Favourable View by the Public

Reason for the Favourable View	B.R.S.	P.H.	Total Sample
Courtesy, helpfulness	6	4	10
Good drivers	4	2	6
Difficulties of job	4	2	6
Driving in bad weather	2	2	4
Car drivers' favourable opinion	2	1	3
Experience of others' attitude	2	1	3
An essential job	1	—	1
A good, honest job	1	—	1
Total	22	12	34

TABLE 49

Reasons for Unfavourable View by the Public

Reason for the Unfavourable View	B.R.S.	P.H.	Total Sample
Status problems	8	3	11
Improper behaviour	7	3	10
Lorries too big and slow	3	2	5
Unseen difficulties in the job	4	–	4
An easy job	1	3	4
Private motorists' opinion	3	–	3
Lorry drivers are tramps	2	1	3
People's attitude at Loading/Unloading points	2	–	2
Lorry Drivers are bad drivers	–	2	2
Newspaper image	–	1	1
An unskilled job	–	1	1
Too many lorry drivers	1	–	1
Others attitude	1	–	1
Lorry Drivers unintelligent	2	–	2
Total	34	16	50

THE FIRMS' SAMPLE
INTERVIEW SCHEDULE

Serial No..........

First of all I would like to ask you some questions about the actual job of driving which you do.

1. Do you regard lorry driving as your regular job?
....

2. Do you like or dislike the actual job of driving?
....

3. Would you say that:
    You like it a lot   *You dislike it a lot*
    You (merely) like it   *You (merely) dislike it*
          You neither like it nor dislike it

4. What are the things about driving which you most like?
....
....
....

5. What are the things about driving which you most dislike?
....
....
....

6. Do you regard the type of driving that you do as:
  (a) Difficult? Why? ....
  (b) Responsible? Why? ....
  (c) Skilled? Why?
  (d) Dangerous? Why? ....

7. Lorry drivers may be trunking, tramping, or shunting,
  (a) Which is the type of driving job which is best to have? Why?
....
....

  (b) What is wrong with the other two types, do you think?
....
....

8. An outsider's view might be that a lorry driver's job is a lonely one. Would you agree? ....
Are there compensations? ....

256

9. Do you have much contact with other lorry drivers? ....
   Where do you meet them? ....

I would now like to ask you some questions about the career of a lorry driver, and about his work in general.
10. Would you tell me about your career.

Occupation	Employer	Place of Employment	Dates	Reason for Leaving

11. If you had the opportunity, would you change the type of work you do?
    ....
12. Do you expect to spend the rest of your working life in driving?
    ....
13. If you could start life all over again, what type of work would you take up?
    ....
14. Would you advise a young man, about to start his working life, to take up lorry driving as a career?...
    ....
15. What do you think people in general think about lorry drivers and their job?..
16. Would you say that you like working for this firm, that you are with at present:
    A lot.   *Neither like nor dislike it.*   *That you dislike it.*
17. What do you like about working for this firm?.........................
    ....
    ....
18. What do you dislike about working for this firm? ....
    ....
19. What do you think of the management of your firm?....................
    ....
20. What qualities does a good transport manager need to have?
    ....
    ....
21. Do you think the pay is high enough for a job like yours?
    ....
    If you were offered more pay to work in a factory, would you go and work in one? ....
    ....
22. From what you know or may have heard about factory work, is there anything you consider attractive or unattractive about factory work?

257

Interview Schedule

Attractive	Unattractive

23. How do you think your job compares with factory work?
    Better. Why? ....
    Same. Why? ....
    Worse. Why? ....
24. Have you ever worked in a factory? ....

We are also studying the effects that a person's occupation has on his family life and his leisure time, so the last few questions are on these aspects of a driver's life.
25. Personal Details.

Age	Conj. Stat.	No. of Children	Ages of Children	Father's Occ.

26. Do you work nights or days regularly? ....
    How many nights are you away from home in the week usually?
    ....
    How long at a stretch are you away? ....
    ....
    Do you normally work an 11 hour shift, or less than this?
    ....
27. What do you usually do with your free time? Who accompanies you?
    ....
    ....
28. Do you belong to any Political or Religious Groups, or to a Trade Union?

Group mentioned	When last attended

29. Do you think that lorry drivers ought to be married or single?
    ....
    ....
30. What does your wife say about lorry driving?
    ....
    ....
    ....

INDEX

259

The International Library of
Sociology
and Social Reconstruction

Edited by W. J. H. SPROTT
Founded by KARL MANNHEIM

ROUTLEDGE & KEGAN PAUL
BROADWAY HOUSE, CARTER LANE, LONDON, E.C.4

CONTENTS

PRINTED IN GREAT BRITAIN BY HEADLEY BROTHERS LTD
109 KINGSWAY LONDON WC2 AND ASHFORD KENT

GENERAL SOCIOLOGY

Brown, Robert. Explanation in Social Science. *208 pp. 1963. (2nd Impression 1964.) 25s.*

Gibson, Quentin. The Logic of Social Enquiry. *240 pp. 1960. (2nd Impression 1963.) 24s.*

Homans, George C. Sentiments and Activities: Essays in Social Science. *336 pp. 1962. 32s.*

Isajiw, Wsevelod W. Causation and Functionalism in Sociology. *About 192 pp. 1968. 25s.*

Johnson, Harry M. Sociology: a Systematic Introduction. *Foreword by Robert K. Merton. 710 pp. 1961. (4th Impression 1964.) 42s.*

Mannheim, Karl. Essays on Sociology and Social Psychology. *Edited by Paul Keckskemeti. With Editorial Note by Adolph Lowe. 344 pp. 1953. (2nd Impression 1966.) 32s.*

Systematic Sociology: An Introduction to the Study of Society. *Edited by J. S. Erös and Professor W. A. C. Stewart. 220 pp. 1957. (3rd Impression 1967.) 24s.*

Martindale, Don. The Nature and Types of Sociological Theory. *292 pp. 1961. (3rd Impression 1967.) 35s.*

Maus, Heinz. A Short History of Sociology. *234 pp. 1962. (2nd Impression 1965.) 28s.*

Myrdal, Gunnar. Value in Social Theory: A Collection of Essays on Methodology. *Edited by Paul Streeten. 332 pp. 1958. (2nd Impression 1962.) 32s.*

Ogburn, William F., and **Nimkoff, Meyer F.** A Handbook of Sociology. *Preface by Karl Mannheim. 656 pp. 46 figures. 35 tables. 5th edition (revised) 1964. 40s.*

Parsons, Talcott, and **Smelser, Neil J.** Economy and Society: A Study in the Integration of Economic and Social Theory. *362 pp. 1956. (4th Impression 1967.) 35s.*

Rex, John. Key Problems of Sociological Theory. *220 pp. 1961. (4th Impression 1968.) 25s.*

Stark, Werner. The Fundamental Forms of Social Thought. *280 pp. 1962. 32s.*

FOREIGN CLASSICS OF SOCIOLOGY

Durkheim, Emile. Suicide. A Study in Sociology. *Edited and with an Introduction by George Simpson. 404 pp. 1952. (4th Impression 1968.) 35s.*

Socialism and Saint-Simon. *Edited with an Introduction by Alvin W. Gouldner. Translated by Charlotte Sattler from the edition originally edited with an Introduction by Marcel Mauss. 286 pp. 1959. 28s.*

Professional Ethics and Civic Morals. *Translated by Cornelia Brookfield. 288 pp. 1957. 30s.*

Gerth, H. H., and **Mills, C. Wright.** From Max Weber: Essays in Sociology. *502 pp. 1948. (6th Impression 1967.) 35s.*

Tönnies, Ferdinand. Community and Association. *(Gemeinschaft und Gesellschaft.) Translated and Supplemented by Charles P. Loomis. Foreword by Pitirim A. Sorokin. 334 pp. 1955. 28s.*

3

SOCIAL STRUCTURE

Andreski, Stanislaw. Military Organization and Society. *Foreword by Professor A. R. Radcliffe-Brown. 226 pp. 1 folder. 1954. Revised Edition 1968. 35s.*

Cole, G. D. H. Studies in Class Structure. *220 pp. 1955. (3rd Impression 1964.) 21s.*

Coontz, Sydney H. Population Theories and the Economic Interpretation. *202 pp. 1957. (2nd Impression 1961.) 25s.*

Coser, Lewis. The Functions of Social Conflict. *204 pp. 1956. (3rd Impression 1968.) 25s.*

Dickie-Clark, H. F. Marginal Situation: A Sociological Study of a Coloured Group. *240 pp. 11 tables. 1966. 40s.*

Glass, D. V. (Ed.). Social Mobility in Britain. *Contributions by J. Berent, T. Bottomore, R. C. Chambers, J. Floud, D. V. Glass, J. R. Hall, H. T. Himmelweit, R. K. Kelsall, F. M. Martin, C. A. Moser, R. Mukherjee, and W. Ziegel. 420 pp. 1954. (4th Impression 1967.) 45s.*

Kelsall, R. K. Higher Civil Servants in Britain: From 1870 to the Present Day. *268 pp. 31 tables. 1955. (2nd Impression 1966.) 25s.*

König, René. The Community. *224 pp. 1968. 25s.*

Lawton, Dennis. Social Class, Language and Education. *192 pp. 1968. 21s.*

Marsh, David C. The Changing Social Structure in England and Wales, 1871-1961. *1958. 272 pp. 2nd edition (revised) 1966. (2nd Impression 1967.) 35s.*

Mouzelis, Nicos. Organization and Bureaucracy. An Analysis of Modern Theories. *240 pp. 1967. 28s.*

Ossowski, Stanislaw. Class Structure in the Social Consciousness. *210 pp. 1963. (2nd Impression 1967.) 25s.*

SOCIOLOGY AND POLITICS

Barbu, Zevedei. Democracy and Dictatorship: Their Psychology and Patterns of Life. *300 pp. 1956. 28s.*

Crick, Bernard. The American Science of Politics: Its Origins and Conditions. *284 pp. 1959. 32s.*

Hertz, Frederick. Nationality in History and Politics: A Psychology and Sociology of National Sentiment and Nationalism. *432 pp. 1944. (5th Impression 1966.) 42s.*

Kornhauser, William. The Politics of Mass Society. *272 pp. 20 tables. 1960. (2nd Impression 1965.) 28s.*

Laidler, Harry W. History of Socialism. Social-Economic Movements: An Historical and Comparative Survey of Socialism, Communism, Co-operation, Utopianism; and other Systems of Reform and Reconstruction. *New edition in preparation.*

Lasswell, Harold D. Analysis of Political Behaviour. An Empirical Approach. *324 pp. 1947. (4th Impression 1966.) 35s.*

Mannheim, Karl. Freedom, Power and Democratic Planning. *Edited by Hans Gerth and Ernest K. Bramstedt. 424 pp. 1951. (2nd Impression 1965.) 35s.*

Mansur, Fatma. Process of Independence. *Foreword by A. H. Hanson. 208 pp. 1962. 25s.*

Martin, David A. Pacificism: an Historical and Sociological Study. *262 pp. 1965. 30s.*

Myrdal, Gunnar. The Political Element in the Development of Economic Theory. *Translated from the German by Paul Streeten. 282 pp. 1953. (4th Impression 1965.) 25s.*

Polanyi, Michael. F.R.S. The Logic of Liberty: Reflections and Rejoinders. *228 pp. 1951. 18s.*

Verney, Douglas V. The Analysis of Political Systems. *264 pp. 1959. (3rd Impression 1966.) 28s.*

Wootton, Graham. The Politics of Influence: British Ex-Servicemen, Cabinet Decisions and Cultural Changes, 1917 to 1957. *316 pp. 1963. 30s.*
Workers, Unions and the State. *188 pp. 1966. (2nd Impression 1967.) 25s.*

FOREIGN AFFAIRS: THEIR SOCIAL, POLITICAL AND ECONOMIC FOUNDATIONS

Baer, Gabriel. Population and Society in the Arab East. *Translated by Hanna Szöke. 288 pp. 10 maps. 1964. 40s.*

Bonné, Alfred. State and Economics in the Middle East: A Society in Transition. *482 pp. 2nd (revised) edition 1955. (2nd Impression 1960.) 40s.*
Studies in Economic Development: with special reference to Conditions in the Under-developed Areas of Western Asia and India. *322 pp. 84 tables. 2nd edition 1960. 32s.*

Mayer, J. P. Political Thought in France from the Revolution to the Fifth Republic. *164 pp. 3rd edition (revised) 1961. 16s.*

Trouton, Ruth. Peasant Renaissance in Yugoslavia 1900-1950: A Study of the Development of Yugoslav Peasant Society as affected by Education. *370 pp. 1 map. 1952. 28s.*

CRIMINOLOGY

Ancel, Marc. Social Defence: A Modern Approach to Criminal Problems. *Foreword by Leon Radzinowicz. 240 pp. 1965. 32s.*

Cloward, Richard A., and Ohlin, Lloyd E. Delinquency and Opportunity: A Theory of Delinquent Gangs. *248 pp. 1961. 25s.*

Downes, David M. The Delinquent Solution. A Study in Subcultural Theory. *296 pp. 1966. 42s.*

Dunlop, A. B., and McCabe, S. Young Men in Detention Centres. *192 pp. 1965. 28s.*

Friedländer, Kate. The Psycho-Analytical Approach to Juvenile Delinquency: Theory, Case Studies, Treatment. *320 pp. 1947. (6th Impression 1967.) 40s.*

Glueck, Sheldon and **Eleanor.** Family Environment and Delinquency. *With the statistical assistance of Rose W. Kneznek. 340 pp. 1962. (2nd Impression 1966.) 40s.*

Mannheim, Hermann. Comparative Criminology: a Text Book. *Two volumes. 442 pp. and 380 pp. 1965. (2nd Impression with corrections 1966.) 42s. a volume.*

Morris, Terence. The Criminal Area: A Study in Social Ecology. *Foreword by Hermann Mannheim. 232 pp. 25 tables. 4 maps. 1957. (2nd Impression 1966.) 28s.*

Morris, Terence and **Pauline,** assisted by **Barbara Barer.** Pentonville: A Sociological Study of an English Prison. *416 pp. 16 plates. 1963. 50s.*

Spencer, John C. Crime and the Services. *Foreword by Hermann Mannheim. 336 pp. 1954. 28s.*

Trasler, Gordon. The Explanation of Criminality. *144 pp. 1962. (2nd Impression 1967.) 20s.*

SOCIAL PSYCHOLOGY

Barbu, Zevedei. Problems of Historical Psychology. *248 pp. 1960. 25s.*

Blackburn, Julian. Psychology and the Social Pattern. *184 pp. 1945. (7th Impression 1964.) 16s.*

Fleming, C. M. Adolescence: Its Social Psychology: With an Introduction to recent findings from the fields of Anthropology, Physiology, Medicine, Psychometrics and Sociometry. *288 pp. 2nd edition (revised) 1963. (3rd Impression 1967.) 25s. Paper 12s. 6d.*
  The Social Psychology of Education: An Introduction and Guide to Its Study. *136 pp. 2nd edition (revised) 1959. (4th Impression 1967.) 14s. Paper 7s. 6d.*

Halmos, Paul. Towards a Measure of Man: The Frontiers of Normal Adjustment. *276 pp. 1957. 28s.*

Homans, George C. The Human Group. *Foreword by Bernard DeVoto. Introduction by Robert K. Merton. 526 pp. 1951. (7th Impression 1968.) 35s.*
  Social Behaviour: its Elementary Forms. *416 pp. 1961. (2nd Impression 1966.) 32s.*

Klein, Josephine. The Study of Groups. *226 pp. 31 figures. 5 tables. 1956. (5th Impression 1967.) 21s. Paper, 9s. 6d.*

Linton, Ralph. The Cultural Background of Personality. *132 pp. 1947. (7th Impression 1968.) 16s.*

Mayo, Elton. The Social Problems of an Industrial Civilization. With an appendix on the Political Problem. *180 pp. 1949. (5th Impression 1966.) 25s.*

Ottaway, A. K. C. Learning Through Group Experience. *176 pp. 1966. 25s.*

Ridder, J. C. de. The Personality of the Urban African in South Africa. A Thematic Apperception Test Study. *196 pp. 12 plates. 1961. 25s.*

Rose, Arnold M. (Ed.). Human Behaviour and Social Processes: an Interactionist Approach. *Contributions by Arnold M. Rose, Ralph H. Turner, Anselm Strauss, Everett C. Hughes, E. Franklin Frazier, Howard S. Becker, et al. 696 pp. 1962. 70s.*

Smelser, Neil J. Theory of Collective Behaviour. *448 pp. 1962. (2nd Impression 1967.) 45s.*

Stephenson, Geoffrey M. The Development of Conscience. *128 pp. 1966. 25s.*

Young, Kimball. Handbook of Social Psychology. *658 pp. 16 figures. 10 tables. 2nd edition (revised) 1957. (3rd Impression 1963.) 40s.*

SOCIOLOGY OF THE FAMILY

Banks, J. A. Prosperity and Parenthood: A study of Family Planning among The Victorian Middle Classes. *262 pp. 1954. (2nd Impression 1965.) 28s.*

Burton, Lindy. Vulnerable Children. *about 272 pp. 1968. 35s.*

Gavron, Hannah. The Captive Wife: Conflicts of Housebound Mothers. *190 pp. 1966. (2nd Impression 1966.) 25s.*

Klein, Josephine. Samples from English Cultures. *1965. (2nd Impression 1967.)*
1. Three Preliminary Studies and Aspects of Adult Life in England. *447 pp. 50s.*
2. Child-Rearing Practices and Index. *247 pp. 35s.*

Klein, Viola. Britain's Married Women Workers. *180 pp. 1965. 28s.*

McWhinnie, Alexina M. Adopted Children. How They Grow Up. *304 pp. 1967. (2nd Impression 1968.) 42s.*

Myrdal, Alva and Klein, Viola. Women's Two Roles: Home and Work. *238 pp. 27 tables. 1956. Revised Edition 1967. 30s. Paper 15s.*

Parsons, Talcott and Bales, Robert F. Family: Socialization and Interaction Process. *In collaboration with James Olds, Morris Zelditch and Philip E. Slater. 456 pp. 50 figures and tables. 1956. (2nd Impression 1964.) 35s.*

THE SOCIAL SERVICES

Ashdown, Margaret and Brown, S. Clement. Social Service and Mental Health: An Essay on Psychiatric Social Workers. *280 pp. 1953. 21s.*

Goetschius, George W. Working with Community Groups. *About 256 pp. 1968. about 35s.*

Goetschius, George W. and Tash, Joan. Working with Unattached Youth. *416 pp. 1967. 40s.*

Hall, M. Penelope. The Social Services of Modern England. *416 pp. 6th edition (revised) 1963. (2nd Impression with a new Preface 1966.) 30s.*

Hall, M. P., and Howes, I. V. The Church in Social Work. A Study of Moral Welfare Work undertaken by the Church of England. *320 pp. 1965. 35s.*

Heywood, Jean S. Children in Care: the Development of the Service for the Deprived Child. *264 pp. 2nd edition (revised) 1965. (2nd Impression 1966.) 32s.*

An Introduction to Teaching Casework Skills. *190 pp. 1964. 28s.*

Jones, Kathleen. Lunacy, Law and Conscience, 1744-1845: the Social History of the Care of the Insane. *268 pp. 1955. 25s.*

Mental Health and Social Policy, 1845-1959. *264 pp. 1960. (2nd Impression 1967.) 28s.*

Jones, Kathleen and **Sidebotham, Roy.** Mental Hospitals at Work. *220 pp. 1962. 30s.*

Kastell, Jean. Casework in Child Care. *Foreword by M. Brooke Willis. 320 pp. 1962. 35s.*

Nokes, P. L. The Professional Task in Welfare Practice. *152 pp. 1967. 28s.*

Rooff, Madeline. Voluntary Societies and Social Policy. *350 pp. 15 tables. 1957. 35s.*

Shenfield, B. E. Social Policies for Old Age: A Review of Social Provision for Old Age in Great Britain. *260 pp. 39 tables. 1957. 25s.*

Timms, Noel. Psychiatric Social Work in Great Britain (1939-1962). *280 pp. 1964. 32s.*

Social Casework: Principles and Practice. *256 pp. 1964. (2nd Impression 1966.) 25s. Paper 15s.*

Trasler, Gordon. In Place of Parents: A Study in Foster Care. *272 pp. 1960. (2nd Impression 1966.) 30s.*

Young, A. F., and **Ashton, E. T.** British Social Work in the Nineteenth Century. *288 pp. 1956. (2nd Impression 1963.) 28s.*

Young, A. F. Social Services in British Industry. *about 350 pp. 1968. about 45s.*

SOCIOLOGY OF EDUCATION

Banks, Olive. Parity and Prestige in English Secondary Education: a Study in Educational Sociology. *272 pp. 1955. (2nd Impression 1963.) 32s.*

Bentwich, Joseph. Education in Israel. *224 pp. 8 pp. plates. 1965. 24s.*

Blyth, W. A. L. English Primary Education. A Sociological Description. *1965. Revised edition 1967.*

1. Schools. *232 pp. 30s.*
2. Background. *168 pp. 25s.*

Collier, K. G. The Social Purposes of Education: Personal and Social Values in Education. *268 pp. 1959. (3rd Impression 1965.) 21s.*

Dale, R. R., and **Griffith, S.** Down Stream: Failure in the Grammar School. *108 pp. 1965. 20s.*

Dore, R. P. Education in Tokugawa Japan. *356 pp. 9 pp. plates. 1965. 35s.*

Edmonds, E. L. The School Inspector. *Foreword by Sir William Alexander. 214 pp. 1962. 28s.*

Evans, K. M. Sociometry and Education. *158 pp. 1962. (2nd Impression 1966.) 18s.*

8

Foster, P. J. Education and Social Change in Ghana. *336 pp. 3 maps. 1965. (2nd Impression 1967.) 36s.*

Fraser, W. R. Education and Society in Modern France. *150 pp. 1963. 20s.*

Hans, Nicholas. New Trends in Education in the Eighteenth Century. *278 pp. 19 tables. 1951. (2nd Impression 1966.) 30s.*
Comparative Education: A Study of Educational Factors and Traditions. *360 pp. 3rd (revised) edition 1958. (4th Impression 1967.) 25s. Paper 12s. 6d.*

Hargreaves, David. Social Relations in a Secondary School. *240 pp. 1967. 32s.*

Holmes, Brian. Problems in Education. A Comparative Approach. *336 pp. 1965. (2nd Impression 1967.) 32s.*

Mannheim, Karl and **Stewart, W. A. C.** An Introduction to the Sociology of Education. *206 pp. 1962. (2nd Impression 1965.) 21s.*

Musgrove, F. Youth and the Social Order. *176 pp. 1964. 21s.*

Ortega y Gasset, José. Mission of the University. *Translated with an Introduction by Howard Lee Nostrand. 86 pp. 1946. (3rd Impression 1963.) 15s.*

Ottaway, A. K. C. Education and Society: An Introduction to the Sociology of Education. *With an Introduction by W. O. Lester Smith. 212 pp. Second edition (revised). 1962. (5th Impression 1968.) 18s. Paper 10s. 6d.*

Peers, Robert. Adult Education: A Comparative Study. *398 pp. 2nd edition 1959. (2nd Impression 1966.) 42s.*

Pritchard, D. G. Education and the Handicapped: 1760 to 1960. *258 pp. 1963. (2nd Impression 1966.) 35s.*

Simon, Brian and **Joan** (Eds.). Educational Psychology in the U.S.S.R. *Introduction by Brian and Joan Simon. Translation by Joan Simon. Papers by D. N. Bogoiavlenski and N. A. Menchinskaia, D. B. Elkonin, E. A. Fleshner, Z. I. Kalmykova, G. S. Kostiuk, V. A. Krutetski, A. N. Leontiev, A. R. Luria, E. A. Milerian, R. G. Natadze, B. M. Teplov, L. S. Vygotski, L. V. Zankov. 296 pp. 1963. 40s.*

SOCIOLOGY OF CULTURE

Eppel, E. M., and **M.** Adolescents and Morality: A Study of some Moral Values and Dilemmas of Working Adolescents in the Context of a changing Climate of Opinion. *Foreword by W. J. H. Sprott. 268 pp. 39 tables. 1966. 30s.*

Fromm, Erich. The Fear of Freedom. *286 pp. 1942. (8th Impression 1960.) 25s. Paper 10s.*
The Sane Society. *400 pp. 1956. (3rd Impression 1963.) 28s. Paper 12s. 6d.*

Mannheim, Karl. Diagnosis of Our Time: Wartime Essays of a Sociologist. *208 pp. 1943. (8th Impression 1966.) 21s.*
Essays on the Sociology of Culture. *Edited by Ernst Mannheim in co-operation with Paul Kecskemeti. Editorial Note by Adolph Lowe. 280 pp. 1956. (3rd Impression 1967.) 28s.*

Weber, Alfred. Farewell to European History: or The Conquest of Nihilism. *Translated from the German by R. F. C. Hull. 224 pp. 1947. 18s.*

9

SOCIOLOGY OF RELIGION

Argyle, Michael. Religious Behaviour. *224 pp. 8 figures. 41 tables. 1958. (3rd Impression 1965.) 25s.*

Knight, Frank H., and **Merriam, Thornton W.** The Economic Order and Religion. *242 pp. 1947. 18s.*

Stark, Werner. The Sociology of Religion. A Study of Christendom.
Volume I. Established Religion. *248 pp. 1966. 35s.*
Volume II. Sectarian Religion. *368 pp. 1967. 40s.*
Volume III. The Universal Church. *464 pp. 1967. 45s.*

Watt, W. Montgomery. Islam and the Integration of Society. *320 pp. 1961. (3rd Impression 1966.) 35s.*

SOCIOLOGY OF ART AND LITERATURE

Beljame, Alexandre. Men of Letters and the English Public in the Eighteenth Century: 1660-1744, Dryden, Addison, Pope. *Edited with an Introduction and Notes by Bonamy Dobrée. Translated by E. O. Lorimer. 532 pp. 1948. 32s.*

Misch, Georg. A History of Autobiography in Antiquity. *Translated by E. W. Dickes. 2 Volumes. Vol. 1, 364 pp., Vol. 2, 372 pp. 1950. 45s. the set.*

Schücking, L. L. The Sociology of Literary Taste. *112 pp. 2nd (revised) edition 1966. 18s.*

Silbermann, Alphons. The Sociology of Music. *Translated from the German by Corbet Stewart. 222 pp. 1963. 28s.*

SOCIOLOGY OF KNOWLEDGE

Mannheim, Karl. Essays on the Sociology of Knowledge. *Edited by Paul Kecskemeti. Editorial note by Adolph Lowe. 352 pp. 1952. (3rd Impression 1964.) 35s.*

Stark, W. America: Ideal and Reality. The United States of 1776 in Contemporary Philosophy. *136 pp. 1947. 12s.*
The Sociology of Knowledge: An Essay in Aid of a Deeper Understanding of the History of Ideas. *384 pp. 1958. (3rd Impression 1967.) 36s.*
Montesquieu: Pioneer of the Sociology of Knowledge. *244 pp. 1960. 25s.*

URBAN SOCIOLOGY

Anderson, Nels. The Urban Community: A World Perspective. *532 pp. 1960. 35s.*

Ashworth, William. The Genesis of Modern British Town Planning: A Study in Economic and Social History of the Nineteenth and Twentieth Centuries. *288 pp. 1954. (3rd Impression 1968.) 32s.*

Bracey, Howard. Neighbours: On New Estates and Subdivisions in England and U.S.A. *220 pp. 1964. 28s.*

Cullingworth, J. B. Housing Needs and Planning Policy: A Restatement of the Problems of Housing Need and "Overspill" in England and Wales. *232 pp. 44 tables. 8 maps. 1960. (2nd Impression 1966.) 28s.*

Dickinson, Robert E. City and Region: A Geographical Interpretation. *608 pp. 125 figures. 1964. (5th Impression 1967.) 60s.*
The West European City: A Geographical Interpretation. *600 pp. 129 maps. 29 plates. 2nd edition 1962. (3rd Impression 1968.) 55s.*
The City Region in Western Europe. *320 pp. Maps. 1967. 30s. Paper 14s.*

Jennings, Hilda. Societies in the Making: a Study of Development and Redevelopment within a County Borough. *Foreword by D. A. Clark. 286 pp. 1962. (2nd Impression 1967.) 32s.*

Kerr, Madeline. The People of Ship Street. *240 pp. 1958. 23s.*

Mann, P. H. An Approach to Urban Sociology. *240 pp. 1965. (2nd Impression 1968.) 30s.*

Morris, R. N., and **Mogey, J.** The Sociology of Housing. Studies at Berinsfield. *232 pp. 4 pp. plates. 1965. 42s.*

Rosser, C., and **Harris, C.** The Family and Social Change. A Study of Family and Kinship in a South Wales Town. *352 pp. 8 maps. 1965. (2nd Impression 1968.) 45s.*

RURAL SOCIOLOGY

Haswell, M. R. The Economics of Development in Village India. *120 pp. 1967. 21s.*

Littlejohn, James. Westrigg: the Sociology of a Cheviot Parish. *172 pp. 5 figures. 1963. 25s.*

Williams, W. M. The Country Craftsman: A Study of Some Rural Crafts and the Rural Industries Organization in England. *248 pp. 9 figures. 1958. 25s. (Dartington Hall Studies in Rural Sociology.)*
The Sociology of an English Village: Gosforth. *272 pp. 12 figures. 13 tables. 1956. (3rd Impression 1964.) 25s.*

SOCIOLOGY OF MIGRATION

Eisenstadt, S. N. The Absorption of Immigrants: a Comparative Study based mainly on the Jewish Community in Palestine and the State of Israel. *288 pp. 1954. 28s.*

Humphreys, Alexander J. New Dubliners: Urbanization and the Irish Family. *Foreword by George C. Homans. 304 pp. 1966. 40s.*

11

SOCIOLOGY OF INDUSTRY AND DISTRIBUTION

Anderson, Nels. Work and Leisure. *280 pp. 1961. 28s.*

Blau, Peter M., and Scott, W. Richard. Formal Organizations: a Comparative approach. *Introduction and Additional Bibliography by J. H. Smith. 326 pp. 1963. (2nd Impression 1964.) 28s. Paper 15s.*

Eldridge, J. E. T. Industrial Disputes. Essays in the Sociology of Industrial Relations. *about 272 pp. 1968. 40s.*

Hollowell, Peter G. The Lorry Driver. *272 pp. 1968. 42s.*

Jefferys, Margot, with the assistance of Winifred Moss. Mobility in the Labour Market: Employment Changes in Battersea and Dagenham. *Preface by Barbara Wootton. 186 pp. 51 tables. 1954. 15s.*

Levy, A. B. Private Corporations and Their Control. *Two Volumes. Vol. 1, 464 pp., Vol. 2, 432 pp. 1950. 80s. the set.*

Liepmann, Kate. Apprenticeship: An Enquiry into its Adequacy under Modern Conditions. *Foreword by H. D. Dickinson. 232 pp. 6 tables. 1960. (2nd Impression 1960.) 23s.*

Millerson, Geoffrey. The Qualifying Associations: a Study in Professionalization. *320 pp. 1964. 42s.*

Smelser, Neil J. Social Change in the Industrial Revolution: An Application of Theory to the Lancashire Cotton Industry, 1770-1840. *468 pp. 12 figures. 14 tables. 1959. (2nd Impression 1960.) 42s.*

Williams, Gertrude. Recruitment to Skilled Trades. *240 pp. 1957. 23s.*

Young, A. F. Industrial Injuries Insurance: an Examination of British Policy. *192 pp. 1964. 30s.*

ANTHROPOLOGY

Ammar, Hamed. Growing up in an Egyptian Village: Silwa, Province of Aswan. *336 pp. 1954. (2nd Impression 1966.) 35s.*

Crook, David and Isabel. Revolution in a Chinese Village: Ten Mile Inn. *230 pp. 8 plates. 1 map. 1959. 21s.*
The First Years of Yangyi Commune. *302 pp. 12 plates. 1966. 42s.*

Dickie-Clark, H. F. The Marginal Situation. A Sociological Study of a Coloured Group. *236 pp. 1966. 40s.*

Dube, S. C. Indian Village. *Foreword by Morris Edward Opler. 276 pp. 4 plates. 1955. (5th Impression 1965.) 25s.*
India's Changing Villages: Human Factors in Community Development. *260 pp. 8 plates. 1 map. 1958. (3rd Impression 1963.) 25s.*

Firth, Raymond. Malay Fishermen. Their Peasant Economy. *420 pp. 17 pp. plates. 2nd edition revised and enlarged 1966. (2nd Impression 1968.) 55s.*

Gulliver, P. H. The Family Herds. A Study of two Pastoral Tribes in East Africa, The Jie and Turkana. *304 pp. 4 plates. 19 figures. 1955. (2nd Impression with new preface and bibliography 1966.) 35s.*
Social Control in an African Society: a Study of the Arusha, Agricultural Masai of Northern Tanganyika. *320 pp. 8 plates. 10 figures. 1963. 35s.*

Hogbin, Ian. Transformation Scene. The Changing Culture of a New Guinea Village. *340 pp. 22 plates. 2 maps. 1951. 30s.*

Ishwaran, K. Shivapur. A South Indian Village. *about 216 pp. 1968. 35s.*
Tradition and Economy in Village India: An Interactionist Approach. *Foreword by Conrad Arensburg. 176 pp. 1966. 25s.*

Jarvie, Ian C. The Revolution in Anthropology. *268 pp. 1964. (2nd Impression 1967.) 40s.*

Jarvie, Ian C. and Agassi, Joseph. Hong Kong. A Society in Transition. *about 388 pp. 1968. 56s.*

Little, Kenneth L. Mende of Sierra Leone. *308 pp. and folder. 1951. Revised edition 1967. 63s.*

Lowie, Professor Robert H. Social Organization. *494 pp. 1950. (4th Impression 1966.) 42s.*

Maunier, René. The Sociology of Colonies: An Introduction to the Study of Race Contact. *Edited and translated by E. O. Lorimer. 2 Volumes. Vol. 1, 430 pp. Vol. 2, 356 pp. 1949. 70s. the set.*

Mayer, Adrian C. Caste and Kinship in Central India: A Village and its Region. *328 pp. 16 plates. 15 figures. 16 tables. 1960. (2nd Impression 1965.) 35s.*
Peasants in the Pacific: A Study of Fiji Indian Rural Society. *232 pp. 16 plates. 10 figures. 14 tables. 1961. 35s.*

Smith, Raymond T. The Negro Family in British Guiana: Family Structure and Social Status in the Villages. *With a Foreword by Meyer Fortes. 314 pp. 8 plates. 1 figure. 4 maps. 1956. (2nd Impression 1965.) 35s.*

DOCUMENTARY

Meek, Dorothea L. (Ed.). Soviet Youth: Some Achievements and Problems. *Excerpts from the Soviet Press, translated by the editor. 280 pp. 1957. 28s.*

Schlesinger, Rudolf (Ed.). Changing Attitudes in Soviet Russia.

1. The Family in the U.S.S.R. *Documents and Readings, with an Introduction by the editor. 434 pp. 1949. 30s.*

2. The Nationalities Problem and Soviet Administration. Selected Readings on the Development of Soviet Nationalities Policies. *Introduced by the editor. Translated by W. W. Gottlieb. 324 pp. 1956. 30s.*

Reports of the Institute of Community Studies

(*Demy 8vo.*)

Cartwright, Ann. Human Relations and Hospital Care. *272 pp. 1964. 30s.*
Patients and their Doctors. A Study of General Practice. *304 pp. 1967.40s.*

Jackson, Brian. Streaming: an Education System in Miniature. *168 pp. 1964.* (*2nd Impression 1966.*) *21s. Paper 10s.*
Working Class Community. Some General Notions raised by a Series of Studies in Northern England. *192 pp. 1968. 25s.*

Jackson, Brian and **Marsden, Dennis.** Education and the Working Class: Some General Themes raised by a Study of 88 Working-class Children in a Northern Industrial City. *268 pp. 2 folders. 1962.* (*4th Impression 1968.*) *32s.*

Marris, Peter. Widows and their Families. *Foreword by Dr. John Bowlby. 184 pp. 18 tables. Statistical Summary. 1958. 18s.*
Family and Social Change in an African City. A Study of Rehousing in Lagos. *196 pp. 1 map. 4 plates. 53 tables. 1961.* (*2nd Impression 1966.*) *30s.*
The Experience of Higher Education. *232 pp. 27 tables. 1964. 25s.*

Marris, Peter and **Rein, Martin.** Dilemmas of Social Reform. Poverty and Community Action in the United States. *256 pp. 1967. 35s.*

Mills, Enid. Living with Mental Illness: a Study in East London. *Foreword by Morris Carstairs. 196 pp. 1962. 28s.*

Runciman, W. G. Relative Deprivation and Social Justice. A Study of Attitudes to Social Inequality in Twentieth Century England. *352 pp. 1966.* (*2nd Impression 1967.*) *40s.*

Townsend, Peter. The Family Life of Old People: An Inquiry in East London. *Foreword by J. H. Sheldon. 300 pp. 3 figures. 63 tables. 1957.* (*3rd Impression 1967.*) *30s.*

Willmott, Peter. Adolescent Boys in East London. *230 pp. 1966. 30s.*
The Evolution of a Community: a study of Dagenham after forty years. *168 pp. 2 maps. 1963. 21s.*

Willmott, Peter and **Young, Michael.** Family and Class in a London Suburb. *202 pp. 47 tables. 1960.* (*4th Impression 1968.*) *25s.*

Young, Michael. Innovation and Research in Education. *192 pp. 1965. 25s.*

Young, Michael and **McGeeney, Patrick.** Learning Begins at Home. A Study of a Junior School and its Parents. *about 128 pp. 1968. about 18s. Paper about 8s.*

Young, Michael and **Willmott, Peter.** Family and Kinship in East London. *Foreword by Richard M. Titmuss. 252 pp. 39 tables. 1957.* (*3rd Impression 1965.*) *28s.*

The British Journal of Sociology. *Edited by Terence P. Morris. Vol. 1, No. 1, March 1950 and Quarterly. Roy. 8vo., £2 10s. annually, 15s. a number, post free. (Vols. 1-16, £6 each; Vol. 17, £2 10s. Individual parts 37s. 6d. and 15s. respectively.)*

All prices are net and subject to alteration without notice

1267 H.B.